For EU product safety concerns:
IN TECH d.o.o., Prolaz Marije Krucifikse Kozulić 3, 51000 Rijeka, Croatia,
info@intechopen.com or visit our website at intechopen.com.

Meet the editors

Dr. Marinela Mircea received a degree in informatics in economy from the Bucharest University of Economic Studies, Romania, a Ph.D. in Economics, and a habilitation degree in Economic Informatics. Since 2003, she has been teaching at the Informatics and Cybernetics Economy Department, Bucharest University of Economic Studies. From 2005 to 2012, she was an employee of the Public Procurement Compartment within the Bucharest University of Economic Studies, where she was the head of the Monitoring and Reporting Office (2007–2012) and engaged directly with the procurement procedures conducted by the university. Currently, she is a full professor at this university. She has published more than 100 articles in journals, magazines, and international conferences on computer science, informatics, and business management. She has authored and coauthored eighteen books. She was a member of more than fifteen research projects and a project manager for two national research projects. Her research interests include programming, information systems, business management, and business intelligence. Prof. Mircea is a member of the Association for the Promotion of Economic Informatics Education, a senior member of the International Association of Computer Science and Information Technology, and a member of the Association of North America Higher Education International.

Dr. Tien Nguyen is an adjunct research professor in Mathematics at California State University, Fullerton (CSUF), Center of Computational and Applied Mathematics (CCAM), where he is the chairman of the CCAM Advisory Board. Concurrently, he also serves as a senior project leader at the Aerospace Corporation. Prior to this position, he was associate director/interim director and principal engineer/technical staff. Previously, he had more than an 11-year successful tenure at NASA-JPL and served as a NASA delegate to the international Consultative Committee for Space Data Systems (CCSDS); many of his works were adopted as CCSDS standards. He also had a very productive 10-year tenure at Raytheon, where he served as a chief engineer, technical director, project manager, and principal investigator for many advanced concept technology (ACT) programs. He became the program area chief engineer for the ACT System Integration product line and retired as a Raytheon engineering fellow. While at Raytheon, Dr. Nguyen was a certified program manager at levels 5/6, EVMS level 2, and Six Sigma. He received his Ph.D. in Applied Mathematics from the Claremont Graduate University, California, and serval master's degrees in pure mathematics, electromagnetic field theory, communications systems theory, and digital signal processing. His current research focuses on the applications of advanced technology enablers developed from industrial revolutions 4.0 and 5.0 for managing future commercial, civilian, and defense programs. He has edited two books on satellite design and complex systems-of-systems modeling and simulation and published more than 250 papers in professional journals, magazines, and national and international conferences. He holds seventeen patents with two pending.

Contents

Preface

From the invention of Gantt charts to help a project managers monitor project progress in the early 1900s to the development of traditional[1] project management (ProM) methodology in the early 1960s, the field of project management has advanced rapidly during the last twenty years. More particularly, the technological advancements during the fourth and fifth industrial revolutions (IRs 4.0 and 5.0), from 2011 to the present, have significantly improved the effectiveness of traditional ProM methods and practices. Many of the technologies developed during IR 4.0, such as the Internet of Things (IoT), Industrial Internet of Things (IIoT), cloud computing, cognitive computing, and machine learning and artificial intelligence (ML-AI), have led to the incorporation of existing IR 5.0 technology enablers into the modern ProM approach to reduce project failures and risks. These IR 5.0 technology enablers include advanced ML-AI, blockchains, banking 4.0, advanced WiFi, 5G communications, digital tween engines, and big data analytics (BDA). These ProM advancements can be referred to as the modernization and enhancement of traditional ProM methodology ensuring all potential program and technical risks are (1) identified during planning and (2) properly addressed and mitigated during the ProM lifecycle process. In summary, the objective of this modernization is to develop effective ProM methods to help project managers and associated execution teams avoid project failures and reduce identified risks. Typical identified risks include schedule, cost, technical performance, and related risks.

This book is a reference book for educators, engineers, scientists, and researchers in the fields of project and program management[2] (PProM). It is a collection of chapters related to recent advancements in PProM approaches and practices. Chapters discuss PProM topics ranging from program management fundamentals to current trends for PProM approaches and practices. The book is organized into four sections that

---

[1] In layperson terms, the traditional PProM methodology is defined as a combination of common program/project management practices and tools concerning logic, program/project planning and management supporting tools (i.e., decision support and analysis tools), systematic combination of rigorous knowledge, methods, and processes that can help program/project managers and teams to plan, develop, monitor, and control a program/project along a continuous program/project lifecycle process from the planning phase to a successful completion. The goal of PPRoM methodology is to provide effective PProM while avoiding program/project failure and reducing risks.

[2] In general, project management is defined as the application of processes, methods, skills, knowledge, and experience to achieve specific project objectives according to the project entrance/exit acceptance criteria within agreed project and technical performance parameters. Using a specific project management approach, a project manager plans, implements project plans, including allocation of project resources, tracks progress, monitors progress, manages risks, communicates with team members, and performs related activities according to the project plan. Program management involves managing a program with multiple, related projects. Since programs are often linked to organizations' strategic initiatives, they are often long running.

address the following key topics in PProM: (1) program management fundamentals, (2) project management maturity modeling, (3) current trends for PProM approaches, and (4) program management interface.

Section 1, "Overview of Program Management", includes one chapter, which is referred to as the introductory chapter. The chapter provides an overview of the program fundamentals and a description of typical program lifecycle management approaches for defense, civilian, and commercial programs. Additionally, the chapter also discusses the current program management trends leveraging advanced ML-AI and related technology enablers.

Section 2, "Project Management Maturity Modeling", also includes one chapter. This chapter proposes a project management maturity model with specific application to the power sector in South Africa (SA). Additionally, this chapter describes a conceptual model for measuring the project management maturity in the SA's power sector. It also addresses the key project parameters that constitute a conceptual model for measuring the maturity of the implemented program management approach.

Section 3, "Current Trends for Program and Project Management Approaches", includes four chapters. The first chapter presents an approach for balancing hedging and flexing for inclusive project management that is adaptable to the dynamic of social and technological changes. The chapter also describes selection criteria and discusses tools that can be used for balancing hedging and flexing for inclusive project management. The second chapter addresses recent advances in the Information Technology (IT) project management approach using fuzzy expert systems (FES). Additionally, this chapter also demonstrates that FES can be used as a reusable management tool to increase IT management effectiveness by leveraging the enrichment of knowledge and databases from past IT projects. The third chapter presents an approach to integrate several key program management discipline areas with emerging data and decision sciences (DDS). This chapter focuses on three key discipline areas related to schedule, cost, and risk management along with recent DDS technology enablers, including BDA, AI, and ML. Finally, the fourth chapter identifies and discusses the challenges associated with program planning and management (PPlaM) for defense advanced concept technology (ACT) programs and presents a newly proposed innovative PPlaM approach addressing these ACT challenges. It describes and discusses the key innovative features of the proposed approach, including the new approaches for (1) quantifying ACT program risks using the simplified Cooper Chart technique, (2) identifying desired ACT program planning activities using the tailored Zachman framework, (3) selecting desired PPlaM activities for balancing cost as well as technical and program management risks from both government and contractor perspectives, and (4) leveraging ML-AI and BDA technology enablers for improving the effectiveness of existing PPlaM supporting tools and processes.

Section 4, "Project Management Interface within a Project Life Cycle", includes one chapter. This chapter emphasizes the improvement of project management success through inter-organizational (IO) interfaces and collaboration between the project's front end and the project's initiation phase. It discusses IO interfaces and the collaboration of a practical for-profit organization between the front-end office, the sales office, and the project management and technical teams. Because the sales office is in the front end, it starts the front-end phase, and the project management and technical teams (ie, the project team) initiate the project initiation phase. The project team usually sets the strategic and operational direction for the rest of the project after the front-end sales office begins the project. Furthermore, the chapter attempts to (1) provide a better understanding of IO interfaces and the collaboration between the sales office and the project team and (2) identify potential deficiencies of existing project planning and management approaches to reduce project failures and improve project management success.

We would like to recognize the contributions of several key people to the creation of this professional technical book and express our deep gratitude to all the authors and coauthors for their contributions and several anonymous reviewers. The success of this book is not only the result of the work of the authors, coauthors, and reviewers but also of the cooperation of several people at IntechOpen who provided constant support. Particularly, we would like to thank IntechOpen Publishing Process Manager, Ms. Paula Gavran for her invaluable assistance, conscientiousness, and relentless support during the review, editing, and publishing processes - without her, this book would not have been possible. We also thank the Commissioning Editor, Ms. Jelena Germuth.

The co-editor of this book would like to thank his colleagues and managers at California State University, Fullerton and the Aerospace Corporation, respectively, for their continuous support. He also wants to thank his wonderful wife, Thu-Hang Nguyen, for her patience, encouragement, and continuous support.

Marinela Mircea, Ph.D.
Professor,
Informatics and Cybernetics Economy Department,
Bucharest University of Economic Studies,
Bucharest, Romania

Tien M. Nguyen, Ph.D.
Adjunct Research Professor,
Chair of the CCAM Advisory Board,
Center for Computational and Applied Mathematics (CCAM),
California State University in Fullerton,
Fullerton, California, U.S.A.
(Also, with Aerospace Corporation)

Section 1

Overview of Program Management

Chapter 1

Introductory Chapter: Program Management Fundamentals and Current Trends

Tien M. Nguyen and Mark B. Hammond

1. Introduction

The five Program Management (PM) fundamentals consist of five key program phases that can be tailored to any type of program life cycles (LCs). These phases include program conceptual phase, planning phase, execution phase, monitoring phase, and program closing phase. These key phases are the basic framework that can help any program managers to lay their foundation for managing any types of programs and associated projects [1–5]. In general, the types of programs and associated LCs can be grouped into three groups, namely, defense program group (DePG), civilian program group (CiPG), and commercial program group (CoPG). This chapter provides an overview of the common practices of these five PM fundamentals, with an emphasis on the discussion of the DePG and CiPD that can easily be extended to CoPG. **Figure 1** describes these three program groups and associated program types in detail.

As depicted in **Figure 1**, DePG can have different program types, namely, traditional US Department of Defense (DoD), defense advanced concept technology (ACT), and DoD rapid acquisition program types. Like DePG, CiPG can have traditional National Aeronautics and Space Administration (NASA), ACT, National Oceanic and Atmospheric Administration (NOAA) weather satellites, and other civilian program types. Unlike DePG and CiPG, CoPG emphasizes on private for-profit programs, such as construction, satellite, and other commercial program types. Examples of construction program type include hotels, hospitals, parks, houses, etc. Examples of satellite commercial program type include Starlink,

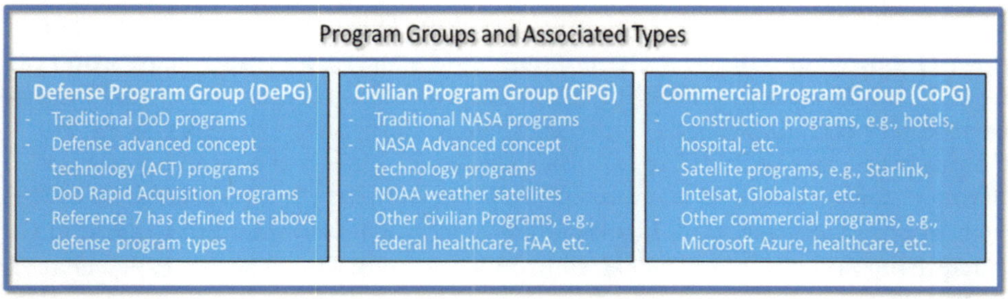

Figure 1.
Description of program groups and associated program types.

Intelsat, Globalstar, Capella Space, etc. Other commercial programs include Microsoft Azure, Amazon Web Services (AWS), commercial healthcare programs, commercial farming programs, etc. The five Program Management (PM) fundamentals mentioned above can be tailored to develop an effective program LC for any program groups and related program types, as described in **Figure 1**. Based on the five PM fundamentals, Ref. [6] and Tien M. Nguyen [7] have discussed and presented the program LC associated with traditional DoD and defense ACT program types with budgets greater than 100 M USD (US dollars) and less than 100 M USD, respectively. To manage each of the program phases specified in program LC, the program managers apply technical and management skills and knowledge, decision support tools, program management processes and techniques to define, plan, execute, and monitor desired program activities to achieve required project requirements.

As pointed out in Carayannis et al. [8], during 1900s–1950s, the program managers leveraged advanced telecommunication systems to gain better communications among the workers and managers allowing for effective resource allocation and mobility. As a result, the automobile manufacturing production schedule had been shortening with enhanced project monitoring and management. Thus, technology has played an important role in improving program planning, execution, monitoring, and management. This chapter also addresses existing state-of-the-art machine learning and artificial intelligent (ML-AI) technology enablers and related PM trends in the improvement of PM activities.

2. Program management fundamentals

As described in Section 1, programs and related projects can be classified into three groups, including DePG, CiPG, and CoPG. As shown in **Figure 1**, for each of these groups, there are different program types associated with it. In general, for DePG, there are several program types, including traditional DoD programs, advanced defense concept technology programs, and DoD Rapid Acquisition Programs. Tien M. Nguyen [7] has addressed the program planning and management (PPM) for the defense advanced concept technology (ACT) programs and further classified the ACT programs into four categories. These categories include ACT Demonstration (ACTD), Defense Advanced Research Projects Agency (DARPA), advanced Contract Research and Development (CRAD), and Small Business Innovation Research and Small Business Technology Transfer (SBIR/STTR) programs [7]. Recently, due to the dynamic of the adversary threats to and rapid changes in technology, DoD has developed a new acquisition program type, which is referred to as rapid acquisition program. This program type focuses on the development of defense systems using rapid acquisition (rapid acquisition LC (RALC)). As discussed in Ref. [9], the proposed RALC requires a new and innovative acquisition framework and processes. Depending on the defense needs, an ACT program can use RALC to acquire a new and innovative technology for an existing defense system. It is important to point out that the characteristics of the program group and associated types will dictate the development of program LCs for acquiring and deploying a desired product or item. The program type's characteristics are the key driver for the tailoring of the five PM fundamentals and related frameworks to construct an efficient program LC. This section describes and discusses the PM fundamentals framework and how one can tailor this framework to generate or select an efficient program LC for a specified program type. **Figure 2** depicts the tailoring process for the program management fundamentals framework to construct an efficient program LC. The section focuses on the DePG and CiPG and provides examples of existing program LCs for traditional DoD and NASA programs. As shown in **Figure 2**, a program LC consists of the five program fundamentals (conceptual, planning, execution, monitoring, and program closing phases) which are the key components of a program LC. From the Government or a buyer perspective, it is important to develop a program acquisition LC to acquire (buy) a new product or item to fill the needs. These program fundamentals should be tailored to align with the Government's needs and associated program's characteristics. The following sections describe the objectives and common practices of these program fundamentals and discuss how we can tailor them to generate an effective program LC.

2.1 Conceptual phase

This conceptual phase is the first phase of the program management fundamentals framework, and it is also referred to as the initial phase. This initial phase is deliberate and features methodological goal setting [10]. Regardless of the program groups and related program types, the objective of this phase is about finding out stakeholders' needs to justify and seeking the approval for the identified effort to acquire a system or an item of interest. To achieve this objective, the program manager requires to understand the required scope of work, budget, and schedule of the effort. For DePG and CiPD, the program manager will approach this phase differently depending on the contractor or Government perspective. From the Government perspective, the program manager must understand the agency objectives and national goals along with the warfighter needs (i.e., stakeholders) and related defense capability needs to

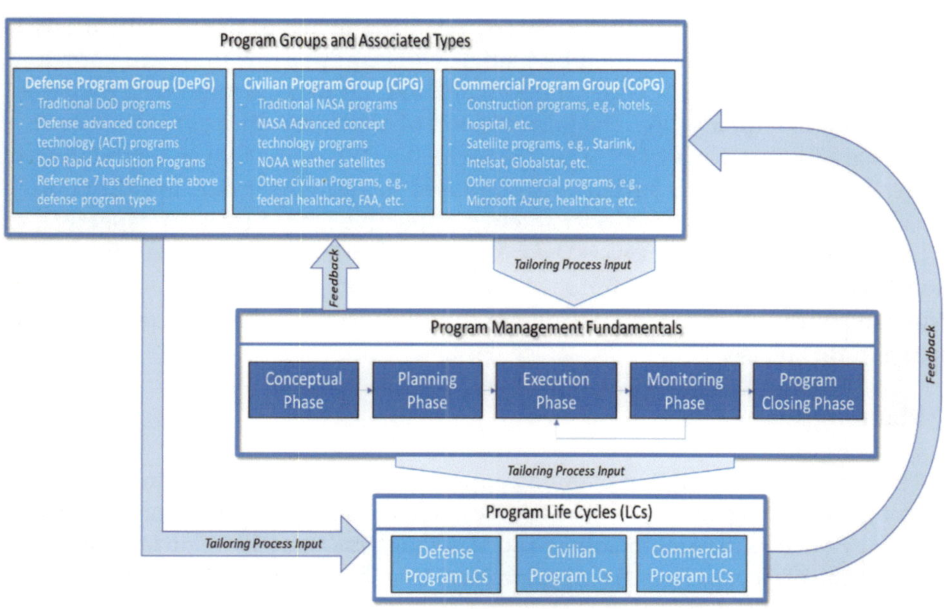

Figure 2.
Program management fundamentals and tailoring process for generating efficient program life cycle.

generate the program roadmap from the conceptual phase to program closing phase. From the contractor perspective, the program manager requires to understand the contractor's business area and the Government[1] program or capability roadmaps.

In practice, for DePG and CiPG, the contractor program manager usually "does not wait" for the request for proposal (RFP) or the broad announcement agency (BAA) to be published, he/she will work with the Government counterpart to shape the RFP/BAA. The focus of understanding of his/her (a.k.a. contractor) business is fundamental for tailoring the concept technology projects/programs for success. The simplest of tools for understanding the contractor's business is the Strength-Weaknesses-Opportunities-Threats (SWOT) analysis. This analysis frequently yields the strengths of the contractor organization, and they can be capitalized on when aligned with a customer's technology roadmap/capability roadmap. And to the extent that the contractor's business recognizes a technology or a capability "trajectory," these can frequently serve as the starting point for the business-customer alignment. In practice, shaping the RFPs/BAAs is a useful practice, especially in the case of DARPA interactions. DARPA's charter is currently expressed as "Creating Breakthrough Technologies and Capabilities for National Security." Originally chartered in response to the Sputnik incident and the Space Race during the Cold War, DARPA's top-level responsibility has not changed, i.e., "avoiding technological surprise in national defense," but DARPA's focus shifts periodically with the propagation of nascent technology waves.[2] A key tool for exploring potential programs with DARPA is the Heilmier Catechism (a.k.a. Heilmier Questions) [11]. It has been said that the Heilmier Catechism is a sort of "recipe" for managing innovation in technology-driven domains and related businesses. An example of a "do not wait for the RFP/BAA" approach is that of "Urgent Needs," frequently expressed as Urgent Operational Needs (UONs) or Joint Urgent Operational Needs (JUONs). The Defense Acquisition University (DAU) defines these as: "Urgent Operational Need (UON) – Capability requirements identified as impacting an ongoing or anticipated contingency operation. If left unfulfilled, UONs result in capability gaps potentially resulting in loss of life or critical mission failure" [12, 13]. When validated by a single DoD component, these are known as DoD component UONs. DoD components, in their own terminology, may use a different name for a UON. The Joint version of UONs recognizes that multiple services are in view for a UON, and hence the JUON designation and validation of the need by a joint force's authority, as opposed to a single service. For the commercial program group, the Government perspective is the buyer's perspective, and the contractor perspective is the seller's perspective. The extension from DePG and CiPD to CoPD is straightforward for the conceptual phase. The characteristics associated with the commercial program type will be the key for the program goal setting in this phase.

2.2 Planning phase

The conventional program planning approach is to identify the desired program planning and management (PPM) activities (a.k.a. tasks) and communicate the plan of these PPM tasks to team members and stakeholders. This PPM plan lays out the "how" of the project so that the program team members understand what they need

---

[1] From the contractor's point of view, this is also referred to as customer.

[2] This explains the recent interest in AI/ML applications for defense.

to do throughout the program LC. During this phase, the program manager develops work breakdown structure (WBS), budget and schedules, anticipating risks, and planning how to manage and mitigate the anticipated risks.

An innovative departure from the conventional program planning technique is described in Tien M. Nguyen [7]. Tien M. Nguyen [7] presents an application of Zachman framework to the program planning phase, especially applicable to DePG and CiPG. The genesis of this approach to planning stemmed from a realization pertaining to technical architecture frameworks, specifically DoD Architecture Framework (DoDAF) [14], which is commonly mandated for defense programs exhibiting complex operational environments. The realization, in a simplified form, is that DoDAF tends to be prescriptive; in contrast, small Research and Development (R&D) programs with budgets less than 50 M USD need to discover the answer to the question "what architectural views matter are impactful for this program?". The use of a Zachman architectural framework is superior in assisting with obtaining this answer quickly before one runs off and expends resources on a stack of conforming DoDAF views, which may not be helpful to the project/program. Although the proposed program planning framework is proposed for the DePG and CiPG with related ACT program types, it is also applicable to CiPG and related types. Regardless of the program group perspective, the program manager can use the proposed Zachman framework for ACT program planning shown in Table 1 of Tien M. Nguyen [7] to develop an effective PPM plan during the planning phase. As pointed out in Tien M. Nguyen [7], one of the key PPM activities is to identify the cost, technical, and program management risks and a plan to balance out these risks by identifying potential risk mitigation techniques. In practice, the program manager is also required to identify potential opportunities associated with these identified risks. The risks, opportunities, and mitigation approaches should be thoroughly analyzed and understood before the program enters the execution phase.

2.3 Execution phase

The execution phase usually occurs after the source selection, i.e., after the government or a buyer selects the best contractor or a seller to perform the contract. Again, regardless of the program group/type perspectives, for this phase, the program manager will put the PPM plan into action. The key approach for implementing this phase is to ensure "resources allocation" to execute the plan. The execution phase starts with a program kick-off where the program manager officially allocates the required program resources and ensures all team leads and their team members receive the resources that they need to have to do their jobs. In general, the resources include allocated budget, program documentations, configuration management, team development and arrangement, required member of technical staff (MTS), stakeholder engagement, quality assurance activities, and program schedule forecasting. The program manager actively works with the program leads to coordinate and assess how the program is running. During this phase, the government and contractor program managers will execute the approved government and contractor PPM plans, respectively. The status of executing these plans will be reported to the government and contractor stakeholders accordingly. In practice, for DePG and CiPG, the contractor stakeholders will also include the government counterparts. Similarly, the seller stakeholders will include the buyer for CoPG.

2.4 Monitoring phase

For DePG and CiPG, the contractor program manager manages the contractor team and monitors the health of the program by tracking the cost, schedule, MTS, technical performance, and program risks based on a set of "success criteria" defined for each program milestone and associated inch-stone. The program status and required program data will be reported to all stakeholders.

For the Government perspective, in addition to executing and managing the government team, the government program manager is also required to monitor the contractor progress. The objective is to ensure that the contractor team progresses according to the contractor program plan approved by all stakeholders. In practice, the execution and monitoring phases occur simultaneously and the contractor gets paid from the government as the program progresses. It's important to recognize up front that Execution and Monitoring (phases) need to be simultaneous; they need to go hand-in-hand. There is an element of "pay as you go" in this approach since the program management functions oftentimes "learn as they go" in the course of ACT projects. The simplest way to incorporate this into the execution phase is via an execution cadence with regular monitoring program metrics and program progress including monthly cadence with a weekly, focused check-in (program progress reviews).

In conjunction with simultaneous Execution and Monitoring, program management needs to periodically ask the question "has the success criteria changed or does it remain the same?" The process of "learn as you go" with ACT types of projects occasionally results in the realization that the target end point and/or the goals have shifted. Early recognition of this situation, and sharing the realization with the customer organization, may result in a shift of a Statement of Work (SOW) and an associated re-baseline of the program plan to align program segments (or phase) with the new objectives.

A key success factor for implementing this phase is to choose appropriate tools and techniques to monitor and disseminate the required program performance metrics. Concerning the DePG and CiPG programs, the Earn Value Management (EVM) system and associated tools are required to monitor the program cost, schedule, and associated program risks [7, 15, 16]. As indicated in Table 5 of Ref. [7], the DePG programs are required to fully implement the EVM system and tools when the programs' budgets exceed 50 M USD. As indicated in Refs. [15, 16], NASA (and NOAA) programs also followed the same EVM requirements as the DePG programs, i.e., full EVM system implementation and tools are required for NASA when the programs' budgets exceed 50 M USD. The extension to CoPG is straightforward, except that the use of EVM system and related tools is not the mandatory requirement. The monitoring approach and related tools will be selected depending on the program's characteristics and related success criteria.

2.5 Program closing phase

In general, the program closing phase is defined as a formal closing process marking the end of the program. In practice, depending on the program groups, the program closing phase can be different. For a traditional program in DePG or CiPG, closing a program can be (i) a delivery of an asset (e.g., a satellite system or a ground satellite tracking station), (ii) holding a final program review to discuss how it went, (iii) archiving program records, and (iv) celebrating the completion of a program. For ACT program in DePG or CiPG, closing a program can be a

DOI: http://dx.doi.org/10.5772/intechopen.113063

transition of a developed technology into a program of record or an existing traditional program [7]. The program closing phase will be tailored for CoPG programs, and the program closing phase is expected to be similar to those for DePG and CiPG programs, and they will be tailored to meet the needs of the buyer.

3. Program life cycles and management approaches for defense, civilian, and commercial programs

Sections 3.1 and 3.2 describe the program LCs for typical DePG and CiPG programs with an emphasis on DoD and NASA traditional and ACT programs, respectively. Additionally, these sections also discuss the DoD and NASA program management approaches to manage and execute the existing program LCs.

3.1 Defense applications

For traditional program type, DoD has tailored the five program fundamentals and developed a very efficient and proven program acquisition LC for acquiring complex defense systems and related technical items to meet their mission critical needs [6, 17–19]. **Figure 3** describes a typical acquisition program LC for DoD traditional programs. Many space-based programs have successfully used this program acquisition LC to acquire complex defense satellite communication (SATCOM), satellite sensing, and global positioning satellite systems. At high level, the LC includes the pre-acquisition and post-acquisition phases. The pre-acquisition phase consists of the tailored version of the conceptual and planning phases to ensure (i) alignment with DoD mission needs and (ii) reduction in the overall acquisition risks. The post-acquisition phase includes the tailored version of the execution, monitoring, and program

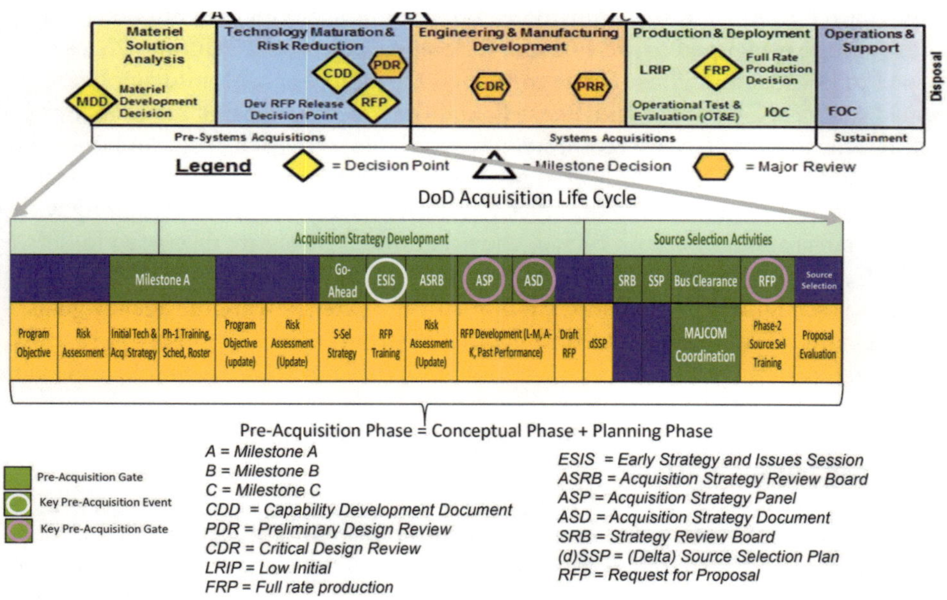

Figure 3.
Acquisition program life cycle for DoD traditional programs.

closing phases to ensure (i) the acquired system deliver the right defense capabilities meeting the warfighter needs and (ii) the manufacturing and deployment risks.

As shown in **Figure 3**, the pre-acquisition phase is also referred to as pre-systems acquisitions, which includes the Milestone A, the acquisition strategy, and the source selection activities. The post-acquisition consists of Milestone B, Milestone C, Initial Operating Capability (IOC) deployment, Full Operating Capability (FOC) deployment, and Disposal activities. The objective(s) and program requirements and related success criteria for each LC phase are discussed in Refs. [17, 20, 21]. To achieve the objectives of the pre- and post-acquisition phases, DoD has also developed a sophisticated and well-structured program management approach to allow the program manager to manage, execute, and monitor these activities with minimum program risk and maximum program opportunity [21, 22]. The program LC shown in **Figure 3** has been developed for acquiring defense products. For acquiring commercial products, DoD has tailored the program LC and program management approaches to align with the scope of work and mission requirements for commercial products [22].

For defense ACT programs, the program LC is very similar to the DoD tradition programs with the four distinct phases, including concept, pre-acquisition, post-acquisition, and transition phases [7]. The concept phase is not part of the pre-acquisition, post-acquisition, and pre-acquisition phases which have been tailored to align with the scope of work and related PPM activities for the defense programs. Ref. [7] discusses the program management approaches and desired PPM activities associated with program planning, program risk assessment, balance cost-technical-and-program risks, and EVM for defense ACT programs.

3.2 Civilian applications

Like DoD, NASA has also developed an efficient and proven program acquisition LC for acquiring complex systems and related technical items to meet their mission critical needs [23]. Similar to DoD, NASA has tailored the five program fundamentals to align with NASA needs for acquiring complex systems for civilian missions. The Concept Phase is mapped to pre-Phase A (concept studies), the Planning Phase mapped to Phase A and Phase B, the combined Execution-and-Monitoring Phase mapped to Phase C-Phase D-and-Phase E, and the Program Closing Phase mapped to Phase F. The objective(s) and requirements associated with each program LC phase are described in Ref. [23]. The desired program management approaches and related PPM activities that can be used to achieve objective(s) and requirements along with success criteria associated with each of the program LC phase are discussed in Refs. [15, 16, 23, 24]. The extension from the defense DoD ACT programs to NASA ACT programs is straightforward. The key factors for the extension are the agency goals/objectives and related mission requirements. The program management approaches and desired PPM activities should be tailored according to NASA goals/objectives and mission requirements.

3.3 Commercial applications

For commercial applications ranging from a simple housing construction project to a complex satellite program like Starlink, there is no existing program LC available that can fit this range of applications. From the buyer's perspective, the program LC can always be derived from the tailoring of the five program fundamentals, as described in **Figure 2**. As shown in **Figure 2**, the input to this tailoring process is the required characteristics associated with a specific type of program that is required to develop an efficient program LC for acquiring a desired product or item. Usually some of the key program characteristics are the buyer's objectives, the program's/project's requirements, and the desired time for the product delivery. These program characteristics will dictate how one will tailor the five program fundamentals to ensure the (i) alignment with each of the program LC phases and (ii) program management approaches and related PPM activities are developed to execute and manage effectively at each phase, i.e., meeting the success criteria for each phase. It should be noted here that the program success criteria should be developed in response to the program objectives and related requirements. The tailoring process also requires the buyer acquisition team to have a deep understanding of the key program management (PM) areas and associated PM disciplines [14]. As pointed out in Ref. [14], there are nine key PM areas and twenty PM disciplines. The nine key PM areas include (i) PM Area 1—Enterprise, Organizational, and Program Goals Management, (ii) PM Area 2—Overall Financial and Program Cost Planning and Management, (iii) PM Area 3—Overall Program Risk Management, (iv) PM Area 4—Overall Program Schedule Planning and Management, (v) Technical Performance Management, (vi) Quality Assurance (QA) Management, (vii) Program Team Forming and Program Team Management, (viii) Internal and External Program Team Communications Management, and (ix) Program Integration Management. The twenty PM discipline areas across the four PM areas include (i) Program goals management, (ii) Systems engineering related to the systems/products/services being acquired, (iii) Specialized engineering related to the products and services being acquired, (iv) Contracts and legal dealing with contractors, suppliers, and stakeholders, (v) Program Financial management, (vi) Business and marketing practices for the newly acquired systems/products/services, (vii) System/product/service technical requirements and associated performance risk management, (viii) System/product/service cost planning and management, (ix) Program schedule planning and management, (x) Program cost planning and management, (xi) System/product/service risk planning and management, (xii) Program risk planning and management, (xiii) System test and evaluation, (xiv) Logistics and supply chain management, (xv) Production, Quality, and Manufacturing (PQM), (xvi) Program and system intelligence and security management, (xvii) Program and system software management, (xviii) Program and system configuration management, (xix) Program and system information technology, and (xx) Other Specialty Program Planning and Management. Note that from the seller's perspective, the program manager and his/her team are required to address the buyer's program LC and related requirements along with required success criteria at each program LC phase.

4. Current program management trends and conclusion

Gartner's research predicted that by 2030, 80% of project management tasks will be (i) run by machine learning and artificial intelligence (ML-AI), (ii) driven by big data, and (iii) processed using natural language processing language[3]. It also predicted certain aspects of the program management will be disrupted, including (i) selection and prioritization of alternative solutions, choices of products, etc., (ii) organizations streamlining and optimizing the role of the project management office

[3] Available from: https://hbr.org/2023/02/how-ai-will-transform-project-management.

(PMO), (iii) faster project definition, and improving project planning and reporting, (iv) virtual project assistant, (v) advanced testing and software, and (vi) creating a new role for program manager. Currently, industry has investigated approaches to integrate program management practices with emerging data and decision sciences (DDS) [14], which is referred to as PM-DDS integration. As discussed in Ref. [14], the key DDS technology enablers that can enhance the program planning, execution, and monitoring during a program LC include big data analytics, artificial intelligence, machine learning, deep learning, neural networks, and artificial intelligent. Tables 1 and 2 of Ref. [14] provide a summary of the proposed PM-DDS integration approaches for integrating DDS processes and ML-AI tools for program cost and schedule management, respectively.

For defense program management, the dynamic of the adversary threats will be the key factor driving the program LC and associated program management approach to ensure the system to be acquired is effective against the threats. Currently, DoD defense programs tend to be smaller in budget with a smaller system that is adaptable to the threats. Concurrently, the rapid acquisition LC is preferable for these smaller programs. For civilian and commercial program management, the rapid change in technology will be the key factor driving the program LC and program management approach. The program LC should be flexible and adaptable to the change in technology. In practice, a majority of defense ACT projects fall below the 50 M USD threshold, and frequently they fall below $20 M USD. EVM is not often mandated in these cases, and subsequently the question becomes, "what aspects of EVM are useful for managing small value ACT programs?" The current trend is to encourage the program manager to seek out and to select the EVM metrics that will be of value for managing and monitoring this type of program. "Tailor/tailor/tailor" is a mantra that can be used in order to prevent overburdening the small value program/project. Tailoring the nonmandatory EVM to match the program scope, limited key performance parameters (KPPs), key performance attributes (KPAs), etc., and then applying that tailored EVM regularly will often yield basic benefits to a program management team.

It is our hope that by reading this chapter, the reader can gain a deeper understanding of the other program management chapters presented in this book. It describes the five program management fundamentals along with the three program groups (DePG, CiPG, and CoPG) and associated program types. A high-level tailoring process presented in **Figure 2** explains how one can tailor the five program fundamentals to generate an effective program acquisition LC. To illustrate the tailoring process, the program acquisition LC for traditional program types is provided for DePG and CiPG. The extension to the development of an effective CoPG program LC is also discussed at high level allowing the readers to gain insight into the existing DoD and NASA program LCs for acquiring complex systems. Finally, the current trends in (i) the use of the state-of-the-art ML-AI technology enablers to enhance program planning, execution, and monitoring, and (ii) the program management practices are also presented.

Conflict of interest

The authors declare no conflict of interest. The opinions expressed in this chapter are those of the authors and they are not endorsed by California State University, Fullerton, California (CSUF) or Aerospace Corp. or Raytheon.

Additional information

Tien M. Nguyen is Adjunct Research Professor, and also, with The Aerospace Corporation. A Raytheon retired Engineering Fellow, Certified Level-5/Level-6 Program Manager, EVMS Level-2, and Six-Sigma.

Mark B. Hammond serves as a member of the CCAM Advisory Board, CSUF. Also, with The Raytheon Company.

Author details

Tien M. Nguyen[1*] and Mark B. Hammond[2]

1 Center for Computational and Applied Mathematics (CCAM), California State University, Fullerton, California (CSUF), California, USA

2 CCAM, CSUF, California, USA

*Address all correspondence to: tmnguyen57@fullerton.edu

References

[1] Heagney J. Fundamentals of Project Management. Fifth ed. Nashville: HarperCollins Leadership Publisher; 2022. Available from: https://vuthedudotorg.files.wordpress.com/2015/10/fundamentalsof-project-management-0814437362.pdf

[2] Kirsi H, Julkaisut L, editors. Project Management Handbook. Vantaa, Finland: Laurea Publications. Laurea University of Applied Sciences. Available from: https://www.researchgate.net/publication/320101542_project_management_handbook

[3] A Guide to the Project Management Body of Knowledge (PMBOK® Guide). Seventh Edition. Newtown Square, Pennsylvania: Project Management Institute. 2020. ISBN: 1628256648. Available from: http://www.cs.bilkent.edu

[4] Johntalaguit. Basic guidelines for program planning and management. Copyright by McNamara C. Authenticity Consulting, LLC. 02 Aug 2023. Available from: https://management.org/programmanagement/business-programs.htm

[5] AcqNotes Website. Program Management. Program Management Overview. 3 May 2021. Available from: https://acqnotes.com/acqnote/careerfields/program-management-overview

[6] AcqNotes Website. Acquisition Topics: Acquisition Process. Acquisition Process Overview. AcqNotes Quick Sheet, Defense Acquisition System. 2022. Available from: https://acqnotes.com/wp-content/uploads/2017/08/Defense-Acquisition-System-Quick-Sheet.pdf

[7] Nguyen TM. Program planning and management for defense advanced concept technology programs. In Edited Volume: Project Management – New Trends and Applications. 24 Sep 2023. DOI: 10.5772/intechopen.112864. Available from: https://www.intechopen.com/online-first/88152

[8] Carayannis EG, Kwak YH, Anbari FT, editors. The Story of Managing Projects: An Interdisciplinary Approach. New York City, New York: Bloomsbury Academic; 30 Jan 2005. ISBN: 1567205062

[9] AcqNotes Website. Acquisition Process, Rapid Acquisitions. 24 Jul 2021. Available from: https://acqnotes.com/acqnote/acquisitions/rapid-acquisitions

[10] Adobe Experience Cloud Blog. Adobe experience cloud team. The Fundamentals of Project Management. 21 Apr 2023. Available from: https://business.adobe.com/blog/basics/project-management-fundamentals

[11] Defense Advanced Research Projects Agency (DARPA) Website. The Heilmeier Catechism. Available from: https://www.darpa.mil/work-with-us/heilmeier-catechism

[12] Monster the M*A*S*H Wiki. M*A*S*H television series characters. 1970 M*A*S*H TV Series Main Characters. Available from: https://mash.fandom.com/wiki/Walter_%22Radar%22_O%E2%80%99Reilly#:~:text=Corporal%20Walter%20Eugene%20%22Radar%22%20O,*A*S*H

[13] Defense Acquisition University (DAU) Website. Urgent Capability Acquisition (UCA). Types of

Urgent Operational Needs (UONs). Available from: https://aaf.dau.edu/aaf/uca/uons/#:~:text=Joint%20Urgent%20Operational%20Need%20(JUON,impacting%20an%20ongoing%20contingency%20operation.&text=These%20types%20of%20UONs%20are%20defined%20in%20CJCS%20Instruction%205123.01H

[14] ACqNotes Website. Acquisition Topics. Acquisition Index: JCIDS Process Overview. Available from: https://acqnotes.com/acqnote/acquisitions/joint-urgent-operational-need-juon

[15] Nguyen TM, Nguyen JDT, Nguyen MTN, Lee CH, Nguyen T. Program Management Integrated with Data and Decision Sciences. In Edited Volume: Project Management - New Trends and Applications. DOI: 10.5772/intechopen.109964. Available from: https://www.intechopen.com/online-first/86949

[16] NASA Website. NASA EVM (Earned Value Management). Available from: https://www.nasa.gov/evm

[17] NASA Website. NASA EVM Implementation Handbooks. 25 Jul 2023. Available from: https://www.nasa.gov/evm/handbooks

[18] DOD DIRECTIVE 5000.01. The Defense Acquisition System. 9 Sep 2020. Available from: https://www.esd.whs.mil/Portals/54/Documents/DD/issuances/dodd/500001p.pdf

[19] Nguyen TM, Guillen A. Resilient Program and Technical Baseline (PTB) - Part 1: A Resilient PTB Framework for Future Space Systems, Aerospace Report NO. TOR-2015-01917. July 9, 2015

[20] Nguyen TM, Guillen AT, Matsunaga SS. A resilient program technical baseline framework for future space systems. Proceedings of SPIE. 2015;**9469**:946907-946901

[21] Cooley WT, Ruhm BC. A Guide for DOD Program Managers. Fort Belvoir, Virginia: Defense Acquisition University (DAU) Press; Dec 2014. Available from: https://acqnotes.com/wp-content/uploads/2014/09/A-Guide-for-DoD-Program-Managers.pdf

[22] Department of Defense. Risk, Issue, and Opportunity Management Guide for Defense Acquisition Programs. Office of the Deputy Assistant Secretary of Defense for Systems Engineering. 3030 Defense Pentagon/. Washington, D.C. Jan 2017. Available from: https://acqnotes.com/wp-content/uploads/2017/07/DoD-Risk-Issue-and-Opportunity-Management-Guide-Jan-2017.pdf

[23] NASA Systems Engineering Handbook. NASA SP-2016-6105 Rev2. Office of the Chief Engineer. Washington, DC: NASA Headquarters; Dec 2007. Available from: https://www.nasa.gov/wp-content/uploads/2018/09/nasa_systems_engineering_handbook_0.pdf

[24] ACQUISITION.Gov website. Part 12 - Acquisition of Commercial Products and Commercial Services. FAC Number: 2023-05. Effective Date: 22 Sep 2023. Available from: https://www.acquisition.gov/far/part-12

Section 2

Project Management Maturity Modeling

Chapter 2

A Conceptual Project Management Maturity Model for the South African Power Sector

Natisha Gareeb and Pantaleo Mutajwaa Daniel Rwelamila

Abstract

The study proposes a conceptual model for measuring project management maturity (PMM) in the SA's power sector. While generic models are available this paper aims to bridge the gap and develop one for the power sector. The research question this paper is trying to answer is: "*What are the parameters that make up the conceptual model for PMM in the SA power sector?*" The study is based on a literature review. The authors reviewed the relevant journals to search for key parameters for measuring PMM. The study proposes a conceptual model for measuring PMM in the SA's power sector. The focus of this paper was limited to the peer reviewed articles and journals.

Keywords: project management, organisational project maturity, projects management maturity, power sector, organisational competencies

1. Introduction

History indicates that modern project management (PM) developed in the Second World War and have developed in some engineering industries. Later year's PM has been adapted in research and development and pharmaceutical industries. Cooke-Davies and Arzymanow [1] found that "industries of origin" have developed more advanced in PM than disciplines that have started later. Knowledge and processes are important contributors to PM capability but are not the only important elements to assess an organisations project management maturity (PMM) [2]. A total approach of what organisational PMM needs to be applied in organisations. Research conducted by Skulmoski [3] affirm there is a lack of research on the competencies most important for certain types of projects. Cooke-Davies and Arzymanow [1] study confirms that the maturity of PM across different industries indicates that a single model cannot be applied in all cases. Jugdev and Thomas [4] states that maturity models are not difficult to imitate and do not lead to sustained competitive advantage; however, they do lead to temporary competitive advantage for some firms and competitive parity for most. Jugdev and Thomas [4] also comment that most maturity models are not firm specific and can be duplicated. Competitors can replicate maturity models because they lack some of the durability characteristics. Killen and Hunt [5] suggest that project and portfolio capabilities must be tailored to the environment and implemented and adjusted over time and that best practice studies indicate correlations between practices and outcomes.

One way the effectiveness of the PM capability in the power sector can be assessed is through the PMM models. This paper presents the key factors that contribute to PMM in the SA power sector. While generic models are available, this paper aims to bridge this gap that exists in literature and develop a conceptual model for the SA's power sector.

The following is a summary of gaps that exist on PMM in current literature review:

- Organisational culture was largely under examined in PM research [6].
- Further empirical studies should build for the mechanisms by which superior PM practices can be developed over time [1]. The authors focused on how PM have developed differently when it was fostered and formed in different environments.
- Barber [7] indicate that the internally generated risks seem to relate inversely to PMM and that an opportunity exists of internally generated risks would be used to drive organisational development.
- Crawford [8] studies on the relationship between PM standards and effective workplace performance find that there is no empirical research that supports or indeed questions the assumptions which is inherent in the way standards have been developed by expert practitioner.
- Studies by De Bruin et al. [9] and Hulya [6] suggest that further research in PMM and how the relation to project performance need to be investigated.
- Killen and Hunt [5] suggest that project and portfolio capabilities must be tailored to the environment and implemented and adjusted over time and that best practice studies indicate correlations between practices and outcomes.
- A single model cannot be applied in all cases across different industries [1].
- Viana et al. [10] indicate in their research that organizational project management maturity models (PMMMs) have been criticized as being ineffective as firms continue to face difficulties in improving their PM practices.
- Alam et al. [11] indicate that there was a lack of organisational factors in PMMM, and the social-cultural skills required by project managers managing projects successfully are under examined.
- The authors Mahasneh and Thabet [12] in their study indicate that there is a social cultural skills gap among construction school graduates indicating that the gap is a result of various factors such as lack of consensus, clear vision, standardization and common language on the social cultural skills gap between industry and academia.
- Marando [13] suggest in their studies that many project managers are not able to successfully lead projects due to a deficiency of the necessary social cultural skills, interpersonal skills include leadership, communication, negotiation, expectations management, influencing, problem-solving, and decision-making.

Considering the following gaps that exist in PMMM it is therefore relevant to form a conceptual model for SA's power sector. Therefore, the purpose of this study is to perform an extensive literature review to determine the key parameters that contribute to PMM in the SA power sector. The research objectives include the following:

- Determine the gaps that is existing in current literature on PMM.
- Determine the key parameters important for PMM.
- Propose a conceptual model for PMM in the SA power sector.

This paper is divided into five sections. Section one provided the gaps that exist on PMM in current literature and section two provides the literature review. The research methodology is provided in section three. The analysis and discussion are provided in section four and the conclusion is provided in section five.

2. Literature review: parameters that affect PMM

To understand the concept of project maturity further, several definitions of the concept will be investigated as followers:

- Hartman and Skulmoski [14] discuss that the maturity of PM tackles the following issues: The competence of the practitioner tries to measure it on a generalised scale and to understand the working environment of the practitioner assesses the business for which the project is being done.
- Schlichter [15] use the word maturity to imply that capabilities must be grown to produce repeatable success in PM.
- According to Andersen and Jessen [16] project maturity indicate that the organisation is perfectly conditioned to deal with its projects and can be used as an indication of or a measurement of the organisation's ability to use projects for different purposes.
- Ibbs and Kwak [17] define PM maturity as a level of sophistication that indicates organisation's current PM practices, processes, and performances.
- There are also links in literature that suggest maturity models also reflect and increasing desire to link PM competence to corporate achievement [4].

Gareeb and Rwelamila [18] paper reveals that most of the models assess PM capability against bodies of knowledge and indicates that there was no model that could be used for the SA power sector. A total approach of what organisational PM maturity will be applied in this research.

Improving the maturity of an organisation was found to be extremely correlated with project success [19]. Earlier research focuses narrowly on the definition of project success as project cost, time, and quality but current literature has adapted this definition to include other factors. There is limited research on the strength of the relationship between the critical factors and success criteria, and even less analysis of the causal effect between these factors and the performance of projects [20]. Han et al. [21] address the distinction between success factors and success criteria and state the following: "*Success factors are factors that influence, constitute as well as determine the success of a project.*" Earlier authors suggest that the success factors (critical success factors/project success factors) are defined as those few key factors necessary to reach goals [22]. Whereas success criteria are more related to the perceived performance based on the formal iron triangle such as time, cost, quality. Although the success criteria are difficult to define because many authors add other dimensions to the success criteria which include customer satisfaction as a success dimension or other dimensions. Two important aspects of project success are related to the technical side of the project and the second aspect relates to the "soft skill "henceforth referred to as social-cultural skills. Crawford and Pollack [23] comment that defining the technical and the social-cultural factors is not always clear. The social-cultural issues have been identified as the key success factors in PM and can have a high impact on the project [24]. Azim et al. [25] focus on the cause(s) of complexity in projects which lists three factors and includes process, product, and people. The author's results indicate the underline importance of "people" not only as factor attributing to project complexity, but also as a key element to project success, thus also highlighting the benefits of social-cultural skills in effective PM. Mishra et al. [26] confirm that despite large work in this area no definite set of factors have been agreed upon that may be due to the organisational or cultural differences through-out the world. Ofori [27] state that generally, critical success factors are a set of project variables or factors that strongly correlate to project success, and whose maximisation or minimisation, depending on whether they are favourable or unfavourable, will lead to project success. Ofori [27] reveals that there is no consensus on what social-cultural factors contribute to project success and indicate that organisational and social-cultural aspects do influence project success because in different project environments different factors are more critical.

The need for developing a conceptual model for the PMMM can have the following benefits:

- Langston and Ghanbaripour [28] indicate that any PM environment needs to support the business for successful project, program and/or portfolio delivery. The author indicates that the basis for achieving consistent excellence in PM is assisted by mature organisational systems and processes.

- Viana et al. [10] point out that PMMMs have significantly contributed to the field of PM as they heighten awareness of competence to assess organizational PM maturity and that an essential input to support organizational development.

- Jugdev and Thomas [4] indicate that PMMM capture the codified knowledge but does not include the intangible assets and if they were included could lead to the competitive advantage of a firm or organisation. Thus, incorporating the correct social cultural factors could add to the competitive advantage of a PMMM.

- Zuo et al. [29] results indicated that social cultural skills of project managers significantly contributed to project success factors and hence the project success. Therefore, if these factors are not included in the PMMM a significant aspect is not included in PMMM assessments and measurement.

- Studies by Campana [30] indicates there is a large shift to recognize the importance of social cultural skills and indicates the critical importance of social cultural skills in PM.

- Assists to spot business or personal opportunities, and it gives advanced warning of significant threats [31].

- It aids in the investigation of the barriers and opportunities in sector and provides several obstacles to effective and efficient commerce [32].

- It reveals the direction of change within the business environment and thus assists shape change rather than work against it [31].

- It provides a framework for the correlation with the production technologies to determine the strengths and weakness of different production pathways. [33]

- Aids in avoidance of starting projects that are likely to fail [31].

- Assistance with assumptions when one enters a new country, region, or market, because it helps develop an objective view of this new environment [31].

2.1 Technical parameter required for success

The most traditional way to establish project success is measured by the technically which include time, cost, and quality [34]. Portny [35] define a project has been successful when it has produced the desired results within the established timeframe with the allotted resources and state that the following three factors are essential to create the greatest chances for successfully completing a project: a clear and specific agreed-upon statement of the desired outcomes, comprehensive lists of all people who are interested in (needed to support, and/or effected by your project) and a complete and detailed listing of all required project work. Browne and O'Donnabhain [36] identifies key issues and concepts relevant to client-project manager relationship using customer service, service quality and customer satisfaction. Hartman and Skulmoski [37] suggest that there are parallels between business and PM research and topics such as leadership, communication, teamwork, success and examining risks alignment. Although the focus of this section is to find technical factors affecting PM the social-cultural factors based on different studies are ranked high. Studies by Nguyen et al. [38] depict the ranking of twenty success factors and the critical success factors indicate that competent project manager, adequate funding throughout the project, multidisciplinary/competent project team commitment to the project, and the availability of resources are ranked extremely high. Again, the social-cultural aspects of the projects are also indicated in the study reveals that commitment to the project, top management support and continuous involvement of stakeholder do rank high as well. Research conducted by Yong and Mustaffa [39] indicates that two of the four factors identify category namely, effective allocation of manpower; urgency in meeting project deadline are of higher importance. The research indicates that financial problem such as delayed payments and financial difficulties are seen to be a major factor that causes delay in the construction project. **Table 1** represents the summary of the literature review that identifies the technical factors required for project success. With a list of several factors of understanding PM standards, risk methodology,

Technical factors	Reference
Project management standards and methodology *Technical specifications and performance **Tools and technique	Lam et al. [40]* Mishra et al. [26]**
Risk assessments methodology	Chen [41]; Besner and Hobbs [42]
Documentation management (keeping proper records) *Adequacy of design details	Nguyen et al. [38] Yong and Mustaffa [39]*
Scope and schedule management. Change control aspects and management *Control of contractor Schedule **Project progress and plans in place ***Project planning	Chen [41] Yong and Mustaffa [39]* Yong and Mustaffa [39]** Griffith [43]*** Zwikael and Globerson [44]*** Lam et al. [40] Mishra et al. [26]
Performance and quality requirements **Quality **Adequacy of design specification	Zwikael and Globerson [44] Schein [45] Yong and Mustaffa [39]** Lam et al. [40]* Roberts et al. [46] Chen [41]* Browne and O'Donnabhain [36] Leveson et al. [47]
Contract and legal management must be in place by the organisation	Ahsan [48]
Top management support *Aligned with the business/project objects thus obtaining top management support	Albu and Panzar [49]; Selders and Ma¨rkle [50]*; Mishra et al. [26] Ofori's [27]
Financial implications/funding and profitability for the organisation *Adequate Funding throughout the project **Financial capability of the client profitability	Nguyen et al. [38]* Yong and Mustaffa [39]** Lam et al. [40]

*The *, **, *** on each factor/theme corresponds to the reference for each.*

Table 1.
Summary of the technical parameter for project success.

documentation control management, understanding how to take make changes in the schedule as well considering the impact of the changes, performance and quality management, contract, legal aspects, top management support and financial management are important for a project manager from a technical side.

2.2 Social-cultural parameter required for success

Social-cultural issues include factors such as benefits, stakeholders, value management, and communications [51]. Studies by Mishra et al. [26] indicate that proper communication has been found a critical success factor in the success of a team. Vance's [52] study consisting of 1800+ system integrators list in Control Engineering's Automation Integrator Guide were asked to share their top tips for ensuring success of an automation project. This study indicated as much as 80% of the project's problems were due to lack of proper communication between the client and the integrator. Mishra et al. [26] study indicates that clearly goals and objectives were the number one ranking in their empirical study on project performance. Ofori [27] study indicate experience and competence of project personnel as ranked number four in their top factors for critical success. Kadefors [53] highlights the importance of trust and project success. Karlsen et al. [54] argue that trust is being particularly important in both organisations and projects, since it is viewed as an essential for stable relationships, vital for the maintenance of cooperation, fundamental for any exchange and necessary for even the most routine of everyday interactions. Pinto and Slevin [55] study also indicate that understanding the mission and goals to measure the outcome as an important success factor. Hartman and Skulmoski [37] depict that multi PM must include inter-project communication, priority setting, planning that align projects with and support corporate strategy. Thus, ensuring outcomes to be understood by the project team members and the criteria for measurement.

Table 2 represents the literature review that identifies the social-cultural factors related to project success. Within a list of several factors for project success are communication and understanding outcomes. Studies on project success identifies success factors, which include communication, clearly defined roles and responsibilities, project team competency and availability of resources, trust and understanding outcomes.

2.3 Organisational competencies

Zwikael [66] comments that different industries face different challenges while managing projects. The author refers to some examples like the software development organisations that must deal with high-technology uncertainty, while construction

Social-cultural factors	Reference
Communication *Clear Communication between client and contractor **Effective team members play a role in communication. ***Strong project commitment ****Communicating effectively on multicultural projects*	Mishra et al. [26]; Vance [52]*; Michalski [56]*; den Otter and Emmitt [57]**; Johannessen and Olsen [58]; Adenfelt [59]; Andersen et al. [60]***; Ochieng and Price [61]****; Zwikael and Globerson [44] Chen [41] Yong and Mustaffa [39]
Clearly defined roles and responsibilities	Portny [35]; Mishra et al. [26]
Project team Competencies and availability of resources *Availability of resources	Cooke-Davies [62] Cooke-Davies and Arzymanow [1] Ofori [27] Thia and Swierczek [20] Nguyen et al. [38]* Yong and Mustaffa [39]*
Trust *Between the client and contractor **Stable pool of project team members	Webber and Klimoski [63]* Pinto et al. [64]; Kadefors [53]; Maurer [65]*; Karlsen [54]
Understanding outcomes: of the project and each team member *Statement of outcomes and deliverables with key measurable criteria **Clear goals and objectives	Portny [35]*; Pinto and Slevin [55]; Hartman and Skulmoski [37] Mishra et al. [26]**

Table 2.
Summary of the social-cultural parameter for project success.

organisations that are usually more troubled with engineering and financial problems. Crawford [8] indicate that the competence of project personnel is important as they are having major impact on project performances and ultimately also impact the business performance. De Oliveria et al. [67] indicates that agility and flexibility represent the way to achieve organisational performance and that maximum project performance is accomplished when efforts are tied together to improve leadership factors and organisational factors. An important organisational success measure is the respondents perceived rate of project success of their organisations compared with competitors organisations in the same sector of activity [68]. Gareis and Huemann [69] indicates that PM competencies must describe, assess, and further develop for the organisation, teams, and individuals in the organisation. Brush et al. [70] describe the resource pyramid of value creation and indicate that firms can have a unique advantage when assets become valuable, rare, inimitable, and non-substitutable. Hartman and Skulmoski [14] state that elements that affect maturity will include technical, business, and social issues.

2.3.1 Strategic organisational PM

Albu and Panzar [49] state that maturity alignment is a concept referring to the extent to which the organisational components (strategy, structure, systems, processes, etc.) reflect similar or close maturity levels, acting in synergy towards the achievement of organisational objectives. Christenson and Walker [71] study concludes that project vision is a critical project success factor. The more immediate contribution remains demonstrating a protocol for getting project teams to focus on the project vision and the likely impact upon that for PM success. Fitsilis et al. [72] suggests that programmes and projects are recognised as one of the most important means of achieving organisations strategic plans. To become durably successful, an organisation should realise its maturity alignment [73]. PMM level cannot be attained or sustained if a certain level of organisational maturity is not reached [74]. Cooke-Davies et al. [75] argue that strategic drivers influence the nature of value expected from PM, and a PM system should be adapted to the specific strategic positioning of each organisation to deliver maximum value. Studies by Andersen et al. [76] found support for the proposition that there is a relationship between project perspectives applied in PM and formal organisational rationality. **Table 3** summaries the Strategic organisational factors.

Strategic Organisational PM	References
Aligning project objective with business objective *Scorecards **Project vision	Albu and Panzar [49]; Selders and Ma¨rkle [50]*; Christenson and Walker [71]**; Fitsilis et al. [72]; Meyer [73]; Andersen et al. [76]
Sustainability of the organisation and best practices *Strategic drivers	[74]; Gareis and Huemann [69]; Cooke-Davies et al. [75] Crawford [8]

Table 3.
Summary of strategic organisational PM.

2.3.2 Organisational culture

Cooke-Davies and Arzymanow [1] definition of organisational culture as: "*Refers to the underlying beliefs, values and principles that serve as a foundation for an organisations management practices and behaviour that both exemplify and reinforce those basic principles.*" Based on the literature review by Cooke-Davies and Arzymanow [1] two important factors on organisational culture is if the culture is unhelpful then it is important to change it and secondly, that irrespective of whether culture helps or hinders the effects of culture must be considered throughout the project. Cooke-Davies and Arzymanow [1] also suggest that the leadership style of a project manager needs to be adapted to the organisational culture and confirm through their literature review that there is a clear correlation between high trust and low cost, and between low trust and high cost. Thamhain [77] results shows that despite cultural differences among organisations a general agreement exists on the factors that drive team performance, one of the most striking finding is the large number of performance factors that is derived from the human side where organisational components that satisfy personal and professional needs seem to have a strong effect on cooperation, commitment, risk management, and ultimately drive overall team performance. Diallo and Thuillier [78] mentions that project success and success dimensions depend on project type and sector. Performance problems on technology-intensive projects involve largely management, behavioural and organisational issues, rather than technical complications [79, 80]. Dvir et al. [81] suggest that project success factors are not common for all projects; different types of projects are affected by different sets of success factors. Therefore, a project-specific approach is appropriate for following studies into the practice and theory of PM [82]. **Table 4** summaries the themes from literature for organisational culture.

Organisational Culture	References
Organisational culture that supports project management process	Cooke-Davies and Arzymanow [1]; Diallo and Thuillier [78]; Killen and Hunt [5]; Mishra et al. [26]; Roberts et al. [46]; Crawford [8]
Support employees to understand cultural diversity	Thamhain [77]; *Belassi and Tukel [79]; *Hartman and Ashrafi [80]; **Branson [83]; Andersen et al. [76]; Deal and Kennedy [84]; Diallo and Thuillier [78]
Organisational structures that support project	*Dvir et al. [81]; **Hyväri [82]; Mishra et al. [26]
Top management support for organisational project culture	Killen and Hunt [5]; Zwikael [66]; *Simons [85] **Cooke-Davies and Arzymanow [1];

Table 4.
Summary of organisational culture.

PESTLE	Analysis of SA's macro environment
Political	Baker [87] suggests that institutionally, the 2006 Electricity Regulation Act should govern the main activities of the electricity sector. However, influence on energy policy and planning is also exerted by SA's Power Sector Parastatal, Treasury, SA's Department of Public Enterprises, metropolitan and municipal governments, and the Inter Ministerial Committee on energy [87]. Besides these entities reducing the effect of the SA's Department of Energy and its regulator (NERSA), the influence of heavy private users (Energy Intensive User's Group) and coal suppliers cannot be ignored [87]. This describes a mix of highly influential political landscape in favour of specific entities that reduce the effect of proper regulation and create numerous policy uncertainties and delays remain. This does not allow for progress, including from energy independent power producers (IPPs) waiting to construct and connect their projects to the country's electric grid. Specific interference by political organisations to suppliers of energy have also been documented [87] and [88].
Economic	The economic policy on supply and demand of electricity falls within the ambit of the SA's Department of Energy and is well documented to be a major driver of growth, reducing poverty, and ensuring social well-being, even of industry [89]. However, lack of cohesive ownership and policy seems to be detracting from the major objectives of various stakeholders, resulting in lack of commitment [87].
Social	Skills remains a critical downfall of the planning, design, supply, and distribution of electricity, as cited by Baker [87] and the SA's Department of Energy [90]. Further, social development along empowerment of independent suppliers can only be addressed through policy.
Technological	SA's Power Sector Parastatal currently generates 95% of the country's electricity [87]. SA's Department of Energy [89] suggests that up to 30% of the country's generation is to come from IPPs, but Baker [87] suggests that the appropriate legislation was never enacted, and no private generation was incorporated to the grid. Most of the country's electricity originates from coal fired power plants in the northeast, many immediately adjacent to privately owned coal mines. The remaining generation comes from pumped storage and imported hydroelectricity, the Koeberg nuclear power station, four gas fuelled turbine stations, and one wind energy power station [87]. In 2005 SA's Electricity Parastatal initiated its expansion programme which includes the construction of two major power plants, the return to service of mothballed coal fired power stations and energy efficiency investments [87].
Legal/regulatory	The Energy Regulator defined by the Electricity Regulation Act 4 of 2006 mandated to ensure adequate supply, distribution, and electrification of all users in a fair and equitable manner. This includes empowering entities to get access to specific sectors and population groups, ensure clarity in policy to operate and integrate to the grid and stipulate environmental and social targets. The cohesiveness of such policy is questioned by policy makers and industry commentators [87]. This together with a lack of governance on managing progress creates a vacuum between planning parties and those organisations charged with delivery. Finally, the scope of legislation for local empowerment and public accountability extends to the regulated energy market and plays a key role to ensure governance and accountability.
Environmental	South Africa pledged to reduce the country's greenhouse gas emissions by 34% by 2020 and 42% by 2025 [91]. Baker [87] suggests that despite the absence of national expertise, South Africa also has an enormous potential for several different renewable energy technologies including: wind, solar water heaters, concentrated solar power, solar photovoltaics, and biomass. SA's Power Sector Parastatal has thus far secured investment in a renewable component consisting only of the 100 MW wind farm now funded by the World Bank [87]. Lack of policy on carbon emission and empowerment of local suppliers to augment the grid is hampering progress.

Source: Gareeb and Rwelamila [18].

Table 5.
PESTLE analysis based on South African macro environment.

No.	Characteristics	Reference
P.S 1	High risk environment	OSHA [92]; Grant and Hinze [93],
P.S.2	Organisational safety culture	McCaffrey [94]; Taylor [95]; Fitsilis et al. [72] OSHA [92]; NERSA [96]; Li and Poon [97]; Weil [98]; Taylor [95];
P.S.3	Sustainability	Oricha and Taiwo [99]; Chambers et al. [100] Goodland [101]; Suberu et al. [102]; Silvius and Schipper [103]; Alzahrani [104]; Păunescu and Acatrinei [105]
P.S.4	Environment impact	Chen et al. [106]; Blaabjerg et al. [107]; Massetti et al. [108]; Silvius and Schipper [103]; Alzahrani [104]; Bai et al. [109]
P.S.5	Compliant with SA's regulations	SA's Department of Energy [90]; NERSA [96]; Karekezi and Kimani [110]; Li et al. [111]
P.S.6	Process capability effectives//high end technology—reliable, sustainable, and environmental effectiveness	Panda and Ramanathan [112]; Oseni [113]; Oseni [114]; Pauschert [115]; Dabre et al. [116]

Source: Gareeb and Rwelamila [18].

Table 6.
Summary of factors related to the power sector industry.

2.4 Country specific factors

A PESTLE is a tool used for macro environmental scanning [86]. Environmental scanning can be defined as the study and interpretation of the political, economic, social, technological, legal, and environ-mental events and trends which influence a business, an industry or even the total market [86]. A PESTLE analysis was conducted by Gareeb and Rwelamila [18] on the SA's macro environment and the full analysis is present in Gareeb and Rwelamila [18]. **Table 5** summarizes the SA specific issues that should be considered when entering the SA environment which is an extraction from the PESTLE analysis. This analysis will be used in this paper to build the PMMM.

2.5 Sector specific factors

The sector specific by Gareeb and Rwelamila [18], include: high-risk environment, organisational safety culture, sustainability, environmental impact, compliance with SA's governing regulations and reliable technologies. **Table 6** summarizes the characteristics of the power sector from Gareeb and Rwelamila [18] been important consideration for the SA's power sector. This analysis will be used in this paper to build the PMMM.

3. Research methodology

This study is classified as a literature review [117]. The literature search in Gareeb and Rwelamila [18] categorised over a 19-year period and using 28 databases indicate that the current models are not completely suitable for SA's power sector (the models tend to be generalizable, and some models are developed for specific countries and areas that are not suitable to the SA environment).

This study proposes a conceptual model for measuring PMM in the SA's power sector. To achieve the goals of this paper a grounded approach was used to develop a conceptual model. First, past and current studies relating to PM success factors for PMM were studied to get a comprehensive understanding of the topic. The next steps included studies that entailed gaps that existed in current PMM literature so that this could be addressed in this study. The literature search continued until saturation of the data occurred. A literature review was used to find the key success factors for PMM as well as gaps that exist in current PMM literature. The data source was the analysis of books, published papers, conference papers, white papers, and specialized material from the relevant institutions.

Finally, the findings and analysis are provided together with the concluding remarks showing the contributions of this study in the PM field. The proposed model will be tested with the relevant case study organisations to determine the validity of the proposed conceptual model.

4. The conceptual model for PMM in the SA power sector

This paper presents a conceptual model for projects taking place in SA's power sector. Section two provided the gaps that existed in current literature on PMM. Organisations are complex environments. It is impossible for researchers to put forward a full detailed picture of these phenomena therefore, a way of representing a simplified version is through a model [118].

To understand the concept of a model, Team [119] defines "model" as: "*A model is a simplified representation of the world.*" KPMG [120] state that models have benefits such as: set process improvement objectives and priorities; improve processes and provide guidance; acts as a guide for improvement of organisational processes and define a starting point; enable the benefits of a community's prior experiences to be shared; create a common language and share a vision. A concept is a bundle of meanings or characteristics associated with certain events, objects, or conditions and used for representation, identification, communication, or understanding [121].

Lilien [122] lists the characteristics of conceptual model as:

- Often a flowchart or simple relationship (graph to indicate the nature of the relationship).
- Generally, of more use to the model builder than the model user (if the user and the builder are not the same).
- Helpful in thinking about reality than in actual decision—making.

This paper presents a conceptual model for projects taking place in SA's power sector.

Section two provided the gaps that existed in current literature on PMM. The proposed PMM model addresses the requirements and complexities identified within the PM environment in a more holistic way (represented in **Figure 1**) for the SA power sector.

Figure 1 indicates the content that exists in literature and highlighted in red indicates what was lacking in current PMM. **Figure 1** presents the requirements of what the key factors for PMM in the SA Power

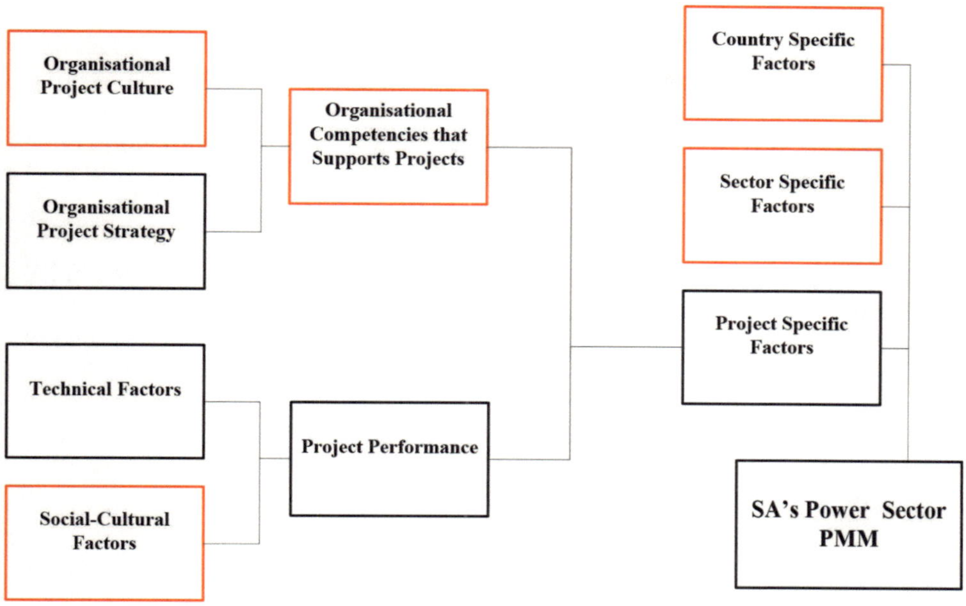

Figure 1.
Conceptual model for PMM for SA's power sector.

Sector should entail. The concept PM maturity was discussed. Diallo and Thuillier [78] mentions that project success and success dimensions depend on project type and sector. Dvir et al. [81] suggests that project success factors are not common for all projects and different types of projects are affected by different sets of success factors. Therefore, a project specific approach is appropriate for following studies into the practice and theory of PM [82].

Studies reveal that project performance is linked to project maturity. Therefore, extensive literature review has been conducted on what constitutes project performance/project success. Empirical correlations of all the factors that affect project success were reviewed. Two important factors were identified that affect project success, namely the technical and the social-cultural factors. This study identifies the critical success factors for successful projects that have an impact on the project maturity

Not only does project performance has links to project maturity but the organisational play a part. There is extensive literature available on the concepts that exist between PM maturity and organisational maturity. Without some degree of organisational maturity, PM maturity would not last or continue.

Therefore, organisations need to have an alignment between the organisational and PM maturity. The project objectives need to be linked into the overall business objects and organisational strategy. This model from a broader perspective takes into account sector specific and country specific factors that have not been established yet.

The proposed PMM model addresses the requirements and complexities identified within the PM environment in a more holistic way (represented in **Figure 1**) for the SA power sector. **Figure 1** indicates the content that exists in literature and highlighted in red indicates what was lacking in current PMM. The framework takes into account what was lacking in current literature on PMM for the SA power sector. **Figure 1** presents the requirements of what the key factors for PMM in the SA power sector should entail.

The conceptual model introduces country specific factors for the SA's environment and sector specific factor for the power sector. If the country specific factors are relaxed and a PESTLE analysis is carried out in the country where projects is taking place, therefore this framework can be adapted to different countries. The success components address the requirements and complexities identified with PM in the more holistic way to the SA power sector.

The proposed conceptual model addresses issues encountered as followers:

- Hulya [6] claims that organisational culture was largely under examined in PM research. This paper considers the organisational culture and the need for the organisational culture to support PM therefore an enabler for PMM eventually. This can be found in **Table 4**.

- Cooke-Davies and Arzymanow [1] state that further empirical studies need to be built for superior PM practices. This study focused on the latest empirical literature.

- Özturan et al. [123] comment that earlier models are a relatively a new proposal and therefore lacks empirical support for determining which competencies contribute most success. **Figure 1** was linked to empirical data. This can be found in the literature review Section 2 of this paper.

- This paper focuses on the country specific factors, sector specific factors and the project specific factors that affect PMM therefore provides a holistic approach for the context of this study. This can be found in **Table 5** where a summarized PESTLE analysis was conducted to determine these components.

- Ibbs and Kwak [124] comment that as new PM knowledge and practice becomes available the models need to be continuously developed and adapted. This study focused on the latest research and Figure 1 address the gaps that is lacking in current literature on considering the PMM requirements for the SA's power sector.

- Organisational development for PMM have been identified in this paper and have addressed the challenges.

5. Conclusion

The crucial factors that underpin the success of the projects are due to social-cultural factors [125]. This paper presents the key factors that contribute to PMM in the SA pwer sector. Section 4 presents the framework for developing a PMM model for the SA power sector. Diallo and Thuillier [78] mentions that project success and success dimensions depend on project type and sector. Dvir et al. [81] suggests that project success factors are not common for all projects and different types of projects are affected by different sets of success factors. Therefore, a project specific approach is appropriate for following studies into the practice and theory of PM [82]. Studies reveal that project performance is linked to project maturity. Therefore, extensive literature review has been conducted on what constitutes project performance/project success. Empirical correlations of all the factors that affect project success were reviewed. Two important factors were identified that effect project success, namely the technical and the social-cultural factors. This study identifies the critical success factors for successful projects that have an impact on the project maturity. Not only the project performance has links to project maturity but the organisational plays a role. There is extensive literature available on the concepts that exist between PMM and organisational maturity. Without some degree of organisational maturity, PMM would not last or continue. Therefore, organisations need to have an alignment between the organisational and PMM. The project objectives need to be linked into the overall business objects and organisational strategy. The contribution for this study provides the conceptual framework from a broader perspective for the SA power sector.

The following was achieved during the research and the following objectives met:

- Firstly, gaps that existed in current PMM were identified and are listed in section two as the starting point of the study.
- Secondly the gaps were addressed through an extensive literature review on PMM and is listed in section four.
- The key parameters that contribute to SA PMM were determined and consist of social-cultural, technical, organisational, sector and country specific and is listed in section two. **Figure 1** provides the conceptual framework for PMM in the SA power sector.

Research limitations—The focus of this paper was limited to the peer reviewed articles and journals on PMM.

Future research—The current research provides the conceptual model for the SA power sector. The next steps are to test the conceptual model with the relevant organisations.

Acknowledgements

The author would like to acknowledge that this paper is part of a doctoral thesis. The author of the thesis is Dr Natisha Gareeb (2018) and is entitled "An Appropriate Project Management Maturity Model for the Power Sector – the Case of South Africa", UNISA, South Africa, Pretoria. The authors would also like to thank our statistician, Juliana van Staden from the University of Witwatersrand.

Disclosure statement

No potential conflict of interest was reported by the authors.

Author details

Natisha Gareeb* and Pantaleo Mutajwaa Daniel Rwelamila
UNISA – University of South Africa, Carlswald, Gauteng, South Africa

*Address all correspondence to: natisha.gareeb@gmail.com

References

[1] Cooke-Davies TJ, Arzymanow A. The maturity of project management in different industries, an investigation into variation between project management models: selected papers from fifth Biennial conference of the International Research Network for organising by projects, Held in Renesse, Seeland, The Netherlands, 28-31 May 2002. International Journal of Project Management. 2003;**21**(6):471-478

[2] Hillson D. Assessing organisational project management capabilities. Journal of Facilities Management. 2003;**2**(3):298-311

[3] Skulmoski G. Project maturity and competence interface. Cost Engineering, ABI/INFORM Global. 2001;**43**(6):11-18

[4] Jugdev K, Thomas J. Project management maturity models: The silver bullets of competitive advantage. Project Management Journal. 2002;**33**(4):4

[5] Killen CP, Hunt RA. Robust project portfolio management: Capability evolution and maturity. International Journal of Managing Projects in Business. 2013;**6**(1):131-151

[6] Hulya JY. The role of project management maturity and organisational culture in perceived performance. Project Management Journal. 2009;**40**(3):14-33

[7] Barber BR. Understanding internally generated risks in projects. Internal Journal of Project Management. 2005;**23**(8):584-590 www.sciencedirect.com

[8] Crawford L. Senior management perceptions of project management competence. International Journal of Project Management. 2005;**16**(7):7-16

[9] De Bruin T, Freeze R, Rosemann M, Kulkarni U. Understanding the main phases of developing a Maturity Assessment Model. In: Campbell, B, Underwood, J, & Bunker, D editors. Australasian Conference on Information Systems (ACIS). Australia, New South Wales, SydneyB. Campbell, J. Underwood, and D. Bunker. Sydney: ACIS; November 30–December 2, 2005:8-19

[10] Viana JC et al. Enhancing organizational project focused thinking model. Production. 2016;**26**(2):313-329

[11] Alam MGA, Brown M, Khan AI. The importance of human skills in project management professional development. International Journal of Managing Projects in Business, Emerald group Publishing Limited. 2010;**3**(3):496-516

[12] Mahasneh JK, Thabet W. Rethinking construction curriculum: A descriptive cause analysis for the soft skills gap among construction graduates. In: 51st ASC Annual International Conference Proceedings; April 22-25, 2015; Texas. Associated Schools of Construction Proceedings of the 51st Annual International Conference Hosted by Texas A&M University in College Station; 2015. Available from: Rethinking-construction-curriculum-A-descriptive-cause-analysis-for-the-soft-skills-gap-among-construction-graduates.pdf (researchgate.net)

[13] Marando A. Balancing Project Management Hard Skills and Soft Skills. Waltham, Massachusetts, USA: Rabb School of Continuing Studies, Division of Graduate Professional Studies at Brandeis University; 2012

[14] Hartman FT, Skulmoski G. Project management maturity. Project Management. 1998;**4**(1):74-78

[15] Schlichter J. Surveying Project Management Capabilities. PM Network. 1999;**13**(4):39-40

[16] Andersen ES, Jessen SA. Project maturity in organisations. International Journal of Project management, Killington. 2003;**21**(6):457-461

[17] Ibbs CW, Kwak YH. Assessing project management maturity. Project Management Journal. 2000;**31**(1):32-43

[18] Gareeb N, Rwelamila PD. Rethinking project management maturity models for the South African power sector. African Journal of Science, Technology, Innovation and Development. 2021. DOI: 10.1080/20421338.2021.1899558

[19] Harter DE, Krishnan MS, Slaughter SA. Effects of process maturity on quality, cycle time, and effort in software product development. Management Science. 2000;**46**(4):451-466

[20] Thia CH, Swierczek FW. Critical success factors in project management: Implication from Vietnam. Asia Pacific Business Review. 2010;**16**(4):567-589

[21] Han WS, Yusof AM, Ismail S, Aun NC. Reviewing the Notions of Construction Project Success. International Journal of Business and Management. 2012;**7**(1):90-101

[22] Rockart J. The changing role of the information systems executive: A critical success factors perspective. Sloan Management Review. 1982;**23**(1):3-13

[23] Crawford L, Pollack J. Hard and soft projects: A framework for analysis. International Journal of Project Management. 2004;**22**(8):645-653

[24] Jaafari A. Management of risks, uncertainties, and opportunities on projects: Time for a fundamental shift. International Journal of Project Manage. 2001;**19**(2):89-101

[25] Azim S, Gale A, Lawlor-Wright T, Kirkham R, Khan A, Alam M. The importance of soft skills in complex projects. International Journal of Managing Projects in Business. 2010;**3**(3):387-401

[26] Mishra P, Dangayach GS, Mittal ML. An empirical study on identification of critical success factors in project based organizations. Global Business, and Management Research: An International Journal. 2011;**3**(3 and 4):356-368

[27] Ofori DF. Project management practices and critical success factors–A developing country perspective. International Journal of Business and Management. 2013;**8**(2):14-31

[28] Langston C, Ghanbaripour AN. A Management Maturity Model (MMM) for project-based organisational performance assessment. Construction Economics and Building. 2016;**16**(4):68-85. DOI: 10.5130/AJCEB.v16i4.5028

[29] Zuo J, Zhao X, Nguyen QBM, Ma T, Gao S. Soft skills of construction project management professionals and project success factors: A structural equation model. Engineering, Construction and Architectural Management. 2018;**25**(3):425-442. DOI: 10.1108/ECAM-01-2016-0016

[30] Campana J. The soft skills of project management: A view from diploma graduates [doctoral dissertation]. Queensland University of Technology; 2010. The soft skills of project management: A view from diploma graduates | QUT ePrints

[31] Rastogi N, Trivedi MK. PESTLE technique – A tool to identify external

risks in construction projects. International Research Journal of Engineering and Technology (IRJET). 2016;**3**(1):384-388

[32] Nandonde FA. A PESTLE analysis of international retailing in the East African Community. Global Business and Organizational Excellence. 2019;**38**(4):54-61

[33] Spyridon A, Johan H, Vasileios A, Gerrit JW. A PESTLE analysis of biofuels energy industry in Europe. Sustainability. 2019;**11**(21):5981. DOI: 10.3390/su11215981

[34] Andersen ES, Dyrhaug QX, Jessen SA. Evaluation of Chinese projects and comparison with Norwegian projects. International Journal of Project Management. 2002;**20**(8):601-609

[35] Portny SE. Improving your project performance with three essential pieces of information. The Journal for Quality and Participations, ABI/INFORM Global. 2010;**33**(3):18-24

[36] Browne M, O'Donnabhain S. The assessment of client satisfaction in the client-project manager relationship: An expectations-artefact model. Quest FOR Team Competence Software Project Management Organizational Change AS A Project Factors Impeding Project Management Learning. 1999;**5**(1):42

[37] Hartman FT, Skulmoski G. Quest for team competence. Project Management. 1999;**5**(1):10-14

[38] Nguyen LD, Ogunlana SO, Do Thi XL. A study on project success factors in large construction projects in Vietnam. Engineering, Construction, and Architectural Management. 2004;**11**(6):404-413

[39] Yong YC, Mustaffa ME. Analysis of factors critical to construction project success in Malaysia. Engineering, Construction and Architectural Management. 2012;**19**(5):543-556

[40] Lam EWM, Chan APC, Chan DWM. Benchmarking the performance of design-build projects: Development of project success index. Benchmarking: An International Journal. 2007;**14**(5):624-638

[41] Chen HL. Predictors of Project Performance and the Likelihood of Project Success. Journal of International Management Studies. 2011;**6**(2):1-10

[42] Besner C, Hobbs B. The paradox of risk management; a project management practice perspective. International Journal of Managing Projects in Business. 2012;**5**(2):230-247

[43] Griffith AF. Scheduling Practices and project success. Cost Engineering. 2006;**48**(9):24-30

[44] Zwikael O, Globerson S. Benchmarking of project planning and success in selected industries. Benchmarking: An International Journal. 2006;**13**(6):688-700

[45] Schein E. Culture: The missing concept in organizational studies. Administrative Science Quarterly. 1996;**41**(2):229-241

[46] Roberts A, Kelsey J, Smyth H, Wilson A. Health and safety maturity in project business cultures. International Journal of Managing Projects in Business. 2012;**5**(4):776-803

[47] Leveson N, Dulac N, Marais K, Carroll J. Moving beyond normal accidents and high reliability organizations: A systems approach to safety in complex systems. Organization Studies. 2009;**30**(2-3):227-249. DOI: 10.1177/0170840608101478

[48] Ahsan K. Determinants of the performance of public sector development projects. International Journal of Management. 2012;**29, 1 Part 1**:77-90

[49] Albu E, Panzar C. A new tool for assessing maturity alignment: The Enterprise maturity matrix. International Society for Performance Improvement. 2010;**49**(9):35-47

[50] Selders M, Ma¨rkle L. Project scorecard. Project Magazine. 2003;**20**(1):15-23

[51] Thiry M. Combining value and project management into an effective programme management model. International Journal of Project Manage. 2002;**20**(3):221-227

[52] Vance JND. How communications help integration projects. Succeed Control Engineering. 2009;**56**(4):42

[53] Kadefors A. Trust in project relationships—inside the black box. International Journal of project management. 2004;**22**(3):175-182

[54] Karlsen JT, Graee K, Massaoud MJ. The role of trust in project stakeholder relationships: A study of a construction project. International Journal of Project Organisation and Management. 2008;**1**(1):105-118

[55] Pinto JK, Slevin DP. Critical success factors across the project life cycle. Project management Journal. 1988;**19**(3):67-75

[56] Michalski L. Effective communication equals successful project management. Pharmaceutical Technology. 2000;**24**(5):84-88

[57] den Otter A, Emmitt S. Exploring effectiveness of team communication: Balancing synchronous and asynchronous communication in design teams. Engineering, Construction and Architectural Management, Bradford, Emerald Group Publishing Limited. 2007;**14**(5):408

[58] Johannessen JA, Olsen B. Projects as communicating systems: Creating a culture of innovation and performance. International Journal of Information Management. 2011;**31**(1):30

[59] Adenfelt M. Exploring the performance of transnational projects: Shared knowledge, coordination and communication. International Journal of Project Management. 2010;**28**(6):529

[60] Andersen ES, Birchall D, Jessen SA, Money AH. Exploring project success. Baltic Journal of Management. 2006;**1**(2):127-147

[61] Ochieng EG, Price ADF. Managing cross-cultural communication in multicultural construction project teams: The case of Kenya and UK. International Journal of Project Management. 2010;**28**(5):449

[62] Cooke-Davies T. The real success factors on project. International Journal of Project Management. 2002;**20**(3):185-190

[63] Webber SS, Klimoski RJ. Client–project manager engagements, trust, and loyalty. Journal of Organizational Behaviour. 2004;**25**(8):997-1013

[64] Pinto JK, Slevin DP, English B. Trust in projects: An empirical assessment of owner/contractor relationships. International Journal of project Management. 2009;**27**(6):638-648

[65] Maurer I. How to build trust in inter-organizational projects: The impact of project staffing and project

rewards on the formation of trust, knowledge acquisition and product innovation. International Journal of Project Management, Kidlington. 2010;**28**(7):629

[66] Zwikael O. Top management involvement in project management exclusive support practices for different project scenarios. International Journal of Managing Projects in Business. 2008;**1**(3):387-403

[67] De Oliveria MA, Valentina LVOD, Possamai O. Forecasting project performance considering the influence of leadership style on organisational agility. International Journal of Productivity and Performance Management. 2012;**61**(6):653-671

[68] Cooper RG, Edgett SJ, Kleinschmidt EJ. Benchmarking best NPD practices – I. Research Technology Management. 2004;**47**(1):31-43

[69] Gareis, R. and Huemann, M. (2000) Project management competences in the project-oriented organization, In Turner JR, Simister, S.J. (eds) The Gower Handbook of Project Management, Gower Publishing: Hampshire, pp 709-721.

[70] Brush CG, Green PG, Hart MM, Haller HS. From initial idea to unique advantage: The entrepreneurial challenge of constructing a resource base. The Academy of Management Executive. 2001;**15**(1):64-78

[71] Christenson D, Walker DHT. Using vision as a critical success element in project management. International Journal of Managing Projects in Business. 2008;**1**(4):611-622

[72] Fitsilis P, Kirytopoulos K, Leopoulos V. Assuring the managerial capability of public organisations implementing projects: The Greek Case. International Journal of Managing Projects in Business. 2011;**4**(2):329-344

[73] Meyer F. Using system dynamics to implement integrated sustainable excellence and performance management systems; 2005. Retrieved November 2013, from: http://www.afscet.asso.fr/resSystemica/Paris05/meyer.pdf

[74] Power B. 2007. Michael Hammer's Process and Enterprise Maturity Model. Retrieved June 2013, from http://www.bptrends.com/publication files/07-07-ART-HammersPEMM-Power-final1.pdf

[75] Cooke-Davies TJ, Crawford LH, Stevens TGL. Project management systems: Moving project management from an operational to a strategic discipline. Project Management Journal. 2009;**40**(1):110-123

[76] Andersen ES, Dysvik A, Vaagaasar AL. Organizational rationality and project management. International Journal of Managing Projects in Business. 2009;**2**(4):479-498

[77] Thamhain HJ. Linkages of project environment to performance: Lessons for team leadership. International Journal of Project Management. 2004;**22**(7):533-544

[78] Diallo A, Thuillier D. The success dimensions of international development projects: The perceptions of African project coordinators. International Journal of Project Management. 2004;**22**:19-31

[79] Belassi W, Tukel O. A new framework for determining critical success/failure factors in projects. International Journal Project Management. 1996;**14**(3):141-151

[80] Hartman F, Ashrafi R. Project management in the information systems

and technologies industries. Project Manage Journal. 2002;**33**(3):5-15

[81] Dvir D, Lipovetsky S, Shenhar A, Tishler A. In search of project classification: A non-universal approach to project success factors. Research policy. 1998;**27**(9):915-935

[82] Hyväri I. Project management effectiveness in project-oriented business organizations. International Journal of Project Management. 2006;**24**(3):216-225. Available from: Project management effectiveness in project-oriented business organizations - ScienceDirect

[83] Branson CM. Achieving organisational change through values alignment. Journal of Educational Administration. 2008;**46**(3):376-395

[84] Deal TE, Kennedy AA. Corporate Cultures: The Rites and Rituals of Organizational Life. 2nd ed. Reading, MA: Addison-Wesley; 1982. pp. 98-103

[85] Simons R. How new top managers use control systems as levers of strategic renewal. Strategic Management Journal. 1994;**15**(3):169-189

[86] Kroon J. General Management. 2nd ed. Pinelands, Cape Town: Pearson South Africa; 1995

[87] Baker L. Governing electricity in South Africa: Wind, coal, and power struggles. Working Paper 015, The Governance of Clean Development Working Paper Series. School of International Development, University of East Anglia UK; 2011

[88] Yelland C. National integrated resource plan, a document to shape our future. Daily Maverick, 23 April 2010; 2010. Available from: http://www.thedailymaverick.co.za/article/2010-04-23-national-integrated-resource-planfor-electricity-a-document-to-shape-our-future [Accessed: March 2014]

[89] South Africa (Republic). White Paper on the Energy Policy of the Republic of South Africa. Pretoria: Department of Energy; 1998

[90] South Africa (Republic). Draft 2012 Integrated Energy Planning Report. Pretoria: Department of Energy; 2012

[91] South Africa (Republic). 2011. The Climate Change Awareness Campaign: South African Government's position on Climate Change. Department of Environmental Affairs and Tourism. Available from: http://www.climateaction.org.za/cop17-cmp7/sagovernment-position-on-climate-change [Accessed: March 2014]

[92] OSHA. 2014. Available from: https://www.osha.gov/SLTC/powergeneration/accessed [Accessed: 26 March 2014]

[93] Grant A, Hinze J. Construction worker fatalities related to trusses: An analysis of the OSHA fatality and catastrophic incident database. Safety Science. 2014;**65**:54-62

[94] McCaffrey DP. OSHA and the Politics of Health Regulation. Albany, New York: Springer Science & Business Media; 2013

[95] Taylor EL. Safety benefits of mandatory OSHA 10 h training. Safety Science. 2015;**77**:66-71

[96] NERSA. 2014. Available from: http://www.ilo.org/oshenc/part-xi/power-generation-and-distribution/item/616-electric-power-generation-transmission-and-distribution-safety-a-us-example [Accessed: 26 March 2014]. www.nersa.org.za

[97] Li RYM, Poon SW. Demand for construction safety. In: Construction Safety. Berlin, Heidelberg: Springer; 2013. pp. 117-121

[98] Weil D. Making OSHA Inspections More Effective: Alternatives for Improved Inspection Targeting in the Construction Industry. Silver Spring, MD: Center to Protect Workers' Rights; 2004

[99] Oricha JY, Taiwo AS. The possibility of incorporating power sector with financial institutions in Nigeria. Advanced Materials Research. 2013;**824**:532-535 Trans Tech Publications

[100] Chambers N, Simmons C, Wackernagel M. Sharing Nature's Interest: Ecological Footprints as an Indicator of Sustainability. Abingdon: Routledge; 2014

[101] Goodland R. Environmental sustainability and the power sector. Impact Assessment. 1994;**12**(4):409-470

[102] Suberu MY, Mustafa MW, Bashir N, Muhamad NA, Mokhtar AS. Power sector renewable energy integration for expanding access to electricity in sub-Saharan Africa. Renewable and Sustainable Energy Reviews. 2013;**25**:630-642

[103] Silvius AG, Schipper R. A maturity model for integrating sustainability in projects and project management. In: 24th World Congress of the International Project Management Association. Istanbul: IPMA; 2010

[104] Alzahrani SS. Developing a project management maturity model to initiate sustainable project performance and modernisation in the Kingdom of Saudi Arabia [doctoral dissertation]. Entrepreneurship, Commercialisation, and Innovation Centre (ECIC), The University of Adelaide; 2015

[105] Păunescu C, Acatrinei C. Managing maturity in process-based improvement organisation companies. Journal of Business Economics and Management. 2012;**13**(2):223-241

[106] Chen Q, Kang C, Xia Q, Zhong J. Power generation expansion planning model towards low-carbon economy and its application in China. IEEE Transactions on Power Systems. 2010;**25**(2):1117-1125

[107] Blaabjerg F, Chen Z, Kjaer SB. Power electronics as efficient interface in dispersed power generation systems. IEEE Transactions on Power Electronics. 2004;**19**(5):1184-1194

[108] Massetti E, Brown MA, Lapsa M, Sharma I, Bradbury J, Cunliff C, et al. Environmental quality and the us power sector: Air quality, water quality, land use and environmental justice. ORNL. 2016:772

[109] Bai L, Wang H, Huang N, Du Q, Huang Y. An environmental management maturity model of construction programs using the AHP-entropy approach. International Journal of Environmental Research and Public Health. 2018;**15**(7):1317

[110] Karekezi S, Kimani J. Status of power sector reform in Africa: Impact on the poor. Energy Policy. 2002;**30**(11-12):923-945

[111] Li RYM, Zuo J, Fanen T. Supply and demand of construction safety regulations in developing countries. In: Construction Safety and Waste Management. Cham: Springer; 2015. pp. 93-109

[112] Panda H, Ramanathan K. Technological capability assessment as an input for strategic planning: Case studies at Electricité de France and Electricity

Generating Authority of Thailand. Technovation. 1997;**17**(7):359-390

[113] Oseni MO. Improving households' access to electricity and energy consumption pattern in Nigeria: Renewable energy alternative. Renewable and Sustainable Energy Reviews. 2012;**16**(6):3967-3974

[114] Oseni MO. An analysis of the power sector performance in Nigeria. Renewable and Sustainable Energy Reviews. 2011;**15**(9):4765-4774

[115] Pauschert D. "Study of Equipment Prices in the Power Sector." ESMAP Technical Paper 122/09. Washington, DC: International Bank for Reconstruction and Development; 2009

[116] Dabre GB, Dutta AA, Kadu AN. Performance Evaluation of Distribution Network and Reduction in Technical & Non-Technical Losses by Using Energy Efficient Equipment and Cost Benefit Analysis in the Power Sector. Amravati: 2014 International Conference on Power, Automation and Communication (INPAC); 2014

[117] Leedy PD, Ormrod JE. Practical Research: Planning and Design, Pearson Education International, Published as Merrill, Upper Saddle River, New Jersey. 9th ed. US: Pearson Education; 2010

[118] Mbengue A, Vandangeon-Derumez I. Causal analysis and modeling. In: Thiétart et al., editors. Doing Management Research. 2001. pp. 267-292. DOI: 10.4135/9781849208970.n12

[119] Team CP. Capability Maturity Model® Integration (CMMI SM), Version 1.1. Pittsburg, PA: Software Engineering Institute, Carnegie Mellon University/SEI-2002-TR-012; 2002

[120] KPMG. Global IT Project Management Survey: How Committed are You? KPMG International; 2005. Available from: Global IT Project Management Survey (totalmetrics.com)

[121] Meredith J. Theory building through conceptual methods. International Journal of Operations and Production management. 1992;**13**(5):3-11

[122] Lilien GL. Model Relativism: A situational approach to model building. The Institute of Management Science, Interfaces. 1975;**5**(5):11-18

[123] Özturan HE, Oral M, Kasap N, Bozkaya B. Information technology and business awareness diagnostic tool. European Journal of Management. 2008;**8**(3):1-8

[124] Ibbs CW, Kwak YH. Project management process maturity (PM)2 model. Journal of Management in Engineering. 2002;**18**(3):150-155

[125] Hall T, Jagielska D, Baddoo N. Motivating developer performance to improve project outcomes in high maturity organisations. Software Quality Journal. 2007;**15**(4):365-381

Section 3

Current Trends for Program and Project Management Approaches

Chapter 3

Balancing Hedging and Flexing for Inclusive Project Management

Wim Leendertse, Bert de Groot and Tim Busscher

Abstract

Current project management often emphasizes hedging through a strictly phased and funneled development of the project scope. However, an increasingly engaged project environment and rise in the complexity of societal challenges cause an emerging demand for more open and interactive ways of managing projects. This requires projects to adopt an integrated management approach that focuses on flexing, which emphasizes the ability of a project to adapt to and co-create with the environment. Overemphasizing flexing, however, may undermine the controlled nature of project management. Therefore, it is necessary to find a form of project management that is both open and interactive without losing control. On the basis of specific project contexts and characteristics, this chapter presents criteria and tools for balancing hedging and flexing for inclusive project management.

Keywords: project management, hedging, flexing, stakeholder participation, project flexibility

1. Introduction

Our society is presented with grand challenges. We have to deal with many issues at the same time, such as climate change, the energy transition, the transition to a circular economy, empowered citizens, the increasing role of digitization, increasing attention to the living environment and nature, etc. This means that projects, which can be seen as interventions in our society, can no longer be separated from their environment. Current project management, however, still follows a hedging approach that is strongly based on the classical step-wise development of a predefined output, where the environment is seen as a threat that must be mitigated. In order to be able to respond to the increasing complexity of the project environment, there is an emerging demand for a more open and interactive approach to project management. We refer to this approach as a flexing approach. While a flexing approach may emphasize the ability of projects to move along with and shape their environment, this also increases the interdependencies between the project and its environment, thereby increasing complexity, leading to less control of the project and potentially causing projects to drift. Therefore, it is necessary to find a form of project management that is open and interactive without losing control. The theory and practice of process management offer valuable insights for this. On the basis of insights from recent project and process management literature, this chapter describes how strategies and instruments of process management can be combined with project management tools and techniques to come to a more open form of management without losing manageability.

2. From hedging to flexing in project management

2.1 What is meant by "project" and "project management"?

Literature has numerous definitions of the term "project." One of the most used definitions was developed by Turner and Müller [1], who define a project as a temporary endeavor in which human, material, and financial resources are organized in a novel way, to undertake a unique scope of work, of given specification, within constraints of cost and time, so as to achieve beneficial change defined by quantitative and qualitative objectives. Following this definition, project management can be seen as the organizational activities, to be carried out by a plurality of specialized persons or groups, in a temporary joint venture that aims to deliver a clearly specified result within a limited period of time, within certain conditions and with finite resources. In short, project management concerns the application of knowledge, skills, tools, and techniques to ensure that project activities meet project requirements [2].

2.2 Limitations of classic project management

Classic project management is strongly focused on manageability and control. It is based on a causal rational paradigm [3, 4], where the process of managing a project is translated in a sequential and linear phasing of activities that should lead to a predefined result. This is further expressed in scope, cost, and time management using dedicated project management tools and techniques, suggesting that the appropriate use of these instruments leads to the intended result. In this paradigm, the project is regarded as a closed system with a clear boundary to its environment. This system is not isolated—there is interaction between the system and its environment—but changes in that environment may have a negative effect on project progress and are considered a potential threat that must be mitigated. Projects are therefore supposed to conduct risk analyses and develop contingency plans to cope with risk. In general, classic project management is based on advanced predictions that must be achieved via a strictly defined path through the correct and effective use of project management tools and techniques. These tools and techniques take the form of methods, rules, step-by-step procedures, frameworks, and models. A search on Google quickly reveals the multitude of project management tools and techniques and a multitude of handbooks that describe these [2, 5, 6]. Organizations such as the International Project Management Association (IPMA) and the Project Management Institute (PMI) even offer dedicated courses to learn these tools and techniques and to certify project managers.

However, due to this closed system perspective, potential opportunities may be missed and the defensive attitude may lead to problems in delivering projects. This limits the contribution that projects can (and should) make to the major societal challenges we are facing today and the potential use of opportunities as tool for adaptation. In addition, society is becoming increasingly engaged, and a sectoral project-oriented process without the engagement of its environment is no longer accepted. Or as Van Buuren et al. [7] argued, the main characteristic and focus of (classic) project

DOI: http://dx.doi.org/10.5772/intechopen.102972

management is its main disadvantage: it tends to focus primarily on the realization of one single project ambition, suffers from a singular logic, and is limited in terms of scope, budget, and time. An answer may be a more open system approach in which the boundary of the system becomes permeable and stakeholders are included as co-actors, especially in more dynamic environments with a relatively high degree of uncertainty. A shift in focus of project management from purely instrumental to more process-oriented.

2.3 From hedging to flexing

Classic project management, based on a hedging strategy, offers hardly any room for adjustments to the project scope, planning, or budget, to respond to changes in the environment. In general, hedging is less satisfactory in dynamic environments when complexity in and around the project is relatively high. In these cases, a process-oriented approach, or flexing, is more appropriate. Flexing is often characterized by a broader scope (integration of challenges), a flexible planning on various timescales (short, medium, and long term), interim monitoring, a partly flexible budget to which several parties contribute (co-financing), and involvement of stakeholders through open dialog and a co-creative approach. Determining the right mix, i.e., a balance between hedging and flexing (which may even change over time), is the key challenge in modern project management. This mix is determined by both the context of the project and the capabilities of the project organization. By "context" we mean the unique conditions in which the project is being managed [8], including the organization's internal context (e.g., other projects, departments, and organizational strategy), and external context (e.g., stakeholders, adjacent environment). **Table 1** shows main characteristics of classic project management and a process-oriented approach [9].

In the next sections, we will first look at the context of a project from a complexity perspective. Higher degrees of complexity of a project and/or its environment require the project to deal with higher levels of uncertainty, which requires more flexibility

	(Classic) project management	**Process management**
Main focus	• A well-thought-out solution to a problem	• Organic development of a solution to a problem or problems through involvement of stakeholders and their interests
Dealing with dynamics	• Through decisiveness and control	• Through resilience, responsiveness and being open to other options
	• Changing circumstances must not affect the course of action	• Changing circumstances are windows of opportunity. • The project has the ability to deal with change (adaptive capacity)
	• Closed system focus	• Open system focus. • Interaction with the project environment for enrichment (opportunities, integration of challenges, engagement)
Context	• A stable, predictable environment	• An unstable, dynamic environment

Table 1.
Main characteristics of (classic) project management and process management (derived from [9]).

of the project. Then we will discuss strategies to open project boundaries and to increase the ability of a project to reach out to its environment through stakeholder engagement, active opportunity seeking, and inclusive planning. Subsequently, we will discuss the ability of the project organization itself to proactively deal with uncertainty. In the final section, we will bring it all together as related building blocks for next-generation project management.

3. Projects and complexity

Complexity is an often-used concept in project development and management. In our daily use, it often refers to the perspective of the project participants on the difficulty of a project. From a more fundamental perspective, complexity revolves around actors or elements in or close to a project that interact with each other in a reciprocal way. For example, nowadays, the project environment in both project development and implementation requires intensive interaction, which may lead to a multitude of interdependent relationships of the project with its environment.

Not all projects are necessarily complex. Some projects can be classified as simple or complicated. The degree of complexity—i.e., a simple, complicated, or complex project—has implications for project management; or at least, it should have. Higher degrees of complexity often imply more uncertainty, more vulnerability for change, and need a management style that can deal with this. In general, simple or complicated projects can be managed on the basis of a hedging project management approach, whereas complex projects need more flexibility and a more flexing project management approach.

On the basis of a recent literature review of international peer-reviewed journals on project complexity, four forms of complexity can be distilled: technical or structural complexity, organizational complexity, contextual complexity, and institutional complexity [10]. Projects may have to deal with any form of complexity. Technical or structural complexity relates to the tasks and substantive aspects of a project. This not only includes the diversity and number of tasks or aspects within a project, but also the interdependencies between tasks or technologies. Organizational complexity relates to the organizational structure of the project or its parent organization. A complex organizational structure is one that consists of several interdependent parts. Institutional complexity is the result of different institutional logics of the actors involved in a project. Institutional logics influence personal definitions and working methods, which are partly shaped by the cultural and political background of the actors. For this chapter, especially the fourth identified type of complexity, the concept of contextual complexity, is relevant. *Contextual complexity* is described in literature as the complexity resulting from environmental influences. The literature review of Busscher et al. [10] revealed several indicators of contextual complexity, which can be used to assess the degree of complexity of a project in a specific context. The following indicators were found in the studied literature: the amount of project stakeholders, the level of sociopolitical interests or influence in project, the degree of support (from stakeholders) for the project, the internal (intra organizational) support for the project, the degree of competition in the market, geographical differences in regulations, the level of influence of contextual developments on the project, and the amount and intensity of social discussions.

As mentioned above, a higher degree of contextual complexity needs more flexibility of the project—or a more flexing style of project management. However, the need for flexibility does not (always) match the possibilities to be flexible in every phase of the project life cycle [11]. For instance, the need for flexibility may be high in the planning phase and the beginning of the execution phase when the design is elaborated and stakeholders are confronted with the concrete effects of the intervention. As the design evolves, the possibilities for flexibility will decrease and will be lower in the end of the planning phase and low in the execution phase and termination phase. Typically, in project management, a change of phase comes with an intermediate decision, which fixes the boundary conditions for the next phase and by doing so reduces the opportunities for flexibility.

4. Strategies, tools, and techniques to deal with contextual complexity

4.1 Stakeholder management and opportunity management

Already in the 1980s of the last century, Cleland (1986) introduced stakeholder thinking into project management. Since then, the importance of *stakeholder management* in project management has increased, i.e., the process of adapting the specifications, plans, and approaches to the different concerns and expectations of the various stakeholders [2]. A stakeholder can be defined as a group or individual that has an interest in the success or failure of a project [12]. Stakeholder management is the process of managing the expectations of anyone who has an interest in a project or will be affected by its deliverables or outputs. Stakeholder management typically has been used as an iterative process of identifying and analyzing stakeholders from a project perspective, defining strategies and accompanying measures, implementing the measures, and evaluating the effectiveness (plan-do-check-act). In this approach, the stakeholders are considered manageable to meet project goals [13]. Together with the development of stakeholder management also *opportunity management* gained increasing attention. Opportunity management can be seen as the inverse of risk management, in the sense that risk management seeks to proactively minimize the probability and/or negative effect of a potential event on a project and opportunity management, in turn, seeks to maximize opportunities that can bring value to a project by connecting project challenges to stakeholder challenges [14]. From a project management perspective, an opportunity is an uncertainty that potentially adds more value to the project than the potential loss of value it may bring along [15]. This interpretation of opportunity management is based on the Mutual Gains Approach as developed at Harvard University in the beginning of this century [16, 17]. Being able to seize opportunities increases the flexibility of the project, since the extra value of an opportunity may be used to, for example, extend the scope of the project or compensate for potential time or cost overruns.

4.2 Co-development

This leaves the question: can one really manage stakeholders and the project environment? As mentioned above, society becomes more emancipated. People take responsibility to design their own environment, and citizens' initiatives are becoming more and more common [18]. The power of interest groups, NGOs, and individual stakeholders is increasing. These developments imply that projects can no longer act autonomously and instead have to work together with stakeholders. Stakeholder and opportunity management thus have to shift to an orientation focused on co-development. In contrast to "management of stakeholders," a "*management for stakeholders*" approach embraces all the stakeholders and tries to reach win-win situations [19]. In line with this approach, participation through co-development is broadly discussed in planning and management literature in the last decades [20–25].

Co-development can be defined as the joint development and improvement of policies and services at an equal level through constructive dialog [26]. Dialog means interactivity, engagement, and a propensity to act on both sides. It is about empathic understanding of both sides and a communication of equals. The intensity of joint activities can differ (see, for example, the classic ladder of participation by Arnstein, 1966), but communication and information exchange are always the basis for any stakeholder involvement. Attuning and adjusting mutual activities can be added on top of communication and information exchange so as to achieve results more efficiently, i.e., mutual coordination. When, in addition to the abovementioned activities, also resources are exchanged, one may speak of cooperation. Collaboration is considered the ultimate form of cooperation, where information, activities, resources, and responsibilities are jointly planned, implemented, and evaluated to achieve a common goal [27]. In all these definitions, joint development in equity, interaction, and dialog influence on agenda setting, high involvement and common goals are main characteristics of co-development.

4.3 Engaging stakeholders and issue management

Co-development in a project environment means that the project engages the stakeholders in a collaborative problem-solving process [28]. The project organization respects and uses the expertise of the stakeholders and is open and willing to share all information necessary for a joint project design. The design is based on problem-specific interaction involving the interests of all relevant stakeholders. The decision-making is based on the weighing of interests in what Aaltonen & Sivonen [29] describe as an adaptation strategy. **Figure 1** shows different corresponding strategies as mentioned in literature the axis from (classic) project management to process management.

Strategic stakeholder Involvement (SSI) is a practical tool to engage stakeholders in co-development [30]. This approach combines traditional stakeholder management, designed to minimize risks caused by parties with different interests, with seizing opportunities through issue management. *Issue management* entails a process of continuously scanning the environment for new issues, which are developments or events that might happen and force stakeholders to take position. Issues come and go and change over time. Central to issue management is the identification of issues that may influence the project or may be influenced by the project and address these in interaction with the stakeholders from a win-win perspective.

4.4 Co-creation and social design

The descriptions above are based on a so-called inside-out perspective, which looks at the environment from within the project. At the same time, the project can also be seen as an instrument that may contribute to solving broader social issues. This perspective works from the outside-in and assumes the project goal and task to be only one of the goals and tasks that have to be tackled in interaction with and between stakeholders, thus opening the box [13].

DOI: http://dx.doi.org/10.5772/intechopen.102972

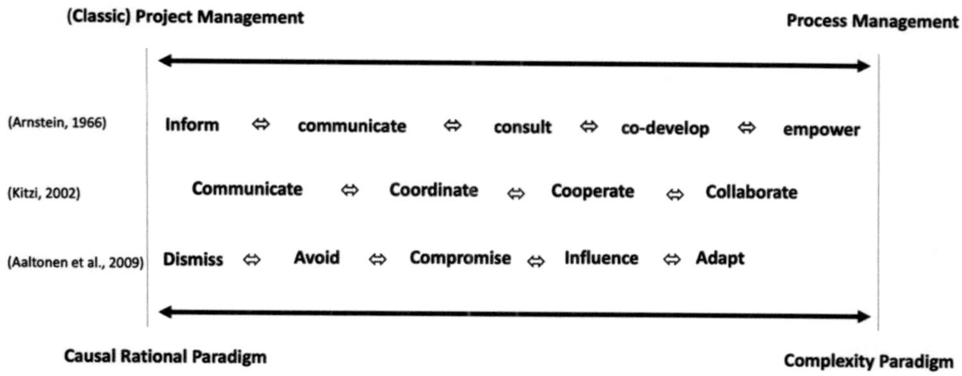

Figure 1.
Strategies for project and process management.

Social design is a design methodology to tackle complex issues, placing the combined social issues as the priority. The basic idea is to break down the walls between disciplines and enable truly interdisciplinary work to take place. The classic approach of project management starts with a (project) problem and organizes the most efficient path to come to a predefined output or outcome, which solves that problem. Social design is based on the process and principles of design thinking developed by the British Design Counsel (www.designcounsil.org.uk), the "Double Diamond" or "4D" model. In this approach, the design process starts with a joint problem definition involving all relevant problems of the project and its context and their stakeholders. The idea is that actors collectively scan a relevant context around the project searching for problems and issues. Based on a joint problem definition, information is gathered and possible combinations are developed in a co-creative process. In contrast to

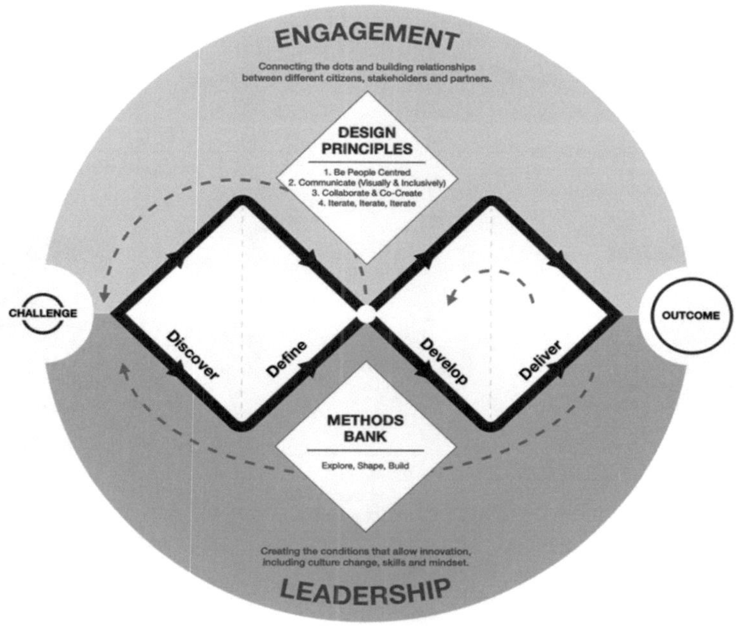

Figure 2.
Process steps of social design (source: British Design Counsel).

the traditional project management life cycle, this process is not linear from problem to solution, but interactively dynamic via diverging and converging stages [20, 31]. **Figure 2** shows the typical steps of a social design process.

Social design may lead to more integrated solutions and a higher degree of acceptance. However, to keep the process manageable, it is necessary to add some hedging elements to the process, for example, by setting milestones, by setting clear and smart boundaries, and by transparently communicating about the boundaries of the decision-making process.

5. Building project flexibility

The project context is essential for the successful management of a project [32]. As mentioned above, project organizations need to be responsive and open up to their context and engage stakeholders to enable project success. This requires considerable flexibility of the project organization, as it includes giving room for co-development and co-creation and at the same time keeping the project manageable [8]. Olsson [33] defines project flexibility as the capability to adjust the project to prospective consequences of uncertain circumstances within the context of the project. Adopting a flexible approach improves not only the project results, but also the evaluation of the project management itself.

The extended Pentagon model of Rolstadås et al. [34] offers a model to connect the project management process to the external context through so-called formal qualities, such as structure and technologies, and informal qualities, such as culture, social relations and networks, and interaction (see **Figure 3**).

The distinction between formal and informal qualities may be viewed as hedging versus flexing, controlling versus emerging, or prescriptive versus adaptive. In this

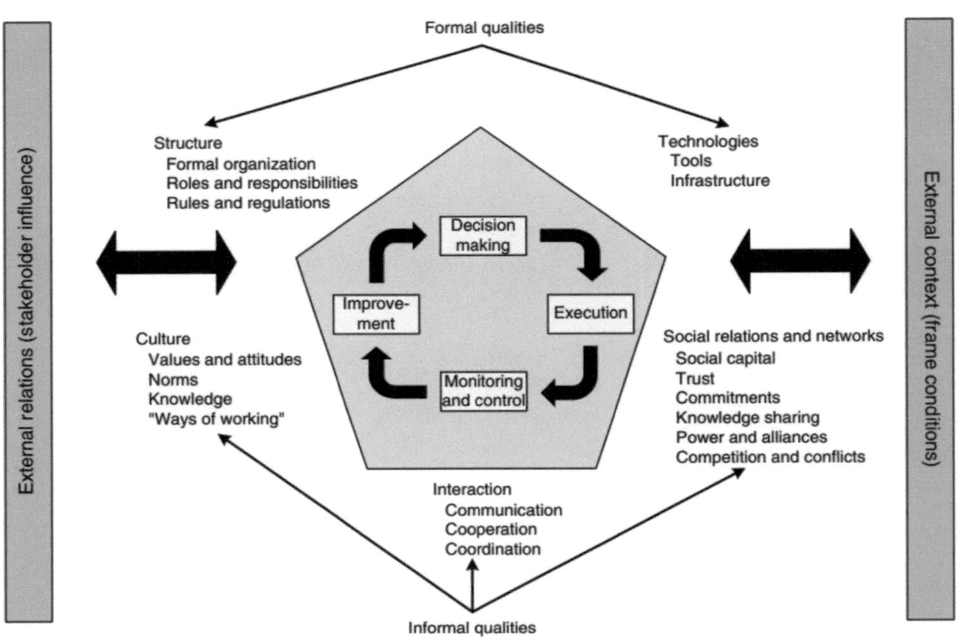

Figure 3.
The extended pentagon model (source: [34]).

model, flexibility is created through the interaction between formal and informal qualities of project organizations. For example, rules may formally be more loosely defined to allow informal qualities to be revealed. Building on this, Sohi et al. [35] delivered a list of flexibility enablers regarding both formal and informal qualities of project organizations as shown in **Table 2**.

Extended pentagon model		**Flexibility enablers**	**Collective learning**
Formal qualities	Structure	• Broad task definition	• Institutional design
		• Functional-based contracts	• Multilevel integration
		• Standardized processes	
		• Stable teams	
		• Self-steering of the project team	
		• Self-assigning of individuals to tasks	
		• Late locking	
		• Short feedback loops	
		• Continuous locking (iterative)	
		• Iterative planning	
		• Iterative delivery	
	Technologies	• Contingency planning	• Information management
		• Visualized project planning and progress	
		• Shared interface management	
		• Joint project office	
Informal qualities	Culture	• Seizing opportunities and coping with threats	• Diversity
		• Possible alternatives	• Scope for change
		• Embrace change as much as needed	• Leadership
		• Team priority over individual priority	• Capabilities of individuals
		• Consensus among team members	
	Interaction	• Open information exchange among different groups	• Rules for dialog
	Social relations and networks	• Trust among involved parties	• Trust and open atmosphere
		• Network structure rather than hierarchical structure	• Informal network
		• Team members as stakeholders	• Learning platforms
		• Continuous learning	

Table 2.
Overview of the extended pentagon model in relation to flexibility enablers and collective learning.

The model is dynamic and involves continuous iterative processes within the project organization and interaction with external stakeholders and contexts. The project team members receive feedback from stakeholders or the context. This feedback is interpreted both individually and collectively. Positive feedback reinforces successful practices, whereas negative feedback will lead to an attempt to alter existing practices. This multilevel process of collective learning is a process of adaptation consisting of changes in common understanding, mutual agreement, and collective action. The ability to build new knowledge, relationships, and practices in response to complex environmental challenges links (collective) learning to flexibility. In fact, collective learning may even be considered a proxy for flexibility. De Groot et al. [36] describe in their article typical identifiers of collective learning in project-oriented organizations as summarized in **Table 2**.

The enablers and indicators shown in **Table 2** resemble the aforementioned characteristics of process management (see **Table 1**). In general, adaptive project management or flexibility requires a more open approach both within the system of a project organization and through interaction with the project context.

While this might be seen to decrease the control of the project, an open approach does not necessarily lead to a loss of control, but to a different form of control. Project organizations still need a solid *structure* with clear roles and responsibilities. However, to enable flexibility, project management may lower barriers between disciplines and promote horizontal and vertical integration through cross-discipline meeting structures and decision-making processes. Project organizations still need *technologies*, such as skills, tools, and techniques to manage the project. However, the corresponding tools and infrastructure may allow for more explicit anticipation of contingencies through, for example, scenario analyses or systems that enable easy access to information throughout the project organization. Finally, there needs to be a *culture* that enables flexibility. Team members may have to get used to a (partially) new way of working. They may be encouraged to look for creative and integral solutions and to view changes as opportunities. In this, important is the organization of *interaction* through *social relations and networks* based on open information exchange leading to trust and effective collaboration within the project organization and with the project's stakeholders.

6. Balancing hedging and flexing for inclusive project management

Classic project management is based on a closed system approach, where the context is typically seen as a threat for the efficient delivering of the project output or outcome, which has to be mitigated through risk management. We referred to this as a hedging approach. However, the increasingly dynamic and engaged society requires an open (inclusive) approach, where challenges are integrated and stakeholders are involved in the development of the project. In general, opening project boundaries may lead to higher contextual complexity. A higher degree of contextual complexity needs more flexibility of the project or a more flexing style of project management. This leads to an important paradox in current project management. To efficiently manage their projects, project managers need (or are forced) to organize interaction with the project context or their community of interest, while involving more stakeholders or integrating more challenges in the project will lead to more (contextual) complexity and more uncertainty. Consequently, an important task for the project manager is to find a balanced mix between hedging and flexing tools and techniques.

DOI: http://dx.doi.org/10.5772/intechopen.102972

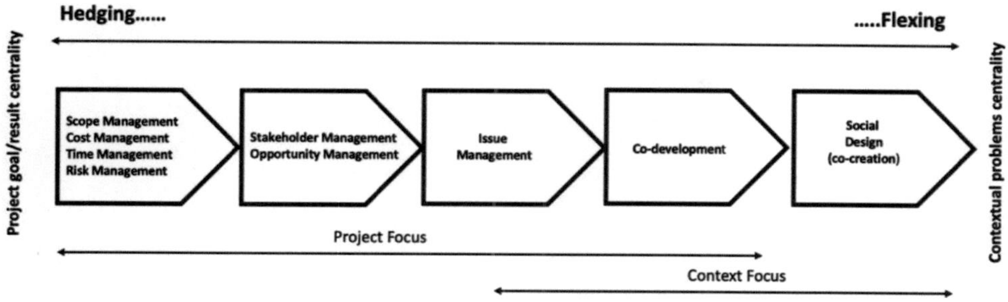

Figure 4.
Building blocks for inclusive project management.

Adding to the challenge is the fact that this mix may change during the project phases, because the need for flexing and the possibilities to implement flexing tools and techniques differ per project stage. In practice, in the planning phase, the need for flexibility is relatively high because the elaboration of the project design confronts stakeholders with the concrete effects of interventions, whereas the possibilities to flex are relatively high in this phase because there are still relatively few agreements, little expenses made, and hardly any concrete results realized. As a project progresses, it becomes increasingly difficult to alter the desired project output due to, for example, ongoing agreements between stakeholders and realized project parts limiting the possibilities for other solutions. However, implementing flexing tools and techniques to engage stakeholders remains also in the latter phases important as (most) projects are realized in a continuously changing environment.

Figure 4 gives an overview of the building blocks that become increasingly important in modern, inclusive project management; arranged in such a way that from the left to the right, tools and techniques offer more flexibility.

7. Conclusion

This chapter has provided an array of tools and techniques that can be used to compose a balanced mix of hedging and flexing for inclusive project management. As such, it provides the building blocks that help to shift the orientation of project managers from a project-problem centrality to a focus on multiple contextual problems and challenges. We argue that project organizations should always strive for project flexibility. Projects, being simple, complicated, or complex, are always potentially confronted with unexpected events. Being flexible may then be the answer to deal with these uncertainties. As discussed above, being able to create diversity and learning are key to increase project flexibility.

Projects are temporary endeavors, which means that they have a beginning and an end. As discussed, in dynamic and engaged contexts, a more open approach of project management may be necessary, which potentially leads to more diversity. However, to come to an end, this diversity has to be converged and funneled by intermediate decision-making or hedging. The real art of modern, inclusive project management is defining a balanced mix of hedging and flexing in every phase of the project.

Author details

Wim Leendertse[1,2*], Bert de Groot[1,2] and Tim Busscher[1]

1 Faculty of Spatial Sciences, University of Groningen, Groningen, The Netherlands

2 Ministry of Infrastructure and Water Management, The Netherlands

*Address all correspondence to: w.l.leendertse@rug.nl; wim.leendertse@rws.nl

References

[1] Turner R, Müller R. On the nature of the project as a temporary organisation. International Journal of Project Management. 2003;**21**(7):1-8

[2] PMI. A Guide to the Project Management Body of Knowledge and the Standard for Project Management. 7th ed. Project Management Institute: Pennsylvania, USA; 2021

[3] Stacey R. Tools and Techniques of Leadership and Management. Meeting the Challenge of Complexity. Routledge: New York; 2012

[4] Stacey R. Strategic Management and Organisational Dynamics. 7th ed. Prentice Hall: London; 2015

[5] Turner R. Gower Handbook of Project Management. 5th ed. Routledge: London, UK; 2014

[6] Morris P, Pinto J, Söderlund J. The Oxford Handbook of Project Management. Oxford, UK: Oxford University Press; 2012

[7] Van Buuren A, Buijs J-M, Teisman G. Program management and the creative art of coopetition: Dealing with potential tensions and synergies between spatial development projects. International Journal of Project Management. 2010;**28**(7):672-682

[8] Martinsuo I, Korhonen T, Laine T. Identifying, framing and managing uncertainties in project portfolios. International Journal of Project Management. 2014;**32**(5):732-746

[9] Edelenbos J, Klijn H-E, Kort M, van Twist M. Project versus process management in PPP projects. Bestuurskunde. 2007;**2007**(1):66-79

[10] Busscher T, Verweij S, Joustra G, Wesselo G. Management of Complexity in Projects of Rijkswaterstaat. Groningen: University of Groningen; 2022

[11] Pinto J. Project Management. Achieving Competitive Advantage. 4th ed. Pearson Education: Harlow, UK; 2016

[12] Freeman R, Harrison J, Wicks A, Parmar B, De Colle S. Stake-holder theory. In: The State of the Art. Cambridge, UK: Cambridge University Press; 2010

[13] Lehtinen J, Aaltonen K. Organizing external stakeholder engagement in inter-organizational projects: Opening the black box. International Journal of Project Management. 2020;**2020**(38):85-98

[14] Hillson. Effective Opportunity Management for Projects: Exploiting Positive Risk. New York: Routledge; 2004

[15] Johansson A, Bjerke Y, Landmark A. Why is it difficult to exploit opportunities in projects? In: Euram Conference 2015 proceedings. 2015

[16] Fischer R, Ury W, Patton B. Getting to Yes. Negotiation an Agreement without Giving in. Random House Group: Croydon UK; 2012

[17] Susskind L. Good for you, Great for me. Finding the trading zone and winning at win-win negotiation. New York: Public Affairs; 2014

[18] Hajer M. The need to zoom out: Understanding planning processes in a post-corporatist society. In: In the Governance of Place: Space and Planning Processes. Taylor and Francis Inc.; 2017

[19] Huemann M, Eskerod P, Ringhofer C. Rethink! Project Stakeholder Management. Newtown Square, USA: Project Management Institute Library; 2015

[20] Ansell C, Torfing J. Public Governance as co-Creation. A Strategy for Revitalizing the Public Sector and Rejuvenating Democracy. Cambridge, UK: Cambridge University Press; 2021

[21] Forester J. Challenges of deliberation and participation. Les Ateliers de l'Ethique. 2008;**2008**(2):20-25

[22] Healey P. Collaborative Planning. Shaping Places in Fragmented Societies. Palgrave MacMillan: New York; 2006

[23] Healey P. Contemporary movements in planning. In: Hillier J, Healey P, editors. Critical Essays in Planning Theory. Vol. 3. London, UK: Routledge; 2017

[24] Osborne S, Strokosch K. It takes two to tango? Understanding the co-production of public services by integrating the services management and public administration perspectives. British Journal of Management. 2013;**24**(1):31-47

[25] Voorberg W, Bekkers V, Tummers L. A systematic review of co-creation and co-production: Embarking on the social innovation journey. Public Management Review. 2014;**17**(9):1333-1357

[26] Leendertse W, Langbroek M, Arts J, Nijhuis A. Generating spatial quality through co-creation. Experiences from the Blankenburgverbinding (The Netherlands). In: Transportation Research Procedia. Elsevier; 2016

[27] Kitzi J. Cooperative strategy: Building networks, partnerships and alliances. In: Dees J, editor. Strategic Tools for Social Entrepreneurs. Wiley & Sons, New York; 2002

[28] Edelenbos J. Proces in Vorm: Procesbegeleiding Van Interactieve Beleidsvorming over Lokale Ruimtelijke Projecten (Process Support of Interactive Policy Making in Local Area Development). Utrecht: Lemma; 2000

[29] Aaltonen K, Sivonen R. Response strategies to stakeholder pressures in global projects. International Journal of Project Management. 2009;**2009**(27):131-141

[30] Wesselink M. Handboek Strategisch Omgevingsmanagement (Handbook Strategic Stakeholder Management). Deventer: Kluwer; 2010

[31] Radulescu M, Leendertse W, Arts J. Living labs: A creative and collaborative planning approach. In: Co-creativity and Engaged Scholarship. Cham, Switserland: A. Franklin, Palgrave MacMillan; 2021

[32] Martinsuo I, Geraldi J. Management of project portfolios: Relationships of project portfolios with their contexts. International Journal of Project Management. 2020;**2020**(38):441-453

[33] Olsson NOE. Management of flexibility in projects. International Journal of Project Management. 2006;**24**(1):66-74

[34] Rolstadås A, Tommelein I, Morten Schiefloe P, Ballard G. Understanding project success through analysis of project management approach. International Journal of Managing Projects in Business. 2014;**7**(4):638-660

[35] Sohi AJ, Bosch-Rekveldt M, Hertogh M. Four stages of making project management flexible: Insight, importance, implementation and

improvement. Organization, Technology and Management in Construction. 2020;**12**(1):2117-2136

[36] De Groot B, Leendertse W, Arts J. Building adaptive capacity through learning in project-oriented organisations in infrastructure planning. Urban Planning. 2020;**5**(1):33-45

Chapter 4

Application of Fuzzy Expert Systems in IT Project Management

Oleksii Dudnyk and Zoia Sokolovska

Abstract

The available statistics show the growing influence of the IT market on the world economy over the last decade. According to expert information, this situation will continue, despite the IT sector's economic crises, uneven development, and periodic fluctuations. The need to involve fuzzy expert systems (ES) in the IT field is stated, based on the high uncertainty level due to specifics of IT project management. The hypothesis of embedding ES in an IT company's business process management to increase the efficiency of operational and strategic decisions is tested. The structure of ES is offered, built on the basis of fuzzy logic using a combined model of the semantic network and implication rules. The operation of the system is demonstrated in the example of managing an IT company's current business processes to maximize its profits. Comparing the conclusions of the ES with the historical decisions of a real company demonstrates the feasibility of implementing the ES. The operation of the developed ES, using the knowledge base formed on the basis of 30 Ukrainian IT companies, confirmed the effectiveness of its use as a tool to support management decisions and increase the IT sector's financial performance.

Keywords: IT market, IT company, expert system, fuzzy logic, IT business processes, management decisions, project management

1. Introduction

One of the distinguishing features of recent years has been the exponential growth of digital data aggregation. This is accompanied by the expansion of big data analytics, artificial intelligence, cloud computing, and digital platforms. As more devices access the Internet and the number of people using digital services grows, the role of digital data and technology is becoming more widespread, and the digital economy is evolving at a breakneck pace [1]. The information and communication technology (ICT) industry is at the heart of much of this activity, supporting the digital economy and serving as a reliable measure of its effectiveness.

ICT plays a crucial role in the economy not only as a source of potential income but also as a vector of cross-growth, making profound changes in various sectors of the economy. Technologies such as the Internet of Things, robotics, artificial intelligence, cloud computing, big data analysis, 3D printing, and many others are already changing the way businesses design, produce and provide services.

Despite how important IT projects are to all aspects of the modern world, their management is not an ideal process. A recent survey conducted by Standish Group showed that 19% of over 50,000 software projects are failed and never completed [2]. At the same time, over the previous 10 years, the percentage of failures varied from 17–22%, which indicates the regularity of this problem in software engineering [3]. In the context of numerous crisis phenomena of the world economy, against the background of these trends, the importance of the main subjects in the IT industry (product and outsourcing IT firms) and tools to improve the efficiency of their operational business processes is growing. One of the innovative directions is the use of technologies like ES in the management processes to better plan and execute project development. Although the use of expert systems in economics and management is not entirely new, the dynamics of research and application of this artificial intelligence apparatus over the past 20–40 years have undergone significant changes and fluctuations—from discovery and active development to a significant decline, and again to the current trend of scientific recovery and the practical interest of specialists in various fields.

Accordingly, the tasks of the analysis of the history of development and use of expert systems in IT project management are set. The expediency and prospects of using the ES in the management of business processes in IT companies as innovative management methods that take into account the vagueness and uncertainty of the information environment of the facilities are proven. The positive impact of the introduction of intelligent technologies, including fuzzy ones, on the management processes of IT companies is demonstrated, which is reflected in the main financial indicators of their operation.

The article is organized as follows. Section 2 confirms the relevance of embedding expert systems in the overall business process management of IT companies. A retrospective of ES research and examples of applications of specific applications in various fields of economics and management are presented. Section 3 discusses the working hypotheses of the study; the ES architecture developed on the basis of fuzzy logic is offered. Section 4 provides a statement of the simulated situation, which is used for expert consultations using the appropriate knowledge base; an example of forming a knowledge base is described based on information provided by 30 IT companies of Ukraine, as well as using the expertise of agile specialists; the conclusions of the fuzzy expert system obtained as a result of its implementation (expert consultations) and historical decisions made by a functioning IT company are presented. Section 5 provides a comparative analysis of the results of the expert system inference conclusions and the real conclusions of a functioning IT company. Section 6 is devoted to outlining potential ways of further research to determine the useful consequences of the implementation of the proposed mathematical apparatus.

2. Historical analysis and overview

2.1 IT project management research analysis

The characteristic features of a software project are a large amount of research and development work, high uncertainty in the type, timing and cost of work, significant risks, and high costs. On top of that software development is associated with a high degree of complexity in a constantly changing environment. Thus, software projects demand effective management using innovative approaches.

Problems of IT project management are researched in many literature sources. Tam et al. in Ref. [4] conducted a survey of 216 agile professionals and identified the main human factors for the success of agile software development projects. In Ref. [5] Fink and Pinchovski presented an empirical study of the bias of the decision to save time in a software development project by increasing the speed of development and proposed methods to combat this bias. In Ref. [6] Hoffmann et al. presented the principles of designing strategically consistent and effective, but flexible portfolios of IT projects. Einhorn et al. in Ref. [7] consider the importance of taking into account the business case throughout the project life cycle and also provides valuable information on ways to avoid common mistakes and achieve the planned strategic benefits of the project. Lin et al. explore in Ref. [8] how to improve the integration of knowledge by actively addressing the problem of project uncertainty and proposes different management regimes, taking into account the types of uncertainty. In Ref. [9] Bjorvatn and Wald conducted an empirical study of the relationship between project complexity and management efficiency and determined the crucial importance of absorption capacity at the team level. Keil et al. in Ref. [10] research the impact of project management constraints on the possible escalation of software projects. In their work, Tavares et al. [11] analyzed different risk management strategies carried out in Scrum software projects and developed a novel risk management framework.

One of the key issues faced by both software developers and customers is to consider the degree of risk inherent in the various stages of IT project deployment. In [12–17] the classification of risks, their sources—related to incorrect determination of project volumes [13], excess of project costs [14], errors in budget planning [15, 16], deviations from deadlines performance [17].

Several works are devoted to automating some parts of IT project management activities. Alba and Chicano in Ref. [18] applied genetic algorithms to optimally allocate resources for IT projects. Uzzafer in Ref. [19] presented a simulation model for strategic IT project management. The results of the simulation determine the budget and schedule required for a project.

In the process of preparing and implementing a software project, the manager is forced to make decisions in conditions of uncertainty, based on incomplete or inaccurate information about the current state and prospects of the project's development. It is possible to improve the quality of the decisions made by integrating an intelligent component—an expert system—into the decision-making process. However, the use of expert systems in the process of IT project management is almost beyond the attention of researchers.

2.2 Expert system research and usage in IT project management

An expert system is a computer program that, based on the rules laid down in its knowledge base, can give reasonable advice and suggest a solution to a problem. The use of the expert system as a decision support tool is justified for solving problems that cannot be solved based on analytical calculations.

Work on the creation of expert systems began in the early 1950s by Newell et al. [20], who developed a common problem solver for solving problems of elementary logic, proving theorems, and playing chess. This approach underestimated the role of specific knowledge in reasoning. Aware of the possibilities, research has been conducted in more specific areas of knowledge, such as medicine and chemistry. The first expert system was developed in 1965 by Feigenbaum et al. [21] and was intended for the analysis of chemical compounds. Since then, the range of applications of expert systems to industrial and commercial problems has become so widespread that they have become one of the most successful commercial areas of artificial intelligence. Some examples of the ES use in various areas of business are discussed below.

One example of the ES application in management is the software application Business Insight [22]—an expert system to support decision-making and strategic planning. Insight business presents the user with opportunities for strategic analysis, business monitoring; identification of key factors influencing business success; strengths and weaknesses of the business; obtaining the results of forecasts for the implementation of various business strategies. Starting with the user's answer to the questions asked by the system during the introduction, it can conduct a number of analyzes, providing the user with practical understanding and advice on his business and marketing strategies. The system also shows the progress of its logic for each comment or recommendation it makes.

In Ref. [23] Rao et al. present an expert system called PAT (productivity assessment technology), which provides a comprehensive analysis of project effectiveness. PAT uses the same logical process as a specialist in this field would identify the causes of good or bad performance. The proposed system also recommends corrective action and provides the user with explanations or justifications for the results.

When discussing the pros and cons of expert systems, most researchers focus on the list of advantages of expert systems and pay less attention to the disadvantages. In Ref. [24] Zarandi et al. focus on the weaknesses of expert systems, namely:

- Lack of ability and flexibility to adapt to changes in the environment.

- Lack of ability to generate a creative answer when there is no answer.

- Lack of ability to summarize their knowledge using an analogy.

- Impossibility to learn: usually, expert systems do not have the opportunity to learn from experience. Many expert systems cannot automatically change their knowledge base, nor adjust existing rules or add new ones.

One of the methods of combating these shortcomings is a combination of expert systems with methods and techniques of machine learning and artificial intelligence. For example, fuzzy logic can be used to manage uncertainty in expert systems and solve problems that cannot be effectively solved by conventional methods [25]. The main purpose of fuzzy expert systems is to use human knowledge to process uncertain and ambiguous data. Fuzzy expert systems have a history of use in various fields, in particular in economics and IT.

One of the potential areas of ES and fuzzy ES applications is IT projects management and their inherent business processes. Information technology projects are particularly prone to failures due to their specific characteristics, such as the lack of clear constraints, the complexity and abstractness of tasks, and the extremely rapid pace of technological progress. These factors increase the uncertainty, inaccuracy, and subjectivity in information technology projects and require the search for new management methods. Here are some examples of the ES application in the field of information technology.

The work of Dufner et al. [26] discusses the PMA expert system (Project Management Advisor), which can improve control over the IT project by evaluating the proposed project plan, identifying anomalies, and providing guidance for correction.

The PMA was developed as part of the CyberCollaboratory [27], built to facilitate collaborative design work. The PMA was approved by industry experts involved in the knowledge acquisition process and evaluated on 11 realistic project plans. The results showed a clear ability to detect anomalies in the project plan. The PMA also provided explanations and suggested corrective action.

Truică and Barnoschi present in Ref. [28] an expert system for recruiting IT specialists, which helps the human resources department to perform the recruitment of qualified specialists, assessing their skills, and offering advice on appointments. The system is designed to work in the field of information technology. Checking the accuracy of the system showed that the system selected the same three best job candidates as the expert person.

The work of Rodríguez et al. in Ref. [29] proposes a new method of risk assessment for the analysis of projects in the field of IT. The proposed method is based on a combination of a fuzzy process of analytical hierarchy and a system of fuzzy inference, benefiting from their advantages and minimizing their disadvantages. The proposed model takes into account different levels of uncertainty, the relationship between groups of risk factors, and the possibility of adding or suppressing variations without losing consistency with previous estimates. A case study of three actual IT projects showed the suitability and consistency of the proposed method results.

However, despite the fact that the field of information technology is very promising for the use of fuzzy expert systems, a review of the literature shows extremely little use of this apparatus in this area.

3. Fuzzy expert system application design

Historical review of the development and use of expert systems show both the prospects of the direction and the lack of attention to it. Next, we will focus on the architecture, methodological platform, and usage of the developed application—a fuzzy expert system. We will prove the possibilities and efficiency of its use in the business process management of a typical IT company.

Further considerations are based on the following hypotheses:

1. Expert systems, as the apparatus of artificial intelligence, can be used as an innovative method of managing economic processes and systems by taking into account the various informal influences of their uncertain environment.

2. Expert systems should be built into the overall business process management of IT companies, which has a positive effect on the effectiveness of operational and strategic management decisions.

3. The use of the expert system applications, based on fuzzy logic, in the process of managing the IT company business processes, increases the level of the main financial indicators, in particular, net profit.

Classical ES architecture based on inference: Database with initial information necessary to get an output; base of facts for the preservation of intermediate results; knowledge base with information on inference process through the knowledge base and fact base, and the core of inference (see **Figure 1**). The most important components that make sense to explore are the knowledge base and the core inference.

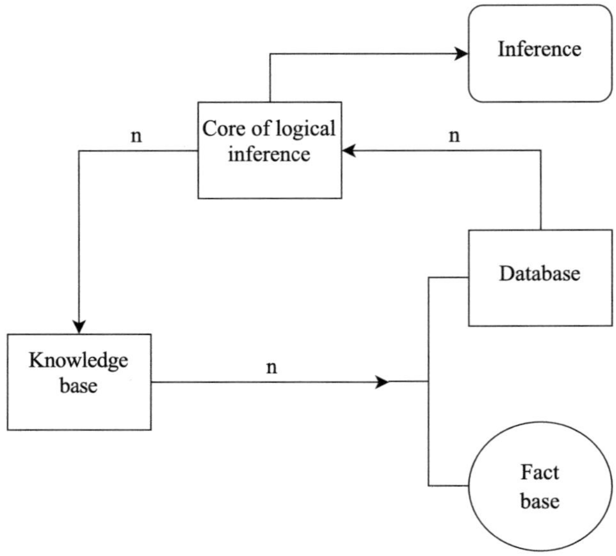

Figure 1.
The classic mechanism of inference.

One of the disadvantages of the classical inference architecture is the constant need to access the database to obtain the necessary information to calculate and maintain the database of facts in the current state. The second disadvantage creates unnecessary questions about the structure and ways to maintain a database of facts, which can be physically part of the knowledge base, which is illogical, or part of the database, which increases the load on the database.

It is possible to get rid of both shortcomings by reviewing how to work with the knowledge base and ways to maintain it. Instead of using crisp inference rules, there is a possibility to use a combination of fuzzy inference rules and simplified linguistic variables, which will be described below. This structure of the knowledge base allows getting rid of the intermediate facts database, which was closely related to the need to store intermediate information in order to have permanent access to the database.

3.1 Knowledge base structure

Before moving on to the use of semantic networks for fuzzy inference core, consider the second important component—the knowledge base. In the terminology of fuzzy expert systems, the knowledge base is a set of inference rules and linguistic variables, on the basis of which the mechanisms of direct and inverse inference work. A production rule can be defined as an IF-THEN structure that links information or facts in an IF part to certain actions or information in a THEN part. Thus, the base of production rules can be composed of an unlimited number of rules of the form:

$$IF\ (X = A)\ THEN\ (Y = C), \tag{1}$$

X, Y are linguistic variables;A, C are fuzzy linguistic equivalents of some crisp value associated with the corresponding linguistic variable.

The second part of the knowledge base is a set of linguistic variables that consists of an unlimited number of variables of the form:

$$X : Initial : [A : Trapezoidal : (A1, A2, A3, A4)|B : Trapezoidal : (B1, B2, B3, B4)], \quad (2)$$

X is a linguistic variable;*Initial/Derivative* indicates that linguistic variable value will be taken, for example, from a database or the value of which will be derived in the process of working with the knowledge base;*A: Trapezoidal:(A1,A2,A3,A4) and B: Trapezoidal:(B1,B2,B3,B4)* are the fuzzy membership functions;*A, B* are sets of values for a linguistic variable *X*;Trapezoidal indicates a trapezoidal type of membership function used to describe the values of a linguistic variable;*(A1,A2,A3,A4), (B1,B2,B3, B4)* are crisp values behind the fuzzy values of *A* and *B*, respectively.

This structure of the knowledge base has several very important features. First, it is possible to expand and reuse. The knowledge base can be expanded with new knowledge in the transition from specialist to specialist. Second, it is a potential opportunity to combine a knowledge base and a database to simplify the creation of a knowledge base based on production rule templates and linguistic variables. In this case, it will be possible to use rule templates instead of the structures of inference rules and linguistic variables described earlier, which will significantly speed up the process of creating a typical content of the knowledge base.

3.2 Inference core: SNePS

Next, we consider the process of fuzzy inference, namely the use of semantic networks for fuzzy inference. Semantic networks have been developed to present knowledge of an intelligent system that uses natural language. For the fuzzy inference problem, it was decided to use the SNePS semantic network processing system from the study of Shapiro and Rapaport [30], which is a denoted directional graph in which nodes represent concepts and arcs represent binary relationships between concepts. A feature of the SNePS semantic network is access to the database once to obtain the initial data. The inference rule can be represented in a graph through the nodes of the rule itself, the formulas of the input and output arguments, as well as the arcs that pass from the nodes of the rule to the nodes of the arguments. We should not forget about the connection between the rules due to the inclusion of linguistic variables from the right or left part of one rule in the right or left part of another rule. If the left part of one rule occurs in the right part of the second, the second rule is called the predecessor. Otherwise—a follower. Consider the following example and semantic network for this set of rules (see **Figure 2**):

R1: IF (A1) THEN (B1)
R2: IF (A2 AND A3) THEN (B2)
R3: IF (B1 AND B2) THEN (C1)

Rule *R1* is an equivalence rule, which means the following—if the predecessor is *TRUE*, then the successor also becomes *TRUE*. Rules *R2* and *R3* are general inference rules, which means that each predecessor must be *TRUE* for the followers to be *TRUE*.

Inference graphs were proposed and developed by Schlegel and Shapiro in Ref. [31] as extensions of propositional graphs. An inference graph is a graph of reasoning that is capable of inverse, direct, and bidirectional inference. It can support parallel processing for reasoning using inference logic. Inference graphs modify propositional graphs by adding channels between nodes along possible inference paths. Channels carry priority messages to transmit new information from one node to another. Message priorities affect the order in which tasks are performed so that messages are executed closer to the inference output and the inappropriate output tasks are canceled. A rule node is capable of performing inference operations using a set of rules known as Rule Usage

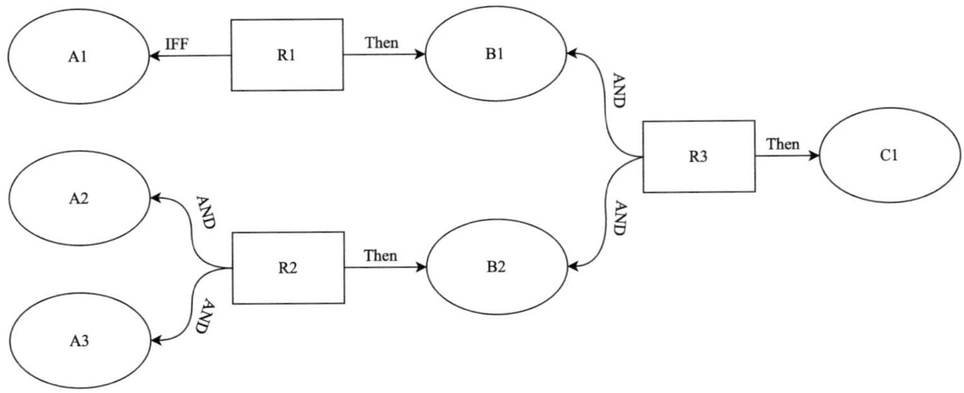

Figure 2.
Semantic network for a set of rules.

Information (RUI) [32]. RUIs contain information about which predecessors are true *TRUE* or *FALSE*, as well as information that explains how these values were derived. When a new RUI is created, it is combined with a set of existing ones. The resulting combination is used to determine whether the inference rule node can be used again.

For fuzzy inference in the developed system, only the direct inference process is used. Therefore, the structure of the inference graphs can be simplified:

1. There is no need for parallel reasoning, so there is no need for priorities for messages.

2. Instead of RUI, it is possible to use the simple status of the rule, which is updated when a new message is received. The status contains the result of counting the statuses of all rule predecessors.

Figure 3 represents a graph from **Figure 2** with the corresponding channels. Channels allow predecessors to report rule nodes when it was calculated and also allow rule nodes to report that they have been calculated. With this use of the semantic network, the dependence on the initial data in the database is reversed so that the core of the inference mechanism, that is, the semantic network, does not need to

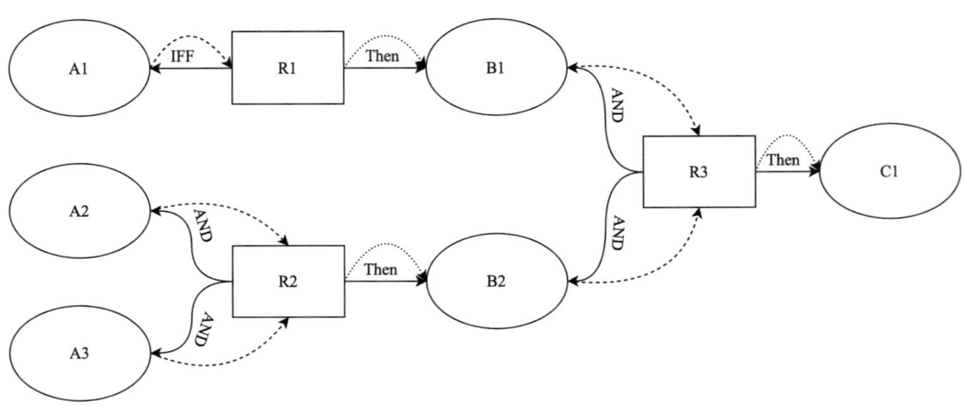

Figure 3.
Semantic network for a set of rules with channels.

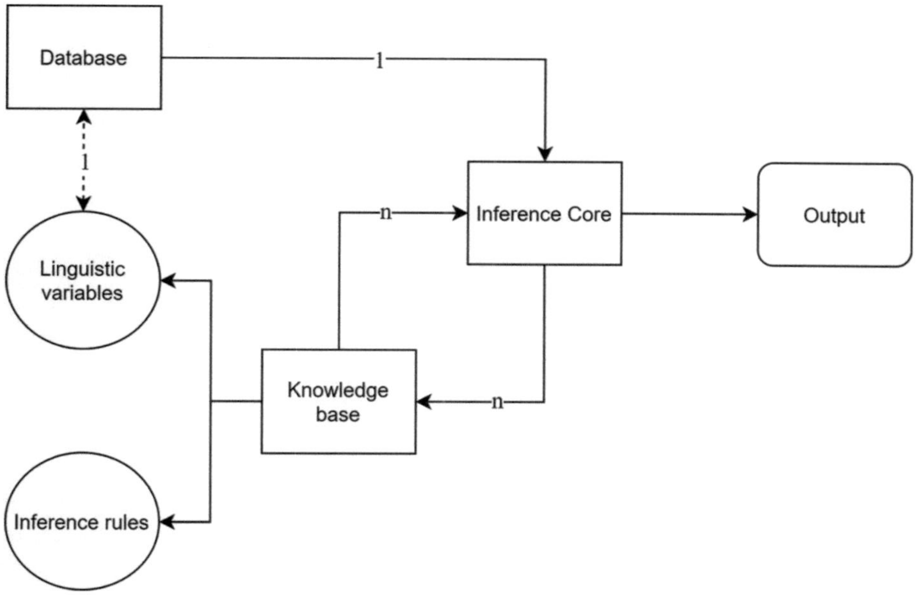

Figure 4.
Modified inference mechanism.

constantly query the data, but only rely on existing initial data and the potential for external expansion during the inference process. Thus, the general architecture of the developed fuzzy ES[1] is shown in **Figure 4**.

More information on the proposed architecture can be found in the authors' work on a detailed review of the methodology for creating a fuzzy expert system application suitable for work in the IT field combined with the Stage-Gate framework [33].

4. Application of fuzzy expert systems in IT project management

On the example of one of the expert consultations, we will demonstrate the work of an expert system based on fuzzy logic using a combined model of the semantic network SNePS (Semantic Network Processing System) and fuzzy inference rules.

Consider the following problem statement for an IT company. The model situation for projects is the availability of five teams (CycleDuo, Templater, Avion, Howl, and Converge) to develop existing and potential projects. A new team (Emerald) was also hired during the year, increasing the total number of available teams to six. The current market situation is to select five projects (Genesis, Crowding, Firantis, Exploration, and Hymera) from two customers (Mazzle, Global State). Also, additional information is provided on costs not directly related to current projects, namely the costs inherent in the maintenance of the office, administrative staff, and the cost of various advertising campaigns. Given the available data, the IT company faces the task of finding the best way to maximize annual profits.

According to the above problem statement, we will demonstrate the results of using a fuzzy expert system based on modeled data and compare those results with

[1] Source code of developed fuzzy expert system could be found at https://github.com/frightempire/FuzzyExpert.

Name	Description
Net revenue	The difference between the company's profit and all costs. From an accounting point of view, net profit is the difference between gross revenue and costs associated with managing the firm.
Total revenue	The total sales of the company and other sources of profit. It is important to note that total revenue differs from net revenue because it does not take into account expenses.
Gross revenue	Income at invoice value received for goods and services over a period of time.
Cost of goods sold (COGS)	Value of goods or services sold during a certain period.
Operating expenses	Amount paid for the maintenance of assets or business expenses, excluding depreciation.

Table 1.
Net revenue calculation indicators.

real historical data. To prove the success of the proposed method, it is necessary to find a way to measure its performance. In this example, it is advisable to consider the criterion of net profit as a measure of the effectiveness of the task of maximizing the company's profits [34]. Next, consider in more detail the process of calculating net revenue.

First, consider the main indicators involved in the calculation of net revenue. **Table 1** provides a general description of these indicators [35].

Let us start with the calculation of gross revenue:

$$\text{Gross revenue} = \text{total revenue} - \text{COGS}, \tag{3}$$

where the value of total revenue can be obtained by summing the planned annual profit from projects in development, and the cost of goods sold in our case is the cost of services, that is, the total cost of compensation for teams working on projects in development.

Given the value of gross revenue, it is possible to calculate the value of net revenue:

$$\text{Net revenue} = \text{gross revenue} - \text{operating expenses}, \tag{4}$$

where operating expenses in our case are the costs of advertising campaigns and assets in the form of office space and administrative staff.

Thus, based on the indicators for which data are available, we can formulate the following method of calculating net revenue:

$$\text{Net revenue} = \text{total revenue} - \text{COGS} - \text{operating expenses}. \tag{5}$$

4.1 Knowledge base creation process

To fill the knowledge base we used a combination of project managers' expertise and leading research results in the field of software project management (described in Section 2). Combining research data with information provided by management specialists from approximately 30 Ukraine IT companies, which describes the general structure of business processes during the management of the project portfolio within the IT company, a knowledge base was formed. Knowledge base corresponds to the IF-THEN structure and is aimed at solving a specific task of maximizing the profits of a typical IT company.

Templates for creating a knowledge base are as follows:

1. *IF (Risk of cooperation with the company X is N1 AND Project Y profit from the company X is N2) THEN ({It makes {no} sense to consider the project Y from the company X)*

2. *IF (Company X is the current customer AND It makes sense to consider the project Y from the company X AND Deviations in company X estimates is N1 AND Project Y profit type from the company X is N2) THEN (Project Y priority is N3)*

3. *IF (It makes no sense to consider the project Y from the company X) THEN (Project Y has no priority)*

4. *IF (Team X will soon complete the project AND Team X compensation is N1 AND Risk of interaction with team X is N2) THEN (Team X priority is N3)*

5. *IF (Team X does not complete the project soon) THEN (Team X has no priority)*

6. *IF (Team X is without match AND Project Y is without match AND Team X priority is N1 AND Project Y priority is N2) THEN (Team X has a match AND Project Y has a match AND Team X corresponds to project Y)*

7. *IF (Team X has no priority OR Project Y has no priority) THEN (Unable to match team X to project Y)*

8. *IF (Team X is without match AND Team X will soon complete the project) THEN (Team X must be disbanded)*

9. *IF (Project X is without match) THEN (Need to look for a new team)*

10. *IF ([Risk of interaction with team X is N]xM OR [...]xM) THEN ({No} risk of remote work)*

11. *IF ({No} risk of remote work AND Office expenses is N1) THEN (It makes {no} sense for remote work transfer)*

12. *IF (Company size is N1 AND The size of the administrative staff is N2) THEN (Need to {reduce, no action, increase} administrative staff)*

13. *IF (Type X advertising campaign expenses is N1 AND The benefits of an type X advertising campaign is N2) THEN (Need to {decrease, no action, increase} a type X advertising campaign)*

4.2 Fuzzy expert system implementation results

As a usage result of a fuzzy expert system, the following recommendations were received from the system:

- To carry out the Genesis project, it is recommended to select the Howl team.
- To carry out the Hymera project, it is recommended to select the Converge team.
- To carry out the Crowding project, it is recommended to hire a new Emerald team.
- To carry out the Firantis project, it is recommended to select the Avion team.
- The Exploration project is not recommended to be taken into development.
- It is recommended to abandon the office space.
- It is recommended to expand the budget for an advertising campaign on social networks.
- It is recommended to leave the budget for the advertising campaign in universities unchanged.
- It is recommended to abandon the advertising campaign through conferences.
- It is recommended to abandon outdoor advertising.

4.3 Modeled historical data

The available historical data were provided by the HYS Enterprise B.V.[2] IT company and is based on an annual breakdown of data close to real data, namely:

- planned annual revenue from potential projects;
- monthly compensation of current teams and administrative staff;
- annual expenses for maintaining an active office;
- monthly expenses to support active advertising campaigns.

Approximate available data on planned annual revenues from projects can be found in **Table 2**. Monthly compensation of teams, annual expenses of supporting assets in the form of office and administrative staff, as well as monthly expenses of active advertising campaigns are provided in **Table 3**.

The value of the annual net revenue was provided already calculated, but for visualization, we will perform this calculation again. This will help to make a similar calculation in the case of expert system usage. Before the calculation, we briefly describe the historically made decisions based on the data described in **Tables 1** and **2**:

---

[2] All data are not real, but close to real. Any similarity to real data is a coincidence. HYS Enterprise B.V. is not responsible for the correctness or sharing of the methods proposed in this work, as well as for the quality of the results obtained on their basis. If any questions about described methods, test data, or results occur, it is recommend to contact the authors.

Mazzle	
Genesis	350,000$
Crowding	250,000$
Global state	
Firantis	285,000$
Exploration	90,000$
Hymera	320,000$

Table 2.
Planned annual revenues from potential projects.

Team compensations (monthly)	
CycleDuo	7000$
Templater	4000$
Avion	12,000$
Howl	8000$
Converge	3000$
Emerald	5000$
Asset support expenses (monthly)	
Administrative staff	15,000$
Office space	18,000$
Advertising campaign support expenses (annual)	
Social networks	12,000$
Conferences	90,000$
Universities	50,000$
Outdoor advertising	15,000$

Table 3.
Expenses by different categories.

- To carry out the Genesis project the Howl team was selected.
- To carry out the Hymera project the Converge team was selected.
- To carry out the Crowding project the Avion team was selected.
- To carry out the Firantis project a new Emerald team was hired.
- The Exploration project was not taken into development.
- It was decided not to abandon the office space.
- The size of administrative staff has been reduced.
- The budget for the advertising campaign on social networks was expanded.

- The budget for the advertising campaign at universities was expanded.
- The conference budget was left unchanged.
- It was decided to abandon outdoor advertising.

First, we calculate the planned total revenue based on the planned annual revenues from the projects. Already existing projects are also taken into account in the calculations regardless of their completion date. Another interesting point is the failure of the Crowding project by the Avion team due to the combination of high risk of interaction with the customer Mazzle and the Avion team. Thus, the Crowding project is not taken into account in the calculations:

$$\begin{aligned}\text{Total revenue} &= 12 \times 1000 \times (150 + 90 + 50 + 45 + 35) + 12 \times 1000 \times (350 + 285 + 320) \\ &= 1,640,000\$.\end{aligned} \tag{6}$$

Now we calculate the annual cost of goods sold, which in this example is the sum of the compensation of the teams involved in the development. Teams involved in the development of current projects that have not yet been completed are also taken into account in this calculation:

$$\text{COGS} = 12 \times 1000 \times (7 + 4 + 12 + 8 + 3 + 5) = 468,000\$. \tag{7}$$

It remains to calculate the operating expenses, which consist of advertising campaigns, office support, and administrative staff expenses:

$$\begin{aligned}\text{Operating expenses} &= 12 \times 1000 \times (18 + 15) + 1000 \times (12 + 50 + 90 + 15) \\ &= 563,000\$.\end{aligned} \tag{8}$$

All indicators necessary for calculation of net revenue are prepared:

$$\text{Net revenue} = 1,640,000\$ - 468,000\$ - 563,000\$ = 609,000\$. \tag{9}$$

5. Results

Here we will consider in what aspects the historical solutions coincide and differ with solutions proposed by the expert system and will demonstrate the effects of those differences. Let us briefly summarize the differences in decision making:

- To complete the Crowding project, it is proposed to hire a new Emerald team as opposed to the Avion team.
- To implement the Firantis project, it is proposed to choose the Avion team as opposed to a new Emerald team.
- It is proposed to abandon the office.
- It is proposed to expand the budget for the advertising campaign on social networks, in contrast to the historical data, which left this budget unchanged.

- It is proposed to leave the budget for the advertising campaign in universities unchanged, in contrast to the historical data that increased this budget.

- It is proposed to abandon the advertising campaign in the form of conferences, in contrast to the historical data, which left this budget unchanged.

Other expert system decisions are similar to decisions from historical data. The first major difference is in finding a team for the Crowding project. The expert system analyzed the risk of cooperation with the customer and existing teams and concluded that due to a combination of high risks it is less risky to hire a new team to implement the project than to appoint one of the existing ones. Thus, the probability of successfully completing the project and avoiding the situation demonstrated in the historical data on the failure of the Crowding project due to incompatibility with the Avion team increases. Given this information, the Avion team was tasked with working on the Firantis project.

The next difference is a proposal to abandon the active office. This decision was made after analyzing the risks of working with current teams and obtaining a low overall risk. The usefulness of current advertising campaigns is analyzed. The budget for the social media campaign has been expanded, which on the one hand increases expenses, but due to high utility and small investments creates the most favorable environment for finding new teams and customers. This in the long run leads to a more rapid expansion of the company and increases the likelihood of finding a customer, which will increase the value of total revenue. Due to the average level of utility and costs, it was decided to leave the budget of university advertising campaigns unchanged. After analyzing the low level of utility and high costs of the campaign through conferences, the expert system made an unequivocal decision to abandon this type of campaign.

Next let us make similar calculations of net revenue, taking into account the implementation of the expert system recommendations. But it should be borne in mind that since the data are historical, the implementation of the expert system is modeled. Based on these calculations, we can observe the impact of these decisions on the value of total profit and operating expenses.

We calculate total revenue based on planned annual revenues from existing and potential projects. In contrast to real historical data, the Crowding project corresponds to a team with a lower risk of cooperation, which suggests a higher probability of successful completion of the project. Thus, in this calculation, the Crowding project is taken into account:

$$\begin{aligned} \text{Total revenue} &= 12 \times 1000 \times (150 + 90 + 50 + 45 + 35) + 12 \times 1000 \times (350 + 250 + 285 + 320) \\ &= 1,890,000\$. \end{aligned} \tag{10}$$

The calculation of the compensation amount of the teams involved in the development does not differ from the calculation of historical data. After all, the same teams are involved in the development. The amount of compensation is:

$$\text{COGS} = 468,000\$. \tag{11}$$

Thus, we immediately proceed to the calculation of operating expenses. The difference from historical data is the proposal to abandon the active office, as well as the advertising campaign through conferences. At the same time, do not change the budget for university advertising campaigns. We are reducing the budget for university advertising campaigns compared to historical data from \$50,000 to \$30,000, which is the size of this budget before expansion. We are expanding the budget for an advertising campaign on social networks in approximately the same proportions from \$12,000 to \$20,000. Refusing an advertising campaign through conferences and office support, we generally have:

$$\text{Operating expenses} = 12 \times 1000 \times 15 + 1000 \times (20 + 30) = 230,000\$. \quad (12)$$

All indicators necessary for calculation of net revenue are prepared:

$$\text{Net revenue} = 1,890,000\$ - 468,000\$ - 230,000\$ = 1,192,000\$. \quad (13)$$

Comparing historical data and implementation results, we can see that the total profit increased by \$250,000. In turn, operating expenses decreased by \$333,000. Thus the total increase in annual net revenue is \$583,000.

6. Conclusions

The role of the main subjects in the industry—IT companies—and the level of management of their business processes are growing. Effective management will help to achieve the strategic goals of companies and strengthen their financial stability. The analysis of the instrumental base for support of management decision-making in the conditions of uncertainty and risk brings to the fore the use of expert systems. At the same time, fuzzy expert systems built using methods and models of fuzzy logic seem to be the most effective.

Historical review of research and applications of this mathematical apparatus has shown only some examples of its use in the field of IT—a "bottleneck" that must be overcome because the feasibility of implementing intelligent technologies is confirmed by many factors. Among the main ones—the ability to present available information in linguistic form, smoothing insufficient or missing information, the institutional memory of the ES with tools to supplement and modify it, the presence of built-in mechanisms (for various architectures and algorithms) decision-making, metacomponent to explain expert advice, a library of precedents for adjusting the adoption of previous management decisions with the involvement of expert data, etc.

Given the need and feasibility of implementing the apparatus of fuzzy ES in IT project management, a fuzzy ES application was developed. The main difference between the developed application and the existing one is the proposal of the architectural model of the ES with a modified mechanism of fuzzy inference. This significantly speeds up the process of fuzzy inference and reduces the duration of expert consultations. The effectiveness of the proposed fuzzy ES application is demonstrated by the example of a modeled situation of maximizing the revenue of an IT company in specific circumstances—the business process environment associated with the implementation of current projects.

Currently, the experimental operation of the developed expert system application is carried out on the basis of a number of IT companies. Topics of expert advice on IT business process management include a wide range of tasks, such as search and monitoring of projects (selection of customers, teams, and other resources), forming a balanced portfolio of the company, assessing the status of projects, ensuring strategic goals and improving (in particular, financial) indicators of its activity, etc.

The experience gained based on the sector of outsourced IT companies allowed us to propose a methodology for embedding the ES application in the overall management loop within the Stage-Gate framework, which increases the efficiency of the system.

Further improvement of the application is carried out in the following areas:

- Expansion of knowledge and databases through definitions that meet the specifics of the IT industry functioning.

- Improving the accuracy and adequacy of the implemented fuzzy inference due to:

    - Combining fuzzy and crisp calculations;

    - Integration with the metacomponent of historical analysis;

    - Increasing the flexibility of the fuzzy model for knowledge base creation.

- Creation of a more developed metacomponent to explain in detail the expert consultations results.

- Development of a user-friendly interface for end-users, taking into account the wishes of IT professionals.

In essence, expert systems belong to the reusable apparatus. Their effectiveness as a management tool increases with the enrichment of knowledge and databases through the introduction of new experiences. The rapid development of the IT industry, specification, and standardization of software development processes at the global level provides a fundamental basis for the exchange, reproduction, and implementation of intelligent technologies with elements of fuzzy logic.

Acknowledgements

We would like to show gratitude to HYS Enterprise B.V.™ for providing modeled historical data for the purposes of this research and validation of the proposed fuzzy ES and its practical relevance.

Author details

Oleksii Dudnyk* and Zoia Sokolovska
Department of Economic Cybernetics and Information Technologies, Odessa National Polytechnic University, Odessa, Ukraine

*Address all correspondence to: dudnyk.o.o@op.edu.ua

References

[1] Digital Economy Report 2019 [Internet]. UNCTAD; 2019. Available from: https://unctad.org/system/files/official-document/der2019_en.pdf [Accessed: December 04, 2021]

[2] Portman H. Review Standish Group—CHAOS 2020: Beyond Infinity [Internet]. 2021. Available from: https://hennyportman.wordpress.com/2021/01/06/review-standish-group-chaos-2020-beyond-infinity/ [Accessed: December 04, 2021]

[3] The Standish Group. CHAOS Report 2015 [Internet]. 2015. Available from: https://www.standishgroup.com/sample_research_files/CHAOSReport2015-Final.pdf [Accessed: December 04, 2021]

[4] Tam C, Moura EJ da C, Oliveira T, Varajão J. The factors influencing the success of on-going agile software development projects. International Journal of Project Management. 2020;**38**(3):165-176. DOI: 10.1016/j.ijproman.2020.02.001

[5] Fink L, Pinchovski B. It is about time: Bias and its mitigation in time-saving decisions in software development projects. International Journal of Project Management. 2020;**38**(2):99-111. DOI: 10.1016/j.ijproman.2020.01.001

[6] Hoffmann D, Ahlemann F, Reining S. Reconciling alignment, efficiency, and agility in IT project portfolio management: Recommendations based on a revelatory case study. International Journal of Project Management. 2020;**38**(2):124-136. DOI: 10.1016/j.ijproman.2020.01.004

[7] Einhorn F, Marnewick C, Meredith J. Achieving strategic benefits from business IT projects: The critical importance of using the business case across the entire project lifetime. International Journal of Project Management. 2019;**37**(8):989-1002. DOI: 10.1016/j.ijproman.2019.09.001

[8] Lin L, Müller R, Zhu F, Liu H. Choosing suitable project control modes to improve the knowledge integration under different uncertainties. International Journal of Project Management. 2019;**37**(7):896-911. DOI: 10.1016/j.ijproman.2019.07.002

[9] Bjorvatn T, Wald A. Project complexity and team-level absorptive capacity as drivers of project management performance. International Journal of Project Management. 2018;**36**(6):876-888. DOI: 10.1016/j.ijproman.2018.05.003

[10] Keil M, Rai A, Cheney Mann JE, Zhang GP. Why software projects escalate: The importance of project management constructs. IEEE Transactions on Engineering Management. 2003;**50**(3):251. DOI: 10.1109/TEM.2003.817312

[11] Tavares BG, da Silva CES, de Souza AD. Risk management analysis in Scrum software projects. International Transactions in Operational Research. 2019;**26**(5):1. DOI: 10.1111/itor.12401

[12] Rosenau MD, Githens GD. Successful Project Management: A Step-By-Step Approach with Practical Examples. 4th ed. United States: Wiley; 2005

[13] Mirza MN, Pourzolfaghar Z, Shahnazari M. Significance of scope in project success. Procedia Technology. 2013;**9**:722-729. DOI: 10.1016/j.protcy.2013.12.080

[14] Bloch M, Blumberg S, Laartz J. Delivering large-scale IT projects on time, on budget, and on value. McKinsey Quarterly. 2012;**27**:2-7

[15] Charette RN. Software Engineering Risk Analysis and Management. USA: McGraw-Hill, Inc.; 1989

[16] Pfleeger SL, Atlee JM. Software Engineering: Theory and Practice. 4th ed. USA: Pearson; 2010

[17] Arnuphaptrairong T. Top ten lists of software project risks: Evidence from the literature survey. In: Proceedings of the International MultiConference of Engineers and Computer Scientists. Hong Kong: IAENG (International Association of Engineers); 2011. pp. 1-6

[18] Alba E, Francisco Chicano J. Software project management with GAs. Information Sciences. 2007;**177**(11): 2380. DOI: 10.1016/j.ins.2006.12.020

[19] Uzzafer M. A simulation model for strategic management process of software projects. Journal of Systems and Software. 2013;**86**(1):21. DOI: 10.1016/j.jss.2012.06.042

[20] Newell A, Shaw JC, Simon HA. Report on a general problem solving program. In: Proceedings of the International Conference on Information Processing. Santa Monica, California, U.S.: RAND Corporation; 1959. pp. 256-264

[21] Feigenbaum E, Buchanan B, Lederberg J. On generality and problem solving: A case study using the DENDRAL program. Machine Intelligence. 1970;**6**:1

[22] McNeilly M, Gessner S. Business Insights™: An expert system for strategic analysis. Planning Review. 1993;**21**(2):32-33. DOI: 10.1108/eb054410

[23] Rao MP, Miller DM, Lin B. PET: An expert system for productivity analysis. Expert Systems with Applications. 2005; **29**(2):300-309. DOI: 10.1016/j.eswa.2005.04.003

[24] Zarandi MHF, Asl AAS, Sotudian S, Castillo O. A state of the art review of intelligent scheduling. Artificial Intelligence Review. 2020;**53**(1):501-593. DOI: 10.1007/s10462-018-9667-6

[25] Zadeh LA. The role of fuzzy logic in the management of uncertainty in expert systems. Fuzzy Sets and Systems. 1983; **11**(1-3):199-227. DOI: 10.1016/S0165-0114(83)80081-5

[26] Dufner D, Kwon O, Doty A. Improving software development project team performance: A Web-based expert support system for project control. In: Proceedings of the Hawaii International Conference on System Sciences. Manhattan, New York, U.S.: IEEE Comp Soc; 1999. p. 6. DOI: 10.1109/HICSS.1999.772622

[27] Dufner D, Kwon O, Hadidi R. Development and implementation of a WEB-enabled CyberCollaboratory for asynchronous teams (Web-CCAT). In: Proceedings of the Thirty-First Hawaii International Conference on System Sciences. Kohala Coast, HI, USA: IEEE; 1998. pp. 330-339. DOI: 10.1109/HICSS.1998.653116

[28] Truică CO, Barnoschi A. Innovating HR using an expert system for recruiting IT specialists—ESRIT. Journal of Software & Systems Development. 2015; **2015**:1-11. DOI: 10.5171/2015.762987

[29] Rodríguez A, Ortega F, Concepción R. A method for the evaluation of risk in IT projects. Expert Systems with Applications. 2016;**45**: 273-285. DOI: 10.1016/j.eswa.2015.09.056

[30] Shapiro SC, Rapaport WJ. The SNePS family. Computers and

Mathematics with Applications. 1992;**23** (2-5):243-275. DOI: 10.1016/0898-1221 (92)90143-6

[31] Schlegel DR, Shapiro SC. Concurrent reasoning with inference graphs. In: Lecture Notes in Computer Science (Including Subseries Lecture Notes in Artificial Intelligence and Lecture Notes in Bioinformatics). New York, U.S.: Springer Verlag; 2014. pp. 138-164. DOI: 10.1007/978-3-319-04534-4_10

[32] Choi J, Shapiro SC. Efficient implementation of non-standard connectives and quantifiers in deductive reasoning systems. In: Proceedings of the Twenty-Fifth Hawaii International Conference on System Sciences. Vol. 1. Manhattan, New York, U.S.: Institute of Electrical and Electronics Engineers (IEEE); 1992. pp. 381-390. DOI: 10.1109/ HICSS.1992.183186

[33] Sokolovska Z, Dudnyk O. Devising a technology for managing outsourcing IT-projects with the application of fuzzy logic. Eastern-European Journal of Enterprise Technologies. 2021;**2** (3(110)):52. DOI: 10.15587/ 1729-4061.2021.224529

[34] Net revenue [Internet]. Farlex Financial Dictionary. Available from: https://financial-dictionary.thefreedictionary.com/Net+revenue [Accessed: November 07, 2021]

[35] Farlex Financial Dictionary [Internet]. Available from https://financial-dictionary.thefreedictionary.com [Accessed: November 07, 2021]

Chapter 5

Program Management Integrated with Data and Decision Sciences

Tien M. Nguyen, John D.T. Nguyen, My T.N. Nguyen, Charles H. Lee and Tam Nguyen

Abstract

Program management (PM) complexity depends on the budget size and program types. In general, the program types can be classified into three categories, namely, defense, commercial, and civilian types. This chapter presents and discusses an approach for integrating the PM discipline areas with emerging data science and decision science[1] (DDS) for any program type. Additionally, we describe the key PM areas and present a corresponding generalized model consists of a list of multiple PM discipline areas that can be tailored for any program types. To demonstrate the PM-DDS integration approach, we focus on three key PM areas and corresponding PM discipline areas related to schedule, cost, and risk management. These three discipline areas are analyzed to identify appropriate program elements that can be enhanced using existing DDS technology enablers (TEs). We also propose a flexible PM-DSS integration framework by leveraging existing machine learning operations (MLOps) framework. The proposed integration framework is expected to allow for enhancing the program planning and execution by reducing the program risk using a wide range of DDS TEs, including big data analytics, artificial intelligence, machine learning, deep learning, neural networks, and artificial intelligent.

Keywords: program management, defense, civilian, commercial, program management model, program risk management, program schedule management, data science, decision (support) science, big data analytics, artificial intelligent, deep learning, neural networks, machine learning operations (ML ops)

1. Introduction

Traditionally, program management (PM) usually addresses a group of several related projects that are meant to achieve an organization's goals and business objectives when integrated them together. A project management is usually deals with a single short-term period of performance (PoP) focused on specific objective(s) and related delivery schedules, quality, and cost controls. In contrast, PM deals with a much longer-term PoP with an emphasis on the integration of all the short-term projects

[1] a. k. a. data and decision sciences and abbreviated as DDS throughout the chapter.

to achieve an overall benefit to the organization. In another word, PM addresses the outcomes of all deliverables obtained from a group of short-term projects.

PM for a sizable budget program (i.e., above 50 Mil USD) regardless of the program type (i.e., defense vs. commercial vs. civilian) is a complex task. As an example, it is usually involved with the nine basic PM areas [1], including (i) managing enterprise, organizational, and program goals, (ii) managing program financial goals, (iii) managing program risk (a.k.a. risk management), (iv) managing program schedule (a.k.a. Schedule Management), (v) managing technical/product performance, (vi) developing and managing program team, (vii) managing performance and quality assurance (QA), (viii) managing internal and external communications, and (ix) managing program integration. These PM areas can be tailored to any specific acquisition system such as DoD acquisition system [2, 3], NASA acquisition system [4], acquisition of commercial products and commercial services for US government agencies [5–7], and commercial procurement process for commercial systems acquisition for private companies [8]. Section 3 provides detailed description of the key PM areas. For defense and civilian acquisition systems, such as US Department of Defense (DoD) and NASA, a program manager can decompose these nine PM areas into at least 13 PM discipline areas [1–7], consisting of (i) system engineering related to the system being acquired; (ii) contracts and legal dealing with contractors, suppliers, and stakeholders; (iii) financial and cost management; (iv) schedule management; (v) system test and evaluation, (vi) logistics and supply chain management, (vii) production, quality, and manufacturing (PQM) management, (viii) program risk management, (ix) intelligence and security management, (x) software management, (xi) business and marketing practices, (xii) configuration management, and (xiii) information technology management. The program manager must have a good understanding of these discipline areas and integrate them to manage them and successfully execute the overall program. In the DoD and NASA, the program manager has the authority to accomplish program objectives for the development, production, and sustainment of systems to meet the user's operational needs and is accountable to the acquisition decision authorities. Section 3 provides a generic model with a comprehensive list of 19 PM discipline areas that can tailored to fit any program types.

The main objective of this chapter is to present an innovative approach for integrating PM with emerging DDS technology enablers[2] (TEs) for improving the program execution and management of any program types. This approach is referred to as the PM-DDS integration throughout this chapter. The approach identifies the five key PM areas that are important to any program managers and a generalized approach to decompose these areas into multiple discipline areas and conducts an analysis of these (discipline) areas for PM-DDS integration. The goal of the analysis is to identify the discipline areas that a program manager can leverage DDS TEs to enhance the overall program planning, execution, and risk reduction. For each area, we will discuss potential ways in which DDS TEs can be used to support the program manager and his team in managing and executing the project more effectively. In addition, the chapter also discusses a simplified, flexible, and adaptable MLOps framework that can help any program managers to identify the desired program discipline areas and related DDS tools to support his program from

[2] In the context of this chapter, the DSS technology enabler (TE) is defined as data science and/or decision science framework, processes, and/or software tools that can enable the data science and decision support (DDS) technologies. An example of DDS technology enable is big data analytics (BDA). An example of a BDA TE is the Data Acquisition processes and software tools or the Data Curation processes and tools.

the start to the end of the program. To limit the scope of work, the chapter only focuses on (i) the program management for acquiring a system, or a product, or a service, and (ii) five key PM areas, namely, program goals, schedule, cost, risk, and technical performance management.

The chapter is organized as follows: (i) Section 2 presents our innovative approach for PM-DDS integration; (ii) Section 3 provides a description of the nine key PM areas; (iii) Section 4 discusses a generalized approach on the decomposition of the multiple discipline areas and provides the decomposed discipline areas associated with the PM areas discussed in Section 3; (iv) Section 5 analyzes and selects a set of discipline areas for applying DDS; (v) Section 6 aligns the selected discipline areas with an appropriate DDS TE and provides some examples to demonstrate how the selected DDS TE can improve the program planning and/or reduce program risk; (vi) Section 7 describes our proposed simple, flexible, and adaptable MLOps framework for use by any program managers; and (vii) the chapter concludes with a summary and proposed way forward.

2. Proposed innovative approach for PM-DDS integration

Our proposed innovative PM-DDS integration approach includes a six-step approach as shown in **Figure 1**. These steps describe how any program manager, regardless of program types, can identify which PM discipline areas can leverage the emerging DDS TEs to improve the execution and management of their programs. A description of these steps is provided below.

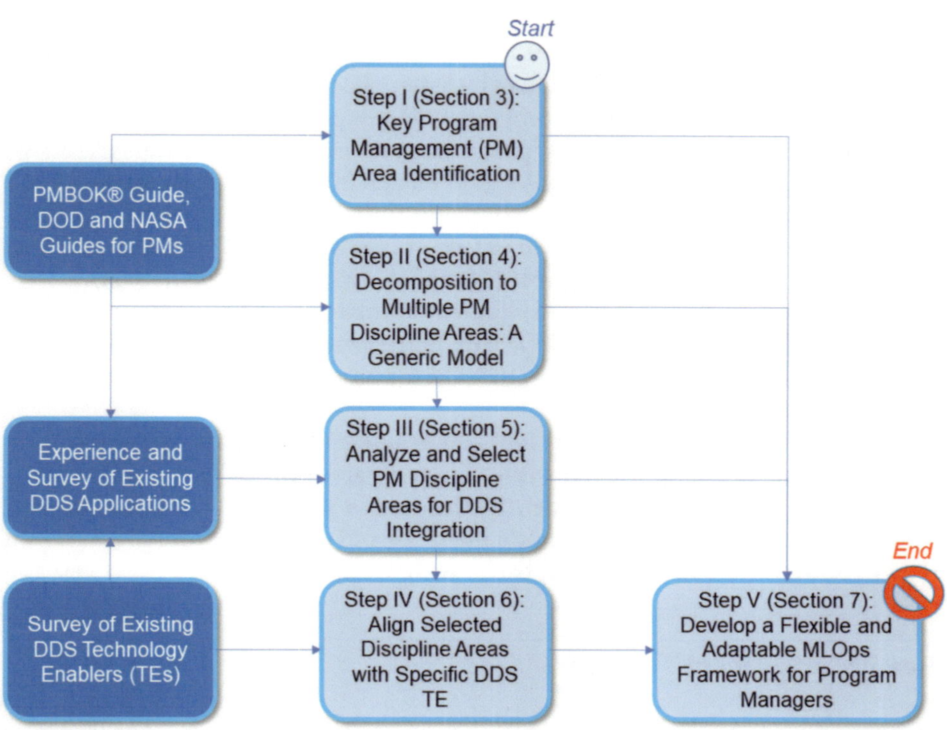

Figure 1.
Proposed PM-DDS integration approach.

Step I: This step leverages existing PMBOK® Guide, NASA PM Guide and Processes, and DOD Guide for Program Managers to identify a set of generic PM areas that are the most important to any program managers. This set of PM areas is also referred to as the key PM areas that can be used for any program types. The detailed description of these key PM areas is provided in Section 3.

Step II: This step discusses a generalized approach to decompose PM areas into multiple discipline areas that any program manager is required to manage throughout the various phases of their program. The generalized decomposition approach can be tailored to any program types. Section 4 provides a detailed description of generalized approach and corresponding PM areas decomposition results.

Step III: To gain a deep understanding of existing DDS technologies, we have conducted a survey on the emerging DDS TEs and their applications on program management. Step III leverages the survey results and our own experience to perform the analysis of the decomposed discipline areas obtained from Step II above. The analysis helps us to select a set of discipline areas that can benefit from the integration of existing DDS TEs for improving the program planning and reduce overall program risk. As indicated in Section 1, the scope of work for this chapter is limited to the five key PM areas, including program goals, schedule, cost, risk, and technical performance management. We will focus our analysis on these five PM areas and related PM discipline areas decomposed from these five areas. Section 5 describes the analysis results on the selected set of discipline areas that can be beneficial from the PM-DDS integration.

Step IV: For each selected discipline area and/or a group of selected discipline areas, Step IV identifies corresponding DDS TE and/or a group of integrated TEs, respectively. The goal of this step is to align each selected discipline areas and/or a group of selected discipline areas with a specific DDS TE or a group of DDS TEs, respectively. The alignment will help us to identify which selected discipline area and/or a group of selected discipline areas can be beneficial by integrating DDS TEs for improved program planning and/or program risk reduction. In practice, this step is the most important step because it helps the program managers to address the question on the integration of DDS technology for enhancing the program execution and effectively reducing the overall program risk. Section 6 provides a summary of the survey results on existing DDS TEs, consisting of big data analytics (BDA), artificial intelligence (AI), machine learning (ML), deep learning, and neural networks. Additionally, Section 6 describes the alignment of the selected discipline areas with specific DDS TEs and/or a group of DDS TEs. Some examples are also provided in Section 6 to demonstrate the use of DDS TEs for improving PM execution and planning.

Step V: Leverages the above four steps and existing MLOps framework and processes to develop a simplified, flexible, and adaptable MLOps framework that can help any program managers to identify the desired program discipline areas and related DDS tools to support his program planning and execution from the start of his program. Section 7 describes the proposed MLOps framework.

3. Key PM areas identification

From our experience and review [1–12], as pointed out in Section 1, the PM areas for any program types that are the most important to any managers can be classified into nine key areas. These nine key areas can be generalized and organized as nine

PM areas. Followings are a brief description of these nine key PM areas. Based on the description, this section provides a set of recommendations for the PM areas that should be beneficial from PM-DDS integration.

i. Enterprise, Organizational, and Program Goals Management: Program goals are usually derived from each organization's goals within an enterprise's overall strategic goals. The program goals should be clearly defined and provide obvious direction for the program team members to follow. The program's goal may be to fix a problem or meet a need among customers (internal or external) or to provide a defense system to the warfighters. The program goals should not focus on fixing a human resource problem in an organization within the enterprise. Managing program goals require the program managers to look at each of the goal within the overall goals as an individual project that they need to execute and manage. For each of these goals (or projects), they need to decompose into sub-goals or project tasks that they need to accomplish to reach that program goal. In the context of program goals management, the program managers can consider each of these goals as an individual project objective and they need to achieve the overall program goals by successfully integrating these individual project objectives. To effectively achieve the program goals, the program managers need to clearly define the key performance indicators (KPIs) for the overall program and related projects. They need to track the projects' KPIs progress and associated program's KPIs to achieve the program goals [9]. It should be mentioned here that a project is usually focused on the development of a unique product, or a service and it has a short period of performance (PoP), while program is usually a much longer PoP that focuses on the integration of the outcomes of each individual projects to create a defense system that meets the overall program benefit to users, or goals or an enterprise service achieving overall program benefit to users.

ii. Overall Financial and Program Cost Planning and Management: The program managers are responsible for planning and managing the overall program finances to ensure that they achieve their budget and program goals. One of the most important financial planning and management issues is the cost planning and management [1–5, 11]. The objective of the program cost planning is to estimate the costs and allocate required budget to the key program's products, services, and tasks defined in the Work Breakdown Structure (WBS), Integrated Master Plan (IMP), and Integrated Master Schedule (IMS). For examples, the products can be a satellite system and related ground tracking subsystems or a residential building. The cost planning activities allow program managers to know where the money will be spent, and on what products, services, and tasks, as well as when those expenditures will occur. The budget planning allows them to know the limit of expenditure for each activity.

iii. Overall Program Risk Management: In general, overall program risk is associated with a measure of future uncertainties related to all program activities preventing the program managers to achieve the program performance goals (or program KPIs), requirements, and objectives (or project KPIs) within defined cost, schedule, and performance constraints. Overall program risk can be associated with all aspects of a program, ranging from program team member's safety issues to actual operational environment, as these aspects are linked to the tasks addressed in the WBS, IMP, and IMS. Program risk management requires the program managers to identify potential risks across the program and quantify these risks to assess and track the potential risk variation in the planned approach and its expected outcome [1–7]. It should be mentioned that the program risk can be classified into two categories, namely, (i) the technical risk associated with the technical requirements associated with a system or a product or a service, and (ii) non-technical risk associated with human resources, supplier, safety, etc.

iv. Overall Program Schedule Planning and Management: The program managers are required to create a WBS and an associated program schedule management plan [1–7]. The overall program schedule plan captures the program start and end dates, program milestones, all individual projects and associated tasks identified in the WBS, timeline for completing individual tasks and related durations, resources for each task, identified predecessors, and dependencies for each task. The objective of the overall program schedule plan is to show the detail of how each individual projects and associated tasks are grouped together to achieve the overall program goals. The plan supports the program managers to effectively execute and manage their program activities through the program life cycle. For examples, some of the benefits of the plan include [1, 2]: (i) providing the basis for effective communications within the government team or stakeholders and with contractors or suppliers, (ii) identifying a baseline for overall program status monitoring, reporting, and program control, (iii) facilitating program management, and (iv) providing the basis for resource analysis and resource leveling, exploration of alternatives, and cost/time tradeoff studies.

v. Technical Performance Management: One of the key challenges to the program managers is to identify the technical risk associated with the system or a product performance that is being acquired by the program. This technical risk is related to the level of uncertainty associated with the performance requirements for the system or product. The level of uncertainty can be quantified in terms of the technology readiness level (TRL) and/or manufacturing readiness level (MRL). The higher the TRL/MRL, the less technical risk associated with the system or product being delivered by the contractor or a supplier to the program. For civilian and commercial programs using commercial of the shelf (COTS) products or services, the TRL and MRL are usually very high, and the risk is very low. But, for advanced development programs, the technical risk is very high, and the program managers are required to develop a technical risk management to manage and track the risk throughout the program phases.

vi. Quality Assurance (QA) Management: In the context of a program that is intended for acquiring a system/product/service, the QA management involves with the approach and process to control and manage QA of the hardware and software products of a system/product being delivered by a contractor to the program. The program managers are required to (i) develop a QA management plan to address the required standardized QA models and related national and/or international standards, and (ii) create QA process for verifying and validating the quality of the delivered systems/products meeting national and international QA standards. As an example, the ISO/IEC 17025 model and related standards addressed general requirements for the competence of testing and calibration laboratories, which is the main ISO/IEC standard used by ISO certified testing and calibration laboratories [12]. This PM area is not the focus on this study and will not be addressed in the remaining sections.

vii. Program Team Forming and Program Team Management: The program managers are responsible for developing, forming, and acquiring the program team of individuals who can carry out each individual project and related tasks [1–6, 13]. The organization of the team can be based on individual project structure with project managers to handle projects' objectives. In the US DOD, the team can also be organized into Integrated Product Team (IPT), where IPT team leaders are responsible for delivering the required products/subsystems. Just as the project team, this IPT team also has their own set of objectives, roles, and responsibilities, which will be aligned to the overall program objectives. This PM area will not be addressed in the remaining sections.

viii. Internal and External Program Team Communications Management: Internal program team communications address the information, data, and ideas exchange within the program team members, project managers, IPT leads, and program manager. The internal communications allow everyone to keep track of their project and associated tasks progress and help the individual project manager and the IPT leads to address technical issues and problems timely. The internal communications also help the program manager to anticipate and mitigate program issues and problems before they occur. External communications with stakeholders, contractors, suppliers, and media are beneficial to program managers. Managing the external communications is very important to the program managers in terms of managing the stakeholders' expectation, contractor's work on achieving the system's/product's qualities, and media's expectation on achieving the overall program goals on time. This PM area is not in the interest of this chapter, and it will not be addressed in the subsequent sections.

ix. Program Integration Management: To achieve the overall program goals, the program managers are responsible for program integration that is required to integrate all the projects under their programs. The integration is required to be performed at the individual project integration level. At this level, the project manager coordinates tasks, resources, stakeholders, and any other project elements, in addition to managing conflicts between different aspects of a project, making trade-offs between competing requests, and evaluating resources. Integrated program management ensures related individual projects are not managed in isolation. This PM area is also not in the interest of this chapter, and it will not be addressed in the subsequent sections.

As mentioned in Section 1, due to page constraint and our focus on the application of DDS technology to program management, this chapter focuses on the four key PM areas that can receive the most benefits from DDS, including (i) program goals, (ii) schedule, (iii) cost, and (iv) risk management. These four PM areas are defined in the bullets above as i, ii, iii, and iv, which correspond to: (i) Enterprise, Organizational, and Program Goals Management using commonly used program KPIs, (ii) Overall Program cost estimate and cost management, (iii) Overall Program risk management, and (iv) Overall Schedule planning and management. Subsequent sections focus on the decomposition of these four PM areas into multiple discipline PM areas for PM-DDS integration.

4. PM area decomposition to multiple discipline areas

In practice, a program manager is the title that is assigned to an individual who is responsible for managing the nine PM areas described in Section 3. The program manager must have the knowledge and a good understanding of the required multiple discipline areas associated with the nine PM areas to successfully execute the overall program. The program manager has the full authority to achieve specific program objectives from the development phase to the sustainment phase. For the US DOD defense programs, the program manager is accountable to the Milestone Decision Authority (MDA). Based on our experience working on NASA, US DOD, commercial programs, and our review of the multiple PM discipline areas associated with the nine key PM areas [1–9], we propose a generalized model for the decomposition of the above nine PM areas into a set of multiple discipline areas. The program manager must fully understand these multiple PM discipline areas to effectively execute the program from the start to the end of the program. Below is a proposed generalized model consisting of 19 PM discipline areas, including:

i. Program goal management,

ii. Systems engineering related to the systems/products/services being acquired,

iii. Specialized engineering related to the products and services being acquired,

iv. Contracts and legal dealing with contractors, suppliers, and stakeholders,

v. Program Financial management,

vi. Business and marketing practices for the newly acquired systems/products/services,

vii. System/product/service technical requirements and associated performance risk management,

viii. System/product/service cost planning and management,

ix. Program schedule planning and management,

x. Program cost planning and management,

xi. System/product/service[3] risk planning and management,

xii. Program risk planning and management,

xiii. System test and evaluation,

---

[3] From here and on, we will use the term "a system" to indicate a system/product/service, which depends on the application. As example, a system can be a satellite system or a commercial building; a product can be a phase array antenna with digital beam forming capability or a complete air condition system for a commercial shopping center; and a service can be a private Wide Area Network (WAN) service to support a military base or a private WAN service supporting a commercial enterprise.

xiv. Logistics and supply chain management,

xv. Production, Quality, and Manufacturing (PQM),

xvi. Program and system intelligence and security management,

xvii. Program and system software management,

xviii. Program and system configuration management,

xix. Program and system information technology, and

xx. Other Specialty Program Planning and Management.

The above 20 PM discipline areas that can be tailored to fit with any program areas and types. Below is a list of four key PM areas and associated PM discipline areas:

- Program Area 1—Enterprise, Organizational, and Program Goals Management using Commonly Used KPIs: PM discipline area associated with this program area is:

- Program Goals Management: For this PM discipline area, let us assume that the program goals are to (i) Meet program budget on time, (ii) Acquire the system/products/service within the specified PoP with specified budget, and (iii) Meet technical performance requirements with acceptable risk. To manage these goals, we want to select DDS frameworks, processes, and tools to integrate them into existing program management processes and tools to support the program manager. These assumptions lead to an important question concerning program management: How the program manager can track and control the three key program areas, namely, cost, risk, and schedule, effectively using the PM-DDS planning processes and tools? Based on our experience and investigation of the existing program management frameworks, the system technical requirements and associated performance risk, cost planning, and risk management are intertwined, and they are the key factors to manage the overall program cost, risk, and schedule effectively. The subsequent sections will address the PM discipline areas related to these three program areas.

- Program Area 2—Overall Program Cost Estimate and Cost Management: PM discipline areas associated with this Program Area 2:

- Program Cost Planning and Management: This PM discipline area is a focus of Section 4.1.

- System (Product/Service) Cost Planning and Management: This PM discipline area covers the System Technical Requirements and associated cost planning and management. This PM discipline area is a lower level than the program cost planning and management and will not be covered in this chapter.

- Program Area 3: Overall schedule planning and management.

- Program schedule planning and management: This PM discipline area is a focus of Section 4.2.

- Program Area 4: Overall program risk management: PM discipline area associated with this program area is as follows:

- Program risk planning and management: This is PM discipline area the focus of Section 4.3.

- System (product/service) risk planning and management: Like PM discipline area 2, This PM discipline area covers the System Technical Requirements and associated risk planning and management. This PM discipline area is a lower level than the program risk planning and management and will not be covered in this chapter.

The following subsections provide detailed description of the above three key PM discipline areas related to program cost, risk, and schedule.

4.1 Program cost planning and management discipline area

Cost planning and management for a product being acquired by a program is critical for the success of the program, especially during the pre-acquisition phase, i.e., planning phase. The cost of a system and its risk depend on the technical requirements. The more uncertainty associated with the technical requirements, the more cost risk. This is especially true for acquiring an advanced state of the art system or when the program management team is not sure about the technical requirements on a specific system they are planning to acquire. In the following section, we discuss this challenge and identify existing DDS TE that can address it.

4.2 Program schedule planning and management discipline area

In Section 3, the program schedule planning provides a program schedule plan captures the program start and end dates for all activities defined in the WBS. The program activities include program milestones, individual projects with associated tasks, timeline for completing individual tasks, related durations, resources for each task, identified predecessors, and dependencies for each task. Based on our review of the existing schedule plan, development and management discipline area includes five steps, namely program activity definition (described in the WBS), activity sequencing, activity duration estimate, schedule development, and schedule control [1–8]. **Figure 2** captures these five steps of the schedule plan development and management, and their detailed descriptions are provided below.

Step 1—Program Activity definition: This step identifies required activities specified in the WBS. This definition step also defines all WBS activities that must be accomplished to achieve the objectives of the overall program. The output of this step includes (i) a list of activities with a complete description of each of the activities

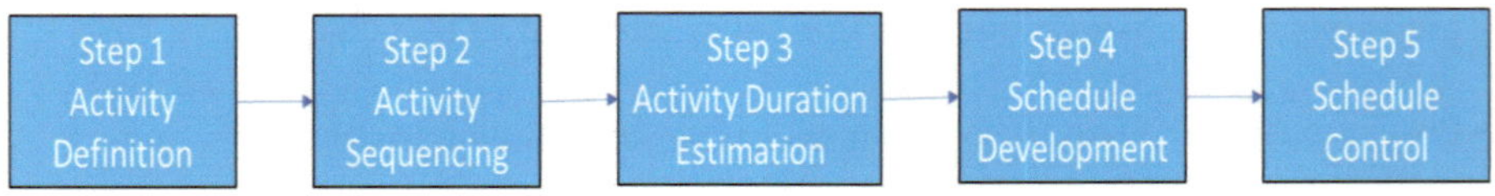

Figure 2.
Five steps for schedule planning and management.

and they are linked to the WBS. The list contains supporting details for each activity, including assumptions and constraints.

Step 2—Activity Sequencing: This step identifies the constraints and relationships among activities. It also defines the priority of the activities and the order of the tasks without causing bottleneck from one activity to the other. To determine the order, this step requires several inputs, including (i) activity list developed in Step 1, (ii) required constraints and related dependencies, discretionary constraints and related dependencies developed by the program management team based on "best practices" or specific sequences desired by management, (iii) external dependencies, and (iv) other constraints and assumptions. For instance, the required constraints and related dependencies can be a prototype must be fabricated before it can be tested, and external dependencies can be the availability of test sites.

Step 3—Activity Time Duration Estimate: It provides an estimate of the time duration required to complete the activities that make up the program. This is an important task that required SMEs who are most familiar with the activity to provide the estimates. At a minimum, there are two key required inputs to this step, namely, (i) the resources required and assigned for the activity, and (ii) the capabilities of the resources assigned. For improving the estimate, this step leverages historical information and lessons earned from past and similar programs and from commercial databases. In practice, the output of this step provides an estimate of the likely time duration to complete each activity. The estimates should include the mean values of the time duration estimate and 1-sigma value around the mean value, for instance, 1 month ±1 week, and corresponding assumptions made in the estimated time durations.

Step 4—Schedule Development: From the estimated time duration obtained in Step 3, this step develops realistic start and finish dates for each activity based on the specified program PoP. The schedule development process is an iterative process considering Step 2—activity sequencing, and Step 3—activity time duration estimates along with resource requirements and availability to display when the activities can be executed, constraints, assumptions, and associated risk. This step provides a set of schedules and associated information for the program, including (i) the IMS and the supporting detailed schedules, and (ii) the best balance possible between competing demands of time and resources. The schedules also consider the risk associated with time, cost, and performance tradeoffs and the impact on the overall program.

Step 5—Schedule Control: This step identifies potential schedule variations and manages actual changes to the developed schedules. The schedule change control system provides a well-defined procedure by which changes can be made and automatically be integrated into the program. The schedule change control system also provides mechanisms for (i) schedule performance tracking, and (ii) the approving and authorizing the required changes. Note that schedule changes come from various factors, including failure to achieve planned dates for specific activities, delayed tests, late delivery of required prototypes, internal program management assessment and replanning, and external direction, such as reallocation of funding.

4.3 Program risk management discipline area

As discussed above, program risk discipline required the program managers to define an approach to measure the future uncertainties in achieving overall program performance goals, requirements, and objectives within defined program cost, schedule, and performance constraints. More specifically, program managers need

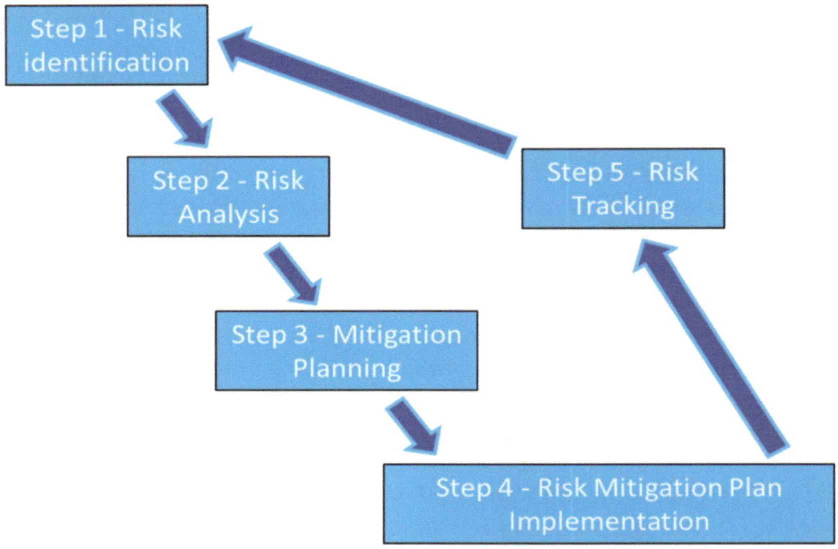

Figure 3.
Program risk management process.

to address risk associated with cyber security threats, human safety, program safety, system risk and safety, technology maturity level (TRL), supplier capability, supply chain management, system design maturation, manufacturing maturity level (MRL), and performance against plan. These program and system risks are usually associated with the program tasks described in the WBS, IMS, and IMP. The program and system risks address the potential variations in the program planned approach and its expected outcomes [1–7]. The US DOD risk management framework is described in Ref. [10]. In general, the risk management process is shown in **Figure 3** below.

As shown in **Figure 3**, the risk management process consists of five key steps, namely, risk identification, risk analysis, risk mitigation planning, risk mitigation plan implementation, and risk tracking. The followings describe these five key risk management activities in detail.

Step 1—Risk Identification: This activity identifies program risks throughout the program life. The risk identification process includes the nine following steps:

- Step 1: Risk program meets with project managers and Integrated Product Team (IPT) to identify a list of potential risk items. There are various methods of identifying risks, including (i) lessons learned, (ii) SMEs, (iii) prior experiences, (iii) TRL determination, (iv) MRL determination, (v) programmatic constraints, (vi) brain storming, and (vii) WBS;

- Step 2: Risks are determined to be acceptable or not by the risk team. For a big program, the risk team usually consists of technical SMEs, risk Integrated Product Team (IPT) managed by the risk manager, project managers, and program manager. Note that all risk items identified in Step 1 above are not necessarily accepted by the program;

- Step 4: Only accepted risks should be recorded and placed into a risk register;

- Step 5: The risk team identifies root causes for each identified risk;

- Step 5: Risk analysis should examine each identified risk to refine the description of the risk, isolate the cause, determine the effects, and aid in setting risk mitigation priorities (Risk Reporting Matrix);

- Step 6: Risk Mitigation Planning should address each risk with action items and due dates.

- Step 7: The risk team meets regularly to (i) assess risks to determine if the risks are burnt down to acceptable levels, and (ii) add new risk items, if necessary.

- Step 8: Identified risks are closed when the risks are burnt down to acceptable levels. In practice, some risk items can be closed quickly; others can be opened until near the end of the program; and some are considered watch items with a pre-planned mitigation plan that only kicks in when a pre-defined negative event occurs.

- Step 9: Document closed risks in the database for lessons learned.

Step 2—Risk Analysis: This activity analyzes each identified risk to ensure the risk description is accurate, isolate the root cause, determine the effects, set risk and associated mitigation priorities. The analysis refines each risk item in terms of its likelihood, its consequence, and its relationship to other risk areas or processes.

Step 3—Risk Mitigation Planning: The objective of the risk mitigation is to reduce or eliminate the impact of risks on a program. The risk mitigation plan (RMP) activity identifies, evaluates, selects, and implements mitigation options to bring the identified risk from unacceptable levels to acceptable levels given program constraints and objectives. The RMP activity also provides detailed description of what mitigation technique should be used, when the risk mitigation should be accomplished, who is responsible for bringing the risk to acceptable levels, and associated cost and schedule. In general, the RMP strategy can be chosen from the four mitigation options, namely, risk avoidance (RAV), risk controlling (RCO), risk transfer and sharing (RTaS), and risk assumptions (RAS) [1, 10].

RAV approach is used when there is alternative activity that can be used for achieving the same outcome of the task without carrying the identified risk. This technique requires the risk team to reconfigure the project such that the identified risk in question disappears or is reduced to an acceptable level. RA approach is recommended when the risk team can control the identified risk by managing the root cause and/or related consequence. RCO approach can leverage the risk database along with a warning system that can provide required warning signs to assess more accurately the impact, likelihood, or timing of a risk. RTaS approach is preferred when the risk team can share the identified risk with a third party like a supplier or subcontractor or an insurance company. RAS approach is recommended as a mitigation strategy by the risk team when the identified risks are small risks. The small risk is defined as the risk that when it occurs the cost of insuring against the risk would be greater over time than the total losses sustained. The RAS strategy accepts the loss, or benefit of gain, from the identified risk when it occurs.

Step 4—Risk Mitigation Plan Implementation: The risk team is responsible for developing and implementing the RMP. The plan ensures successful risk mitigation occurs and the timing for the burnt down risks is based upon the RMP. In practice, the implementation plan (i) determines what planning and associated budget and requirements along with contractual changes are required to burn down the risks, (ii) provides a plan for coordination between program management team and all stakeholders, (iii) directs the program teams to execute the defined and approved RMP, (iv) provides a summary of the registered risk reporting requirements for on-going monitoring, and (v) documents the change history.

One of the key activities in the implementation step is the risk assessment activity. The risk assessment activity is performed by the risk team to identify and analyze the risk by its category. In practice, the key risk categories include performance, schedule, and cost risks. Thus, it is essential that the RMP implementation approach should also be accomplished by risk category, and it is important for this process to be worked through the risk IPT structure and and/or projects' risk structure.

Step 5—Risk tracking: The risk tracking is also known as risk monitoring. It is defined as an activity that can track and evaluate the performance of risk mitigation actions against established metrics throughout the pre- and post-acquisition process. This objective of this activity is to (i) evaluate the performance of RMP actions against a pre-defined metrics, and (ii) execute the RMP or develop further risk mitigation choices, as appropriate. The results obtained from this activity provide required information on how the risks are burnt down ensuring the success of the RMP. The objective of the risk tracking activity is to ensure that the program team to (i) communicate risks status to all affected Stakeholders, (ii) monitor RMP, (iii) review RMP status updates, (iv) display RMP dynamics, (v) track RMP status within the risk reporting matrix, and (vi) alert management as to when RMP should be implemented or adjusted.

5. PM discipline areas analysis for DDS integration

This section provides a summary of our survey results and our experience on the analytical and simulation tools to support the three PM discipline areas discussed in subsections 4.1 (program cost management), 4.2 (program schedule management), and 4.3 (program risk management) above. The objective of this section is to (i) analyze these three PM discipline areas and the identified supporting tools, and (ii) select a set of the activities within each of the PM discipline areas that can benefit from the integration of existing DDS TEs. The objective of the PM-DDS integration is to improve the efficiency of the program planning and reduce the overall program risk for achieving the cost, schedule, and technical performance. The following subsections focus on the analysis of PM-DDS integration for program cost, schedule, and risk management discipline areas.

5.1 DDS integration with program cost management

Based on our survey of existing cost tools, the available cost tools implemented the four commonly used cost-estimating techniques [2, 5, 7, 14], including (i) Analogy technique that based on historical data for an analogous product or system or subsystem; (ii) Engineering Build-up technique, where a system or a product is broken into lower-level components (e.g., individual parts or assemblies), each of which is costed separately for direct labor, direct material, and other costs; (iii) Parametric technique that uses regression or other statistical methods to estimate the cost and its relationship between historical cost of a system and a product; and (iv) Actual cost estimation technique that leverages actual cost experience or trends from prototypes, engineering development models, and/or early production items used to project estimates of future costs for the same system. These cost tools can provide cost estimate with associated confidence level. The confidence level specification helps the program managers to understand the likelihood that actual costs would fall below estimated costs. This means that the greater the confidence level, the higher the estimated cost. Note that in the US DOD, it is mandatory for the program managers to conduct an independent cost estimate that is performed by different organization that is not part of the program organization. Some of the cost tools available are as follows:

- SEER: is an estimating cost tool used by civilian, commercial, and defense programs to generate independent cost estimates for manufacturing, sanity checks, and the analysis of contractor cost estimates [15].

- aPriori Cost Estimating Software Tools: aPriori provides a set of tools to generate manufacturing cost models for setting accurate cost targets accurately and timely. The tools also can provide the estimate model procurement costs for new designs without waiting for supplier quotes [16].

- DOD COCOMO Software: COCOMO software is a Constructive Cost Model consisting of a suite of tools focused on software cost estimation that was originally published in 1981 [17–19]. The COCOMO software tool is specifically designed for DOD defense program but can be extended to civilian and commercial applications.

For acquiring advanced systems with high uncertainty associated with the technical requirements, the cost and schedule estimates of the proposed system during the pre-acquisition phase become a challenge for the system design team, cost team, and risk management team. These three teams need to develop an optimal system solution based on multiple design criteria, including market uncertainty, technological uncertainty, technical risk, performance risk, cost risk, and schedule risk. The program manager needs to come up with a payoff-and-cost function that can balance out the performance, cost, and schedule risks with the market uncertainty and technological uncertainty. This is a multi-criteria decision problem that requires the designer to come up with a satisfactory and safe decision. Recently, a war-gaming concept using game theory was proposed to analyze alternative system solutions by playing out the Government's acquisition objectives against the Contractor's bidding motivations [20, 21]. As pointed out in Ref. [22], the game scenarios simulating various system solutions sometimes lead to conflicting and non-converging solutions. An advanced multiple-criteria decision mathematical model also proposed in Ref. [22]. This model employed the ELECTRE II model to resolve the non-convergence game scenarios encountered in the war-gaming model. Thus, the ELECTRE II model described in [22] when combined with proposed Advanced Game-based Mathematical Framework (AGMF), Unified Game-based Acquisition Framework (UGAF), and a set of War-Gaming Engines (WGEs) described [20] can address the cost estimate for an advanced system with low level of TRL (i.e., high technical requirements uncertainty). The recommended PM-DDS integration approach for cost planning includes big data analytics (BDA) approach with BDA data acquisition and data curation TEs, and artificial intelligent and machine learning (AI-ML) TEs. AI-ML TEs include (i) data mining techniques and tools (DMTT), (ii) data exploitation using multi-objective reinforce learning and adaptive neural network (MORL-ANN) tool, and (iii) predictive analytics techniques using MORL-ANN tool. For cost management, the recommended PM-DDS integration approach for performing the cost management includes three key components, BDA approach with BDA TEs listed above, AI-ML TEs listed above, and the Earn Value Management System (EVMS) to track and manage the cost [23, 24].

5.2 DDS integration with program schedule management

This section analyzes and discusses the five program schedule activity steps defined in Section 4.2.

Step 1—Program Activity Analysis: The techniques commonly used in activity definition are as follows: (i) decomposition process involved the successive breakdown of program elements into smaller, more manageable components, which eventually described the activities to be scheduled. This technique is essentially the same as the one used in the WBS development; and (ii) a template process that is an activity list or WBS element from another similar program that can serve as a model for the current program and provide a starting point for defining specific activities. Based on our current analysis of the existing techniques used for this Step 1 activity, it is difficult to integrate existing technique and tools with the current DDS technology and associated TEs.

Step 2—Activity Sequencing Analysis: Step 2 activity has been using several techniques and tools to develop the logic diagrams reflected the desired activity sequencing. Existing network scheduling techniques and tools include (i) Critical Chain Method (CCM), (ii) Critical Path Method (CPM), (iii) Precedence Diagram Method (PDM), and (iv) Program Evaluation and Review Technique (PERT) [1–7, 25–27]. The recommended PM-DDS integration approach for conducting the activity sequencing estimate includes three key components consisting of BDA TEs, AI-ML TEs, and existing activity sequencing tools (i.e., CCM, CPM, PDM, and PERT). The recommended integration approach is expected to improve the program planning efficiency.

Step 3—Activity Duration Estimate Analysis: The following techniques are commonly used in estimating activity durations: (i) Expert judgment guided by historical information, (ii) Analogous estimating based on the experience of similar programs, (iii) Parametric estimating based on formulas describing relationships among program parameters and time, and (iv) Use of simulation to develop distributions of the probable duration of each activity. Like the above Step 2 analysis, the recommended PM-DDS integration approach for conducting the activity time duration estimate also includes three key components consisting of BDA TEs, AI-ML TEs, and existing four activity duration estimate techniques described above. This recommended integration approach is also expected to enhance the program planning efficiency.

Step 4—Schedule Development Analysis: Several techniques and related tools are useful to developing schedules. These tools contain the capability to perform mathematical analyses calculating theoretical start and finish dates for each activity based on the overall sequencing of the program activities. Two of the more commonly known analysis techniques and related tools are: (i) CPM and (ii) PERT. Other scheduling development techniques and related tools that are also available to generate schedule plan using resource constraints, such as time, human resource, budget, and material. These tools provide another avenue to manage the effect of these constraints. A few of these techniques and related tools are schedule compression, and resource leveling. Like the above Steps 2 and 3 analyses, the recommended PM-DDS integration approach for generating a schedule plan also includes three key components consisting of BDA TEs, AI-ML TEs, and existing schedule development techniques and tools described above. This recommended integration approach when combined with the above integration approaches is also expected to increase the overall program planning efficiency.

Step 5—Schedule Control Analysis: The analysis of Step 5 on schedule control and management showed that the Line of Balance (LOB) process and related tools are currently used by program managers to manage the overall program control process [28, 29]. The LOB process and tools are used to collect program data, measure, and display the actual program status related to timing, phasing of the project activities, cost, related background, and accomplishments measured against a specific program management plan. The displayed results provide program management team desired program information that helps the team to (i) compare actual progress with a formal objective program plan, (ii) examine the deviations from the established plans and evaluate their degree of severity with respect to the remainder of the project, (iii) receive timely program information concerning potential trouble areas and indicate the areas that required immediate corrective action, and (iv) forecast future program performance. The recommended PM-DDS integration approach for schedule control and management also includes three key components consisting of BDA TEs, AI-ML TEs, and existing LOB tool. This recommended integration approach is expected to reduce the overall schedule risk and enhance the program execution by identifying and correcting potential trouble areas before they occur.

Figure 4 illustrates the proposed PM-DDS integration approach. This figure shows that the program schedule management can be integrated with existing DDS technology enablers for enhancing program planning and execution for risk reduction.

5.3 DDS integration with program risk management

This section analyzes and discusses five program schedule activity steps defined in Section 4.2.

Step 1—Risk Identification Analysis: Our analysis shows that the commonly used techniques and tools for risk identification include (i) objectives-based risk identification (OBR-ID), (ii) scenario-based risk identification (SBR-ID), (iii) taxonomy-based risk identification (TBR-ID), and (iv) common-risk checking

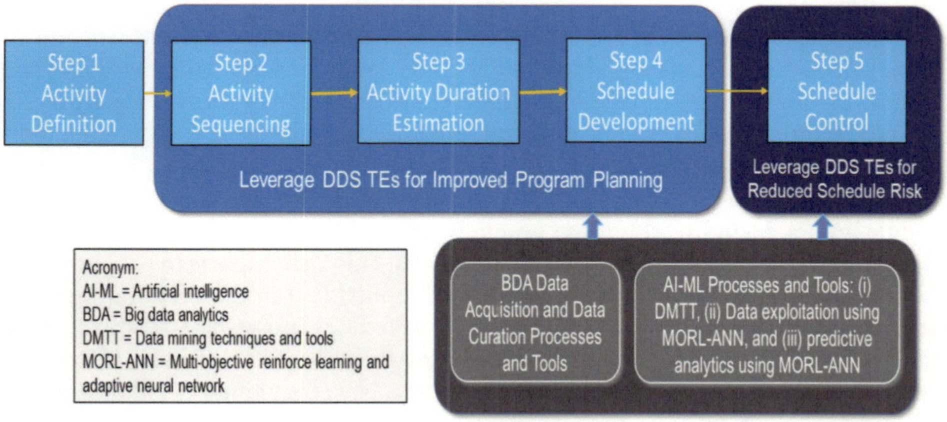

Figure 4.
PM-DDS integration approach for schedule planning and management.

(CRC). The OBR-ID technique and related tools identify the risk associated with the objectives defined by organizations and project teams [1–7]. Any event that may endanger achieving an objective partly or fully is identified as risk. SBR-ID technique and related tool perform scenario analysis using different pre-defined scenarios. The scenarios may be the alternative ways to achieve a pre-defined objective, or an investigation of the interaction of external forces in, for example, a market or battle. An undesired scenario that may occur in the future is identified as a risk, and any event that may trigger it is considered a risk trigger.

The TBR-ID technique and related tools are used to breakdown possible risk sources. Leveraging the taxonomy and knowledge of best practices, a set of questionnaires is compiled for review by SMEs. The answers to the questions reveal potential risks and are compiled in the program risk registry. CRC tools can leverage industry databases to provide lists of known risks associated with known activities, products, program elements. Each risk in the program risk registry can be checked for application to a specific situation.

The recommended PM-DDS integration approach for conducting the risk identification activity includes three key components consisting of risk databases with data acquisition and data curation TEs, AI-ML TEs, and existing risk identification techniques and related tools. The recommended AI-ML TEs include (i) DMTT, (ii) data exploitation using MORL-ANN tool, and (iii) predictive analytics techniques using MORL-ANN tool. This recommended integration approach is expected to improve the program management planning by reducing the uncertainty associated with the risk identification process.

Step 2—Analysis of Risk Analysis Activity: Based on our analysis of Step 2 on the risk analysis activity, the current risk analysis processes and related tools are focused on (i) system performance risk analysis, (ii) schedule risk analysis, and (iii) cost risk analysis [30]. The output of these processes and related tools consists of (i) assigned likelihood (probability of occurrence) and related consequence (the environmental impact if a risk event occurs) results to each risk using the criteria in the risk reporting matrix, (ii) consequence results in terms of performance, schedule, and/or cost impact using defined criteria, (iii) the risk matrix reporting the risk results, and (iv) documented risk results in the program risk register.

The system performance risk analysis tools typically focus on analyzing the technical requirements related to operational environment, TRL and/or MRL associated with systems/products being acquired, standards, material readiness, etc. Section 5.1 discusses available tools for addressing technical requirements with low TRL (i.e., high technological uncertainty level) and/or low MRL (i.e., market availability is low). For technical requirements with low TRL and/or MRL, the recommended tools include ELECTRE II, AGMF, and WGEs.

Existing schedule risk analysis tools are focused on the analysis of the (i) baseline schedule inputs, including durations and network logic; (ii) technical and schedule uncertainty inputs to the program schedule model; (iii) risk impacts to program schedule based on the program technical SMEs' inputs; (iv) IMS incorporating the potential impact from all contract and supplier schedules and associated stakeholders' activities; and (iv) schedule excursions reflecting the effects of cost risks, including human resource, budget, and schedule constraints. Note that when the identified risk impacts the critical path, then this risk affects both schedule and cost, and this risk should be registered as a schedule risk. Section 5.2, Step 5, discussed required analysis tools using PM-DDS integration approach for efficient schedule control and management. The integrated tools can effectively identify potential trouble areas in the IMS and indicate the areas that required immediate corrective action.

Currently, the cost risk analysis tools available focused on the cost analysis of the life-cycle-cost (LCC) by (i) building on technical and schedule assessment results, (ii) translating performance and schedule risks into LLC, and (iii) deriving LCC estimates by integrating technical assessment and schedule risk impacts on resources. The cost analysis tools are also capable of creating budgetary requirements consistent with fiscal year planning and determining the adequacy and phasing of funding supports the technical and acquisition approaches. The tools can document the cost basis and risk impacts and provide program LCC excursions from near-term budget execution impacts and external budget changes and related constraints. The recommended PM-DDS integration approach for performing the cost risk analysis is identical to Section 5.1 above, i.e., also includes the cost analysis tools described above, BDA data acquisition and data curation TEs, and AI-ML TEs. AI-ML TEs include (i) DMTT, (ii) data exploitation using MORL-ANN tool; and (iii) predictive analytics techniques using MORL-ANN tool.

Step 3—Risk Mitigation Planning Analysis: Current risk mitigation planning (RMP) tools focused on the four mitigation techniques, namely, (i) risk avoidance (RAV), (ii) risk controlling (RCO), (iii) risk transfer and sharing (RTaS), and (iv) risk assumptions (RAS). Existing RMP tools are mostly customized to specific programs. Most of the existing RMP tools are stovepiped and do not leverage analytical tools that have recently been developed using BDA and AI-ML technologies and associated TEs. To effectively conducting the RMP activity, we recommend integrating existing BDA and AI-ML tools into existing mitigation techniques. BDA tools include data acquisition and data curation processes and tools. The AI-ML tools include (i) DMTT, (ii) data exploitation using MORL-ANN tool, and (iii) predictive analytics techniques using MORL-ANN tool. This recommended PM-DSS integration approach is expected to improve the program management planning and execution.

Step 4—Risk Mitigation Plan Implementation analysis: Our survey of the risk mitigation plan (MRP) implementation tools shows no tools available and the MRP implementation is usually conducted by the risk team with support from SMEs across the program related organizations. As discussed in Sub-Section 4.4, RMP captured the key risk categories including performance, schedule, and cost risks, and the risk team is responsible for implementing the plan with the support of the program.

Step 5—Risk Tracking Analysis: Our survey of the risk tracking tools showed that the tools are focused on the tracking of the performance of RMP actions against a pre-defined metrics. The tools are also capable of executing the RMP to generate alternative risk mitigation choices, as appropriate. The tools track the burnt down activity to ensure the success of the RMP. To effectively generate alternatives risk mitigation choices, we recommend integrating existing BDA and AI-ML tools into existing risk tracking tools. BDA tools include data acquisition and data curation processes and tools. The AI-ML tools include (i) DMTT, (ii) data exploitation using MORL-ANN tool, and (iii) predictive analytics techniques using MORL-ANN tool.

The recommended PM-DSS integration approach for conducting the risk tracking is expected to improve the program management planning and execution by providing alternative mitigation choices to burn down the risk before it occurs. **Figure 5** depicts our proposed PM-DDS integration approach for conducting program risk management more effectively. For improving the program planning, we recommend incorporating BDA and AI-ML process and tools to support risk identification, risk analysis, and risk mitigation planning. To reduce the program risk, we recommend incorporating BDA and AI-ML process and tools to support risk tracking.

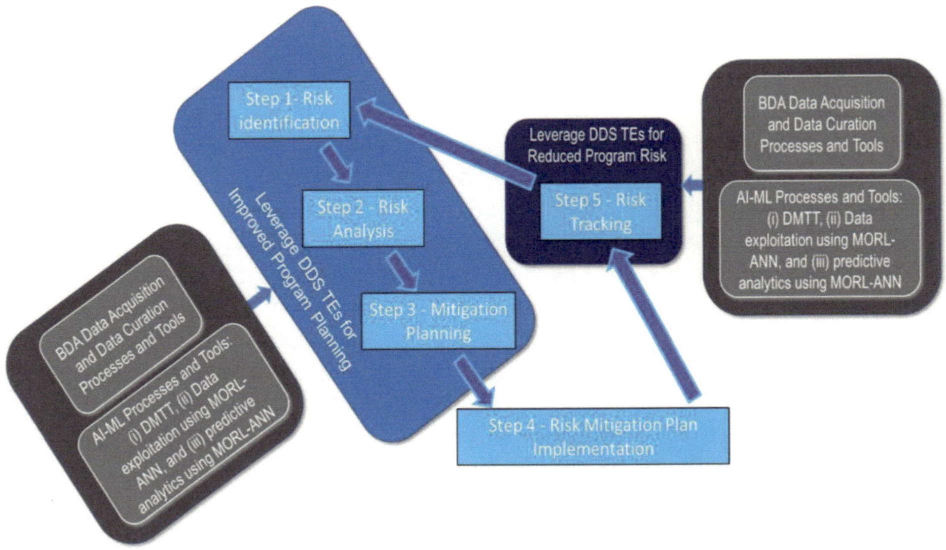

Figure 5.
PM-DDS integration approach for program risk management.

6. Selected DDS TEs alignment with PM discipline areas

This section provides the alignment between the selected sets of DDS TEs and the PM discipline areas identified in our analyses presented in Section 5 above. From the nine key PM areas discussed in Section 3, Section 4 decomposed them into a generalized model of 19 PM discipline areas and selected only three PM discipline areas that were aligned with the selected five PM areas (i.e., program goals, schedule, cost, risk, and technical performance management). **Table 1** provides a summary of the proposed PM-DSS integration approach for the program cost management (PCM) discipline. The table aligns existing PCM framework/process/model with DDS framework/process/model for the recommended PCM integration.

The use of artificial neural network tools to predict the actual cost of a project to enhance EVMS is discussed in Refs. [35, 36] and easily extended to the program cost prediction. **Table 2** summarizes our recommended PM-DSS integration approach for the program schedule management (PSM) discipline. The table aligns existing PSM framework/process/tools with DDS framework/process/model for the recommended PSM integration.

Like **Table 2**, **Table 3** provides a summary our recommendation for the PM-DSS integration approach for the program risk management (PRM) discipline. This table aligns existing PRM framework/process/tools with DDS framework/process/model for the recommended PRM integration.

As discussed in Refs. [24, 31–33], EVMS is a systematic process that uses earned value as the primary tool for integrating program cost, schedule, technical performance, and risk to manage a program. Program managers can leverage EVMS tools to determine and track the actual program status at any given point during program PoP. This activity can be done very effectively if the tools have successfully implemented required program constraints, program rules and process, and organizational rules. The implementation of EVMS requires a disciplined approach. Recently, BDA and AI-ML processes and tools have been successfully integrated into EVMS. Current

PCM framework, process, models, and tool	Recommended DDS framework/process/tool	Recommended implementation approach	Remark
EVMS Framework	ML Library, BDA framework with Data Acquisition and Data Curation Models and Tools	Leverage related cost historical data bases for integrating EVMS models with BDA tools for managing cost	See [24, 31, 32] for basic EVM, [33] for implementation
EVMS Process and Models			
Cost Analogy Model/Tool	Data mining technique & tool (DMTT); data exploitation using MORL-ANN tool; and Predictive analytics techniques using MORL-ANN tool	Implement MORL-ANN using MATLAB DDPG tool	See [34] for DDPG; See [35] for using ANN
Cost Engineering Build-up Model/Tool		For high technological risk with high market uncertainty: ELECTRE II model + AGMF + UGAF+ WGEs	See examples in [20, 22] for ELECTRE, AGMF /UGAF/WGEs
Parametric Cost Model/Tool		Implement MORL-ANN using MATLAB Deep Deterministic Policy Gradient (DDPG) tool	DOD COCOMO Software Tool [18]
Actual cost Estimation Model/Tool			See [34] for DDPG

Table 1.
DDS process and tool for PCM integration.

PSM framework, process, models, and tool	Recommended DDS framework/process/tool	Recommended implementation approach	Remark
EVMS Framework	ML Library, BDA framework with Data Acquisition and Data Curation Models and Tools	Leverage-related schedule historical data bases with EVMS and BDA tools for managing Schedule	See [24, 31, 32] for basic EVM, [33] for implementation
EVMS Process and Models			
Activity Sequencing: CCM, CPM, PDM, PERT methods and Tools	DMTT; Data exploitation using ML-AI tools; and Predictive analytics techniques using ML-AI tools, including MORL-ANN, decision tree, and support vector machine (SVM), cumulant calculator.	Implement MORL-ANN using MATLAB DDPG tool	See [34] for DDPG; See [25, 27] for CCM, CPM, and PERT. [37] addresses ML-AI methods for project duration planning and forecasting. See [38] for cumulant calculator
Activity Duration Estimate: Analogous Estimation, Parametric Estimation, Monte Carlo Simulation methods and tools		Decision tree, SVM, and cumulant calculator	
Schedule Development: CPM and PERT models and tools		Implement MORL-ANN using MATLAB DDPG tool	See [27] for CPM
Schedule Control: LOB process and tools			See [28] for LOB

Table 2.
DDS process and tool for PSM integration.

analysis results show that when these BDA and AI-ML tools are properly integrated with EVMS, the tools can certainly assist the program managers to execute their programs more effectively by anticipating the cost, schedule, program, and technical risks and mitigating these risks before they occur.

PRM framework, process, models, and tool	Recommended DDS framework/process/ tool	Recommended implementation approach	Remark
Risk Identification: OBR-ID, SBR-ID, TBR-ID, CRC models and tools	ML Library, BDA framework with Data Acquisition and Data Curation Models and Tools DMTT; Data exploitation using MORL-ANN tool; and Predictive analytics techniques using MORL-ANN tool	Leverage related schedule historical data bases with BDA tools for managing Schedule. Recommend to implement MORL-ANN using MATLAB DDPG tool	See [24, 31, 32] for basic EVM, [33] for implementation See [34] for DDPG. [39] addresses the differences between ML, AI, deep learning, and neural networks
Risk Analysis: system performance risk, schedule risk analysis, and cost risk analysis models and tools			
Risk Mitigation Planning: RAV, RCO, RTaS, and RAS models and tools	DMTT; Data exploitation using MORL-ANN tool; and Predictive analytics techniques using MORL-ANN tool	Implement MORL-ANN using MATLAB DDPG tool	See [34] for DDPG; See [40, 41] for risk tracking tools
Risk Tracking Analysis: Periodic Risk Status Reporting, Periodic reporting of risk mitigation plans tools			

Table 3.
DDS process and tool for PRM integration.

7. Proposed flexible and adaptable PM-DSS integration life cycle framework leveraging MLOps

Successful PM-DSS integration requires planning, structure process, and proper selection of DSS models and tools. This section focuses on how to leverage the concept of MLOps, and its existing framework described in [42–46] for the development a PM-DSS integration framework. The proposed framework should be easy to use and tailored to any program types.

As pointed out in Refs. [42–46], the objective of MLOps is to reduce the technical friction associated with the development of AI-ML models and tools from an idea into production in the shortest possible time to market with as little risk as possible. But the objective for the PM-DSS integration framework is to reduce the integration risk between a set of BDA, and AI-ML tools with the selected PM discipline areas. The framework focuses on the start of the program to the deployment of the integrated tools with the lowest possible risk. In addition, the framework should also address the operational phase where the program team can leverage the integrated PM-DSS products to execute the program effectively. More specifically, using the program data displayed by the integrated tools, the program team can use proactive risk management method to improve the program planning and execution by reducing overall program risk. **Figure 6** depicts a proposed PM-DSS integration framework leveraging existing MLOps life cycle framework. This proposed integration framework is easy to tailor to any program types and can be adaptable to any PM discipline areas and any set of BDA and AI-ML models and tools.

As shown in **Figure 6**, the proposed framework has a life cycle that consists of seven key stages, including (i) PM-DSS integration specification, (ii) related

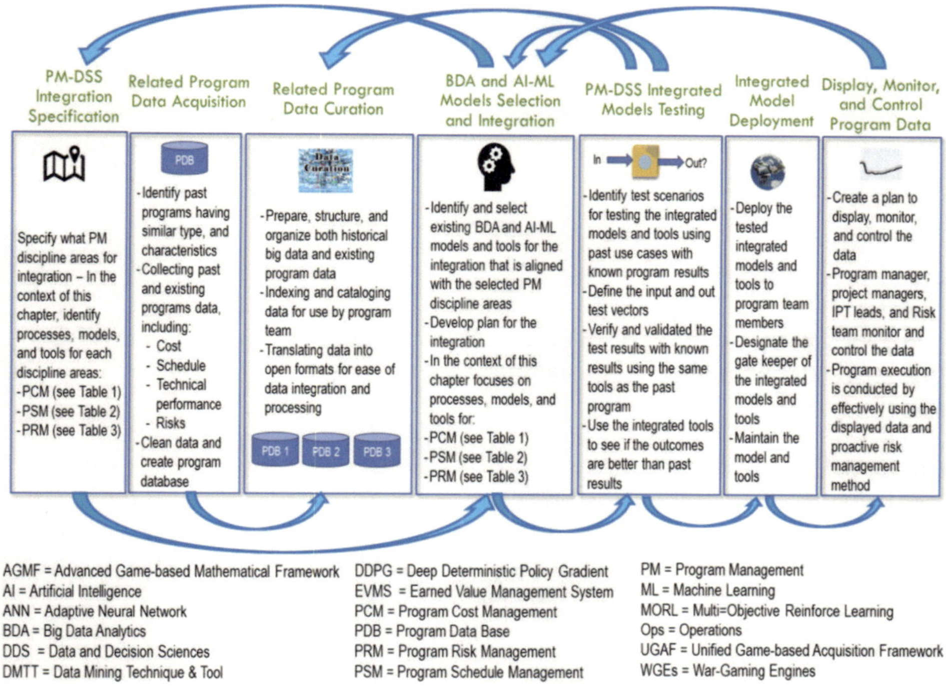

Figure 6.
PM-DDS integration life cycle framework.

program data acquisition, (iii) related program data curation, (iv) BDA and AI-ML models selection and integration, (v) PM-DSS integrated models testing, (vi) integrated model deployment, and (vii) display, monitor, and control program data. A high-level description of these key stages is provided in **Figure 6**. The feed-forward and feedback arrows are shown to describe the transition of each stage and the dependent of each stage.

8. Conclusion

This chapter describes an approach for integrating existing DDS models and tools with any PM processes, models, and tools for improving program planning and more efficient program execution by reducing overall program risk. A detailed description of the nine key PM areas along with the decomposed generalized 20 PM discipline areas were provided. This chapter proposed a PM-DSS integration approach for three PM discipline areas that were aligned with the selected four key PM areas, including program goals, schedule, cost, and risk. For the integration of each PM discipline area, a list of BDA and AI-ML models and tools were identified and suggested for the integration. In addition, the chapter proposes a flexible and adaptable PM-DSS integration life cycle that can be used to deploy BDA and AI-ML models and tools for improving program planning and execution.

Finally, when writing this chapter, the authors were intentionally focused on the high-level PM discipline areas and DDS technology enablers without technical depth. Only common DDS technology enablers that are known to the authors were selected for the integration. In practice, each PM discipline area deserves a whole book to address it in technical detail. There are many open PM-DSS integration problems and technical relevance associated with each activity step described in this chapter. The authors hope that the program management experts, data scientists, decision scientists, and mathematicians would benefit from this paper and its applications to these open problems.

Acknowledgements

The authors would like to thank their CSUF colleagues for their support of this work, particularly Professor Sam Behseta.

Conflict of interest

The authors declare no conflict of interest. The proposed approach and opinions expressed in this chapter are those of the authors and they are not endorsed by CCAM and Mihaylo College of Business & Economics, CSUF.

Notes/thanks/other declarations

The first author would like to thank his wife, Thu-Hang Nguyen, for tremendous patience and support during the preparation and writing of this chapter.

Program Management Integrated with Data and Decision Sciences
DOI: http://dx.doi.org/10.5772/intechopen.109964

Author details

Tien M. Nguyen[1*†], John D.T. Nguyen[2], My T.N. Nguyen[2], Charles H. Lee[3] and Tam Nguyen[3]

1 California State University, Fullerton, California, USA

2 JDTN Consulting Services, California, USA

3 CSUF, Mathematics Department, Mihaylo College of Business and Economics, USA

*Address all correspondence to: tmnguyen57@fullerton.edu

† Adjunct Research Professor, CSUF, Center for Computational and Applied Mathematics. Also with the Aerospace Corporation, California. A retired Engineering Fellow at Raytheon. He was a Raytheon Certified Level-5/-6 Program Manager, EVMS Level-2, and Six-Sigma.

References

[1] Program management overview. Available from: https://acqnotes.com/acqnote/careerfields/program-management-overview

[2] A guide for DOD program managers, defense acquisition authority. 2014. Available from: https://acqnotes.com/wp-content/uploads/2014/09/A-Guide-for-DoD-Program-Managers.pdf

[3] DOD acquisition system. 2020; Available from: https://www.esd.whs.mil/Portals/54/Documents/DD/issuances/dodd/500001p.pdf

[4] Policy for NASA acquisition. 2020. Available from: https://nodis3.gsfc.nasa.gov/displayDir.cfm?t=NPD&c=1000&s=5C#:~:text=NASA's%20strategic%20acquisition%20process%20supports,advance%20the%20Agency's%20statutory%20objectives

[5] Project Management Handbook. Available from: https://www.researchgate.net/publication/320101542_project_management_handbook

[6] A Guide to the Project Management Body of Knowledge (PMBOK® Guide). 2000 Edition; Available from: http://www.cs.bilkent.edu.tr/~cagatay/cs413/PMBOK.pdf

[7] Basic Guidelines for Program Planning and Management. 18 January 2022; Available from: https://managementhelp.org/programmanagement/business-programs.htm#anchor4294894489

[8] Acquisition of Commercial Products and Commercial Services. 2022. Available from: https://www.acquisition.gov/far/part-12

[9] Top 12 Performance Management Goals & Objectives. Available from: https://www.clearpointstrategy.com/top-performance-management-goals-and-objectives/

[10] Department of Defense Risk, Issue, and Opportunity Management Guide for Defense Acquisition Programs. January 2017. Available from: https://acqnotes.com/wp-content/uploads/2017/07/DoD-Risk-Issue-and-Opportunity-Management-Guide-Jan-2017.pdf

[11] Cost Control in Building Design and Construction. July 2022. Available from: https://www.designingbuildings.co.uk/wiki/Cost_control_in_building_design_and_construction

[12] ISO/IEC 17025, Wikipedia. Available from: https://en.wikipedia.org/wiki/ISO/IEC_17025

[13] Program team: The program team: what they do and why it matters; Available from: https://medium.com/loud-updates/the-program-team-what-they-do-and-why-it-matters-64cdda6782ef

[14] DOD Cost Estimating Guide. Available from: https://www.cape.osd.mil/files/Reports/DoD_CostEstimatingGuidev1.0_Dec2020.pdf

[15] SEER Cost Tool. Available from: https://galorath.com/products/seer-for-software/

[16] aPriori Cost Estimating Software. Available from: https://www.apriori.com/should-cost-analysis/?gclid=EAIaIQobChMI97Hqw4bZ-gIVFR6tBh3AJA0eEAAYASAAEgIT2_D_BwE

[17] Paul TB. COCOMO software cost estimating model. 2008. Available from:

https://www.unf.edu/~broggio/cis6516/CocomoPresentation.ppt

[18] COCOMO II - Model definition manual, center for software engineering, USC. 2000. Available from: https://www.rose-hulman.edu/class/cs/csse372/201310/Homework/CII_modelman2000.pdf

[19] Lane JA, Boehm B. Modern tools to support DoD software intensive system of systems cost estimation. Available from: https://citeseerx.ist.psu.edu/viewdoc/download?doi=10.1.1.365.8978&rep=rep1&type=pdf

[20] Tien M. Nguyen, Andy Guillen, Sumner Matsunaga, Hien T. Tran, Tung X. Bui, War-gaming applications for achieving optimum acquisition of future space systems. In: Simulation and Gaming. London, UKINTECH-Open Science-Open Minds: London ISBN: 978-953-51-3800-6. DOI: 10.5772/intechopen.69391. 2018

[21] Nguyen TM, Tran HT, Guillen AT, Bui TX, Matsunaga SS. Acquisition war-gaming technique for acquiring future complex systems: Modeling and simulation results for cost plus incentive fee contract. Journal of Mathematics. 2018;**6**:1-29. DOI: 10.3390/math6030043. Available from: www.mdpi.com/journal/mathematics

[22] Nguyen TM, Freeze T, Bui TX, Guillen A. Multi-criteria decision theory for enterprise architecture risk assessment: Theory, modeling and results. Proceedings, Sensors and Systems for Space Applications XIII. 2020;**11422**:114220. DOI: 10.1117/12.2559317

[23] Earned Value Management Handbook. Princes Risborough, Buckinghamshire: Association for Project Management; March 2013. Available from: https://apmv1livestorage.blob.core.windows.net/legacyimages/earned%20value%20management%20handbook_secure.pdf

[24] NASA Earned Value Management Handbook. Washington D.C.: National Aeronautics and Space Administration, NASA Headquarters; November 2019. Available from: https://www.nasa.gov/content/earned-value-management-handbook

[25] Procurement 101: Process, types and optimization guide 2022. 2022. Available from: https://kissflow.com/procurement/procurement-process/

[26] A critical look at critical change project management. Available from: https://www.researchgate.net/publication/3228307_A_Critical_Look_at_Critical_Chain_Project_Management

[27] Critical Change Project Management. Available from: https://ensembleconsulting group.com/wp-content/uploads/2018/07/CCPM-Executive-Guide.pdf

[28] Line of Balance (LOB). Available from: https://acqnotes.com/acqnote/tasks/line-of-balance

[29] Vargas RV, Moreira FF. Scheduling optimization with line of balance and start-finish relations. In: PMI® Global Congress 2015—EMEA. London, England. Newtown Square, PA: Project Management Institute; May 2015. Available from: https://www.pmi.org/learning/library/scheduling-optimization-balance-10614

[30] Risk and Safety Management. Available from: https://acqnotes.com/acqnote/tasks/risk-analysis

[31] Earned Value Management: The Basic. Available from: https://www.ecosys.net/knowledge/earned-value-management-basics/

[32] Simplilearn, Understanding Earned Value Management and Formulas, August 2022; Available from: https://www.simplilearn.com/earned-value-management-and-its-formulas-article

[33] Office of Under Secretary of Defense, Joint Space Cost Council Better Earned Value Management System Implementation. October 2017; Available from: https://www.acq.osd.mil/asda/ae/ada/ipm/docs/JSCC_Better_EVMS_Implementation_Study.PDF

[34] MATLAB Deep Deterministic Policy Gradient (DDPG) Agents. Available from: https: //www.mathworks.com/help/reinforcement-learning/ug/ddpg-agents.html

[35] Iranmanesh SH, Zarezadeh M. Application of artificial neural network to forecast actual cost of a project to improve earned value management system. International Journal of Social, Behavioral, Educational, Economic, Business and Industrial Engineering. 2008

[36] Garling R. Artificial intelligence and earned value in project management, a [Master thesis], American Military University. 2020. Available from: https://richgarling.com/#_Toc36301150

[37] Wauters M, Vanhoucke M. A comparative study of artificial intelligence methods for project duration forecasting. Expert Systems with Applications. 2016;**46**:249-261. DOI: 10.1016/j.eswa.2015.10.008

[38] Lee S, H, Kim K-Y, Shin Y. Effective feature selection method for deep learning-based automatic modulation classification scheme using higher-order statistics. MDPI Applied Science. 2020. DOI: 10.3390/app10020588

[39] AI vs. Machine learning vs. deep learning vs. neural networks: What's the difference?. 22 May 2020. Available from: https://www.ibm.com/cloud/blog/ai-vs-machine-learning-vs-deep-learning-vs-neural-networks

[40] Raz T, Michael E. Use and benefits of tools for project risk management. International Journal of Project Management. 2001;**19**:9-17. Available from: https://www.diva-portal.org/smash/get/diva2:708652/fulltext01.pdf

[41] Hayford F, Ahmed S. Tools and techniques for project risk management: Perspective of micro to small scale construction firms in Ghana, [Master thesis], Stockholm, Sweden. 2013, Available from: https://www.diva-portal.org/smash/get/diva2:708652/FULLTEXT01.pdf

[42] Valohai, MLOps Basics. Available from: https://valohai.com/mlops/

[43] Kirenz J, Gröger C, Lutsch A. Data Platform Architectures & Machine Learning Operations (MLOps). Hochschule Der Medien. HdM Stuttgart; 2021. Available from: https://www.kirenz.com/slides/data-platform-mlops.pdf

[44] Kreuzberger D, Kühl N. Machine learning operations (MLOps): Overview, definition, and architecture. Available from: https://arxiv.org/ftp/arxiv/papers/2205/2205.02302.pdf

[45] Liu Y, Ling Z, Huo B, Wang B, Chen T, Mouine E. Building a platform for machine learning operations from open source frameworks. In: 3rd IFAC Workshop on Cyber-Physical & Human Systems CPHS 2020. Beijing, China: ScienceDirect, Elsevier; 3-5 December 2020. DOI: 10.1016/j.ifacol.2021.04.161

[46] Munir M. How artificial intelligence can help project managers. Global Journal of Management and Business Research: Administration and Management. 2019;**19**(4):29-35. Online ISSN: 2249-4588 & Print ISSN: 0975-5853

Chapter 6

Perspective Chapter: Program Planning and Management for Defense Advanced Concept Technology Programs

Tien M. Nguyen

Abstract

The complexity of program planning and management (PPM) for defense programs and related projects depends on the program types and associated budget size. In general, the defense program types can be classified into three categories, namely, normal program of record (POR), new program with traditional and/or well-defined acquisition strategy, and advanced concept technology (ACT) program. This chapter offers a new perspective on the development of an effective PPM plan for ACT programs. For the ACT program type, the traditional PPM is usually not applicable and required to be handled differently according to the uncertainty associated with the technical requirements and associated technology and corresponding cost risks. The chapter provides an overview of typical ACT PPM and associated planning, execution, and management activities from both government and contractor's perspectives. In addition, the chapter attempts to (i) quantify the risks associated with ACT programs in terms of innovation indicators using simplified Cooper chart, and (ii) develop a set of recommended PPM activities that can be used as a basic framework for conducting the planning and execution of PPM of ACT programs.

Keywords: advanced concept technology, program planning and management, defense, acquisition, requirement, technology risk, cost risk, innovation, Cooper chart

1. Introduction

In practice, the complexity of planning, managing, and executing a defense program depends on the budget size and program type. In the US, for a new traditional or a POR with large budget, usually above 100M USD, the government PM plans the program using the DOD acquisition system [1, 2] and DOD Instruction (DODI) 5000.02 [3]. The PM follows the planning and execution of the program according to the DOD guide for PMs [4]. In addition to the DOD guide for PMs, the government PM also uses additional DOD guidebooks to (i) identify the potential technical, management, and related program issues and risks [5], and (ii) investigate the use of modular open system approach to reduce the interfaces technical risk and the associated cost [6]. When the new traditional program with large budget involved with the acquisition of commercial products and/or commercial services, the government PMs seek guidance from the federal acquisition regulation (FAR) Part 12 [7] for the development of a PPM plan. This type of large programs is usually required to go through the normal acquisition process, which leverages mature technology and related technology enablers (TEs). In practice, the level of mature technology is defined using the Technology Readiness Level (TRL) scale ranging from TRL-1 to TRL-9 [8]. TRL-1 is defined as the basic principles have been observed and reported, and TRL-9 is for an actual system is proven through successful mission operations. Practically, TRL-8 is usually considered to be matured, because at this TRL the actual system is completed and qualified through test and demonstration.

Unlike the traditional program and/or POR, for advanced concept technology (ACT) programs with small budgets (less than 100M USD) are usually not acquisition programs. This type of advanced defense programs includes DOD ACT Demonstration Program (ACTD) [9, 10], advanced contract research and development (CRAD) programs from DOD Laboratories (Labs) (e.g., Air Force Research Lab (AFRL), Naval Research Lab (ARL), Army Research Lab (ARL), etc) [11], and Defense Advanced Research Projects Agency (DARPA) programs [12, 13]. In addition to these ACT programs, US government also manages ACT programs with emphasis on the development of advanced TEs in critical technology areas by domestic small businesses [14]. These ACT programs are referred to as Small Business Innovation Research and Small Business Technology Transfer (SBIR/STTR) programs. For these ACT programs, the government PMs are required to use different DOD acquisition process that is different from the normal acquisition process for traditional programs and/or POR. The development of a PPM plan for ACT programs is quite different from traditional/POR programs with large budgets. In practice, when selected as the prime contractor (a.k.a. developer) for executing an ACT program, the contractor program manager (PM) is also required to develop a PPM plan, and execute and manage the plan, according to the government PPM requirements.

The primary objective of this chapter is to provide an overview on the development of an effective PPM plan and executing the plan from both government and contractor perspectives. The chapter also provides a set of recommendations that can be used as a basic framework for the development and executing a PPM plan. The chapter has eight main sections, and it is organized as follows:

- Section 2 describes the type of ACT programs/projects and their characteristics,
- Section 3 presents a typical ACT program acquisition life cycle from both government (a.k.a. US department of defense (DOD)) and contractor perspectives,
- Section 4 presents a recommended tailored Zachman framework that can be used for ACT program planning activities,
- Section 5 recommends an approach to quantify the technology and market risks associated with ACT programs using the innovation indicators and Cooper chart,
- Section 6 recommends a set of PPM activities for balancing cost, technical and program management risks from both government and contractor perspectives,

- Section 7 describes the use of Earned Value Management System (EVMS) for tracking and managing ACT program risks,

- Section 8 discusses the use of machine learning and artificial intelligent (ML-AI) and recommends ways to improve the development and executing of a PPM plan, and

- Section 9 concludes with a summary of the chapter.

2. Characteristics of ACT programs/projects

Figure 1 captures typical DOD ACT program types discussed in Section 1. For US DOD, the defense ACT program types can be classified into four categories, namely, ACTD, DARPA, CRAD, and SBIR/STTR programs. The ACTD programs usually range from a few millions USD to 10+ mils USD [10], which are initiated by DOD to determine a proposed mature technology enabler (TE) that will be used to improve specific defense capabilities before entering the normal DOD acquisition process. The period of performance (PoP) for the assessment of the proposed TE is typically between 2 to 4 years, and the TE under ACTD program implementation is usually at TRL-7 (or even at TRL-8) with a goal to achieve higher TRL before entering formal acquisition process. Note that TRL-8 and TRL-9 indicate low and the lowest possible technology risk level, respectively. From the government PM perspective, ACTD program requires to identify (i) a mature TE that aligns with a priority military need for achieving specific defense capabilities, and (ii) a corresponding government sponsor in urgent needs of these capabilities. From the developer (contractor) PM perspective, ACTD program requires the execution team to be ready and prepare a detailed plan to conduct the demonstrations and/or exercises with required key performance parameters for the military utility assessment. The plan must also address all related risks for the demo/exercises.

Figure 1.
A general description of ACT program types.

The CRAD programs are usually more advance than the ACTD programs, since they are more focus on the advancement of scientific and technical knowledge and apply that knowledge to achieve specific goals set by the sponsored agency and national goals [11]. Practically, most of CRAD programs usually start at TRL-1. Like ACTD programs, CRAD program funding has similar budget ranging from a few millions USD to 10+ mils USD. PoP for CRAD programs also range from 2 years to 4 years. From the government PM perspective, CRAD program requires to (i) find a critical technology area and related TEs that are aligned with the agency needs and national goals, and (ii) supply a clear, concise, and complete statement of work (SOW) or a request for proposal (RFP) describing the area for basic research and the end objectives for development and applied research. The technical and contracting personnel must individually tailor the SOW/RFP to allow for contractor to exercise innovation and creativity while achieving objectives of the R&D [11]. From the contractor PM perspective, the CRAD program requires the contractor execution team to be ready and prepare a detailed PPM plan to address the SOW/RFP requirements and associated challenges. The contractor PPM plan must also provide supporting evidence to demonstrate the contractor's technical capabilities to achieve the end objectives.

The DARPA program type is quite different than ACTD and CRAD programs because they are focused the development of breakthrough technology [12]. As stated in the DARPA website, the objective of DARPA programs is to transform revolutionary concepts and even seeming impossibilities into practical defense capabilities. Typical DARPA program ranges from a few millions USD funding and up to 100M[1] USD [13]. Practically, DARPA program PoP ranges from 1 to 3 years for proof of revolutionary concepts. From DARPA perspective, DARPA program requires to (i) identify a revolutionary and breakthrough technology that aligns with DARPA needs (or national needs), and (ii) provide a clear, concise, and complete Broad Agency Announcement (BAA) or an RFP describing the area for research and development pushing the leading-edge technology and the end objectives. The BAA/RFP should address how DARPA rewards risk by clearly define criteria for evaluating the proposed DARPA programs using a set of questions known as the "Heilmeier Catechism" [15]. From the contractor PM perspective, DARPA program requires the contractor execution team to be ready and prepare an innovative PPM plan to address the BAA/RFP requirements with emphasis on the answers to Heilmeier's questions. The plan must clearly describe the innovative features of the proposed solution and provide supporting evidence to demonstrate the contractor's technical capabilities to achieve the program objective.

Last but not least, the SBIR/STTR programs are usually focused on the critical technology areas that are aligned with the government agencies' objectives and national goals. Typical SBIR/STTR programs are usually emphasis on the basic and applied research for advancing the state-of-art, increasing knowledge, or understanding of specified technology and related TEs rather than focusing on a specific system or hardware solution. Typically, these programs have three phases, namely, Phase 1, Phase 2, and Phase 3. Phase 1 funding ranges from 150K to 175K USD, Phase 2 funding from 750K to 1M USD, and Phase 3 funding ranges from 2M or higher depending on

---

[1] In practice, for defense ACT programs, the program manager is required to (i) go through official program management and EVMS training programs, and (ii) be certified at specific certification level corresponding to the ACT program budget.

the commercialization matching funds. Typical PoP for Phase 1 is usually from 6 months to 1 year, Phase 2 is 2 years, and Phase 3 is 2 to 4 years depending on the funding and industry partner's plan for the integration with existing partner's products or planned systems.

3. ACT program life cycle: government vs. contractor perspectives

Practically, a detailed ACT program life cycle varies depending on the ACT program types, agency objectives and national goals. Thus, the development of a PPM plan also varies accordingly depending on government and contractor perspectives. This section provides an overview of typical ACT program life cycle and discusses the roles of the PMs and desired PPM activities from both government and contractor perspectives. In general, the ACT program life cycle can be expressed in four phases, namely, concept, pre-acquisition, post-acquisition, and transition phases as shown in **Figure 2**. The figure is derived from the traditional DoD program acquisition life cycle [1–3]. It also captures the roles of government and contractor PMs for each phase.

As shown in **Figure 2**, the government PM role with required PPM activities covers the entire ACT program life cycle from the concept phase to the transition phase. While the contractor PM role with PPM activities begins after the pre-acquisition from the post-acquisition to the transition phases. Theoretically, the contractor PM role starts at the post-acquisition phase after the ACT contract is awarded. But in practice, the contractor PM role starts at the release of the BAA/RFP/SOW. For large ACT programs (i.e., 10^{+}M USD), at the release of the BAA/RFP/SOW, the contractor PM is usually working with the contractor capture team (CCT) under the leadership of a business capture manager to prepare and generate proposal and cost volume for the bids. The contractor capture and program managers with support from their program chief engineer will work with the government PM to gain a deep understand of the agency objectives, national goals, and corresponding program requirements to properly address them during the preparation of the proposal and cost volume.

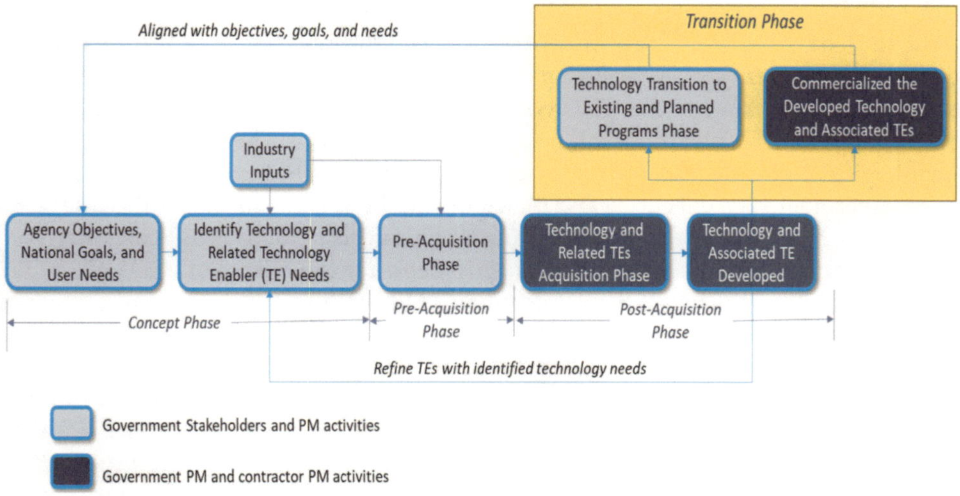

Figure 2.
ACT program life cycle derived from traditional DoD program life cycle [1–3].

As mentioned earlier, the PPM activities begin at the concept phase and pre-acquisition phase for the government team and contractor team, respectively. In practice, for the contractor team, the PPM activity begins at end of the pre-acquisition phase after the lease of the BAA/RFP/SOW and the execution of the PPM plan starts at the beginning of the post-acquisition phase after the contract award and continues throughout the transition phase. As shown in **Figure 2**, the role of the contractor PM changes slightly during the transition phase. When the technology and associated TE developed by the program is selected for transition to existing POR and/or planned acquisition program, the contractor PM and his technical team will continue to work with the new government PM to integrate the newly developed TEs into the new program execution plan. When the newly developed TE is selected for commercialization, the contractor PM will continue to work with the government PM and the industry partner to commercialize the products. For SBIR/STTR programs, the funding for the commercialization of the ACT products is usually through a matching fund with support from an industry partner. Note that for ACTD program, if the selected technology and associated TE are successfully demonstrated, the contractor PM will continue to work with the new government PM.

During the concept phase, the government PM works with the government team to develop a PPM plan. The team includes potential stakeholders, technical personnel, contract personnel, and operational users. The government team ensures that the PPM plan will (i) provide required operational capabilities to meet the user needs, and (ii) meet the end objectives and national goals. The user's needs must be identified and approved by appropriate government decision makers and associated stakeholders. After the approval, the government PM will conduct industry survey (a.k.a. market survey) to collect necessary technical inputs and related data to identify appropriate technologies and related TEs to address the user's needs. The government PM with support from the team will work with government acquisition authority to make the decision on new ACT programs/ projects based on the collected inputs and data. A positive decision allows to turn on the pre-acquisition process and start the new ACT programs/projects. During this pre-acquisition phase, the government PM with support from government technical and contract personnel will identify and analyze the program risk, including technical performance, cost, and schedule risks and prepare the BAA/RFP/SOW. The government PM generates and releases the BAA/RFP/SOW to public for bids. After the release of BAA/RFP/SOW, the government PM forms the source selection team (SST) consisting of subject matter experts (SMEs) in specific technology areas related to the ACT topics, cost, contract, and schedule. The SST will review and select the best proposal(s) for the contract award. The post-acquisition phase begins after the contract award, and the government PM executes and manages the ACT contract (i.e., executing and managing the PPM plan) to ensure the contractor team meets the contract requirements from technical, cost, and schedule perspectives.

The contractor team begins the PPM activities after the release of BAA/RFP/SOW. The team usually works with the government PM to (i) understand the ACT program requirements, and (ii) prepare the proposal addressing all required requirements and submits the bid. As mentioned earlier, for large ACT programs (10^{+}M USD), the contractor PM works with the business capture manager to accurately address all ACT program requirements with high probability of winning the contract award. For this type of program, the contractor capture team (CCT) will develop an effective PPM plan to ensure high probability of win. The CCT team consists of SMEs across contractor's organization, including engineering, contract, cost, and schedule departments. After the contract award, the contractor PM will work with the government

PM to adjust the proposed contractor's PPM plan to ensure alignment with the government's PPM plan. The contractor PM will work with his contractor execution team to execute the adjusted PPM plan. The contractor PM reports the program progress and milestone accomplishments to the government PM. The role of the contractor PM will slightly change during the transition phase depending on the transition path. As shown in **Figure 2**, when the transition path goes to existing and/or planned DOD program that followed normal DOD acquisition process, the contractor PM is required to work with the existing government PM and the new government PM[2] and the new government execution team to develop an integration plan. At this time, the contractor team is required to (i) gain a good understanding of the proposed system being acquired, and (ii) develop an integration plan to integrate the newly developed TEs into the proposed system. The contractor PM and the contractor execution team are usually required to provide technical support over the life cycle of the DOD program being transitioned into. When the transition path goes to the commercialization path, the contractor PM will work with the ACT government program PM and the interested industry partner to develop detailed plan and associated products using the newly developed TEs. For this transition path, the contractor PM is required to understand the industry partner products and the to be developed products.

The remaining of this chapter provides an overview of the ACT program PPM activities for both government and contractor perspectives.

4. ACT program planning: the Zachman framework

As pointed out in ref. [16], there is a set of twenty multiple PM discipline areas, including (i) Program goals management, (ii) Systems engineering related to the systems/products/services being acquired, (iii) Specialized engineering related to the products and services being acquired, (iv) Contracts and legal dealing with contractors, suppliers, and stakeholders, (v) Program Financial management, (vi) Business and marketing practices for the newly acquired systems/products/services, (vii) System/product/service technical requirements and associated performance risk management, (viii) System/product/service cost planning and management, (ix) Program schedule planning and management, (x) Program cost planning and management, (xi) System/product/service[3] risk planning and management, (xii) Program risk planning and management, (xiii) System test and evaluation, (xiv) Logistics and supply chain management, (xv) Production, Quality, and Manufacturing (PQM), (xvi) Program and system intelligence and security management, (xvii) Program and system software management, (xviii) Program and system configuration management, (xix) Program and system information technology, and (xx) Other Specialty Program Planning and Management. For ACT programs, depending on the PM's perspective, the PM is required to select a subset of these PM discipline areas for the development of an effective PPM plan. From the government perspective, at the minimum, the PM must develop a PPM plan that addresses the eleven out of the twenty PM discipline areas listed above, including (i), (ii), (iii), (iv), (v), (vii), (viii), (ix), (x), (xi), and (xii).

---

[2] In practice, the government PM for the existing and/or planned acquisition program is different from the government PM for the ACT program.

[3] The term "a system" in ACT program context means a new system concept that leverages advanced TEs being developed under the ACT program, which depends on the application.

From the contractor perspective, the PM also requires develop a PPM plan that addresses the same PM discipline areas except Bullet (i), namely "program goals management." Note that for the PM discipline area (iv), namely the "contracts and legal dealing with contractors, suppliers, and stakeholders," the contractor PM is required to address the contracts and legal dealing with the government PM and its subcontractors, including the suppliers. Based on our experience working on ACT program planning from both contractor and government perspectives, the Zachman framework can be tailored to effectively develop the PPM plan:

- For Government Perspective: The government PPM plan includes acquisition strategy, execution, program management, and transition plans; and

- For Contractor Perspective: Contractor PPM plan includes bidding strategy, execution, program management, and transition plans.

To develop an effective PPM plan, the Zachman framework can be tailored as recommended in **Table 1** to address the PPM activities across the PM discipline areas (i), (ii), (iv), (v), (vii), (viii), (ix), (x), (xi), and (xii) from both government and contractor PM perspectives. Like standard Zachman framework, the recommended tailored-Zachman framework also organizes around the points of view taken by the various players. The players include government PM and contractor PM. From the government perspective, the PM undertakes the planning of an ACT program to ensure alignment with the agency objectives and national goals. Hence, the government PM role is to develop a PPM plan, prepare, generate and release BAA/RFP/SOW that is fully support by the industry. From the contractor perspective, the PM will work with his technical team to identify and apply specific technologies and related TEs to solve the ACT problems described in the government released BAA/RFP/SOW. In summary, each of these players can look at the same PM discipline areas but with different perspectives. The government perspective is to ensure meeting the agency's ACT development objectives and national goals within allocated budget with minimum program risks. The key program risks are defined in terms of technology and market uncertainties that will be discussed in the next section.

Like standard Zackman framework, the roles of the players are represented by rows in a matrix shown in **Table 1**, and the columns represent the issues/topics that will be examined by the players. More specifically, the columns represent [17, 18]:

- ACT program data to be used by an DOD agency and/or desired operational users (what),

- Newly proposed functions (how),

- Operational environment and/or existing network where the newly developed ACT capability will be conducted/deployed (where),

- DOD Agency and associated operational users involved (who),

- Operational events that trigger the defense activities (when) – Note that this event related to the "Business Model for Defense Applications (BMDA)," and

- Motivations and constraints which determine how the BMDA behaves (why).

	ACT program data (What)	Newly proposed function (How)	Operational environment/ existing network (Where)	People: DOD agency/ User (Who)	Time (When)	Motivation /Defense needs (Why)
Objectives/ Scope	List of things important to sponsored DOD agency	List of new functional capabilities vs. Existing functions	List of operational environment and locations where to-be system operates	List of agency involved and users	List of ACT program events / mile-stones	List of agency objectives, goals, and strategies
Business & Operational Model for Defense Applications (BOMDA)	Entity relationship diagram (including attributed relationships)	New BOMDA vs. existing BOMDA	ACT Logistics network (nodes and links for to-be deployed ACT system)	Organiza-tional chart with roles, skill sets, and issues.	ACT program master schedule	Business and operational ACT plan
Information System Model (ISM)	Data model associated with ACT program	ACT data flow diagram vs. existing ISM	Distributed ACT system architecture	User interface (roles, data, access)	Depen-dency diagram, program life cycle	Business and ACT system operational rule design
Technology Model (TM)	Data architecture, map to legacy data	ACT system design vs. existing design	ACT System architecture (hardware, software types)	User interface (how ACT system behaves); security design	ACT Control flow diagram (control structure)	Business ACT system operational rule design
Detailed Representation (DR)	Data physical design	Detailed ACT program design	To-be ACT network architecture	Screens, security design (who can see what?)	ACT system timing definitions	ACT system operational Rule specification
Functioning ACT System (FAS)	Existing working system Data model associated with ACT program	ACT executable program planning	Existing vs. to-be ACT Communications facilities	Opera-tional user training	ACT program mile-stones	Enforced business and ACT system operational rules

Table 1.
Tailored Zachman framework for ACT program planning [17, 18].

The set of cells shown in **Table 1**, constructed by the roles of the players and the issues/topics to be examined by the players. These ceels describe all the ACT planning topics/issues that are required to be addressed by the government and contractor PMs. The government PM will use this tailored Zachman framework to conduct the PPM activities under government perspective discussed. The contractor PM can also use this tailored framework but with contractor perspective. Unlike the government perspective, the contractor perspective focuses on meeting the government requirements stated in the released BBA/RFP/SOW with minimum cost (i.e., maximum profit) and lowest ACT program risks. The ACT program risks will be addressed in the next section.

The description of the rows in the first column shown in **Table 1** is given below:

- Objectives/Scope: Definition of the organization's direction and business/agency purpose. From government perspective, this is the DOD agency's objectives and national goals for the ACT programs in planning. From the contractor perspective, this is concerned with the things that define the contract objectives and business goals under the contract pursuit. The contractor's objectives and business goals must be aligned with the government perspective.

- Business and Operational Model for Defense Applications (BOMDA): From the government perspective, this defines the existing business/agency and operational user model for defense applications, including its structure, functions, organization, and so forth. From the contractor perspective, this defines the to-be BOMDA that is compatible with existing government BOMDA.

- Information System Model (ISM): This defines the BOMDA, but in more rigorous information terms, where the BOMDA describes business/agency and user operational functions, and ISM describes those things about the to-be developed ACT system to collect and maintain information and begins to describe desired information to be collected by the to-be ACT system.

- Technology Model (TM): This describes the to-be ACT system how the new technology and associated TEs may be used to address the information processing needs identified in the ISM.

- Detailed Representations (DR): This is typically a contractor view of the program listings, database specifications, networks, and so forth that constitute a to-be ACT system that will meet the government's requirements. Government team usually generates a government reference architecture (GRA) with related DR information for assessment of contractor's ACT system solution.

- Functioning ACT System (FAS): The to-be ACT system is final implemented and made part of an existing defense system or a commercialized product.

5. Quantification of ACT program risks using innovation indicators

This section emphasizes on the analysis of ACT program risks for the development of an effective PPM plan. From a PM's perspective, regardless of government or contractor, it is important to understand and mitigate the program risks. As discussed in Section 4, the technology and market[4] uncertainties are the key attributes for the

[4] Note that the market uncertainty represents the measure of the uncertainty associated with the availability of the hardware/software (HW/SW) components associated with the selected technology and related TEs. Low market uncertainty means there are related SW/HW components available in the market and these components are required to modify/upgrade to meet the required ACT program requirements. High market uncertainty means no HW/SW components are available in the market.

Innovation Indicator Level (IIL)	ACT program risk		Remark
	Technology risk	Market risk	
IIL-1	L	L	Technology and market risks are quantified based on the technology and market uncertainties associated with the selected technology and its TEs. The government PM can use the request for information (RFI) process and tools to collect and assess the uncertainties from industry
IIL-2	M	M	
IIL-3	L → M	H	
IIL-4	H	L → M	
IIL-5	H	H	

Table 2.
Newly proposed ACT program innovation indicators.

assessment of ACT program risks. Practically, the technology and market uncertainties can be used to translate into the technology and market risks, respectively. To plan and manage these risks, the PMs are required to quantify these risks based on the technology and market uncertainties provided by the manufacturers. Let us classify the uncertainty (i.e., risk) levels as Low (L, blue color), Medium (M, green color), and High (H, red color), and define the innovation indicators associated with these uncertainty levels as follows:

- Innovation Indicator Level 1 (IIL-1): This innovation indicator level indicates both the technology and market uncertainties that are low risk level (L).

- Innovation Indicator Level 2 (IIL-2): The IIL-2 indicates both the technology and market uncertainties that are medium risk level (M).

- Innovation Indicator Level 3 (IIL-3): The IIL-3 designates high market uncertainty that is high market risk (H) level and technology uncertainty ranging from low-to-medium risk level (L-M)

- Innovation Indicator Level 4 (IIL-4): IIL-4 indicates market uncertainty ranging from low-to-medium (L-M) risk and technology uncertainty at high (H) risk level.

- Innovation Indicator Level 5 (IIL-5): IIL-5 indicates both the technology and market uncertainties are at high risk level (H).

Table 2 summarizes the technology and market risk levels associated with the five proposed innovation indicator levels. Our next step is to associate these innovation indicator levels with the desired innovative solutions required for various types of ACT programs as described in **Figure 1**.

In practice, private and for-profit enterprises (PaFoPEs) are usually invested into their internal research and development (IRAD) projects[5] to (i) defend and extend their current capabilities to sustain the position in existing market, (ii) prepare for a venture launch by continuously improving existing products, (iii) look-out for a market for their new products (scouting option) by incremental changes of

[5] This is a.k.a. industry IRAD projects, which in internally funded by private and for-profit enterprises to improve their existing products or launch a new products or prepare to capture new programs.

Innovation indicator level (IIL)	IIL mapping to IRAD and ACT programs		Remark
	Industry IRAD project	**Government funded ACT project/program**	
IIL-1	Defend and extend	ACTD, CRAD	Low technology and market (T&M) risks
IIL-2	Venture launch	CRAD, SBIR/STTR	Medium T&M risks
IIL-3	Scouting option		Medium technology and High market risks
IIL-4	Position option	CRAD, SBIR/STTR, DARPA	High technology and Medium market risks
IIL-5	stepping-stone Option	DARPA Program	High T&M risks

Table 3.
Newly proposed mapping of IILs to industry IRAD and ACT projects/programs.

technology, (iv) position for a newly developed radical technology and related products that can transform industry and potentially creating a new market (position option), and (v) develop disruptive technology that can disrupt existing products and market (stepping-stone option) [19–23]. In fact, these types of PaFoPEs' IRAD projects are usually classified based on the technology and market risks that can be mapped to the IILs presented in **Table 2**. For government ACT programs listed in **Figure 1**, they are classified in terms of TRLs that can be linked to the technology risk shown in **Table 2**. Thus, ACT programs can also be mapped to the IILs presented in **Table 2**. **Table 3** captures the mapping of the IIL levels to industry IRAD projects and government ACT projects/programs.

As shown in **Table 3**, the ACTD type of ACT programs focuses the technology demonstration of mature TEs with high TRLs (i.e., L technology risk). The CRAD type of ACT programs can range from low-to-high TRLs (i.e., H-to-L technology risk). Typically, the SBIR/STTR program type focuses on the development of TEs ranging from medium-to-high TRLs (i.e., M-to-L technology risk). Finally, the DARPA programs/projects focus on the development of disruptive technology with low TRLs (i.e., H technology risks). The mapping shown in **Table 3** reflects these facts. Note that the mapping of SBIR/STTR, CRAD, and DARPA are based on our experience working on these ACT programs/projects.

The mapping presented in **Table 3** can be captured using a simplified Cooper chart approach [19–23] as shown in **Figure 3**. In this figure, the chart has two axes, namely, x-axis represents the market uncertainty indicator, and the y-axis is the technology uncertainty indicator with a scale from low to high corresponding to L-to-H risk. As mentioned earlier, the technology and market uncertainty indicators are translated directly to technology and market risks. The technology risk is indicated by the TRL as discussed above.

Note that the market risk presented in **Table 2** can be translated into the manufacturing readiness level[6] (MRL) [24, 25]. The five IILs presented in **Table 2** are

[6] The MRL concept was developed by the US DOD to assess the maturity of a manufacturing process throughout its conception, development, deployment and support progression phases. As defined in Refs [24, 25], MRLs, the MRL scale ranges from MRL-1 to MRL-10, with MRL-1 being the least mature and MRL-10 being the most mature.

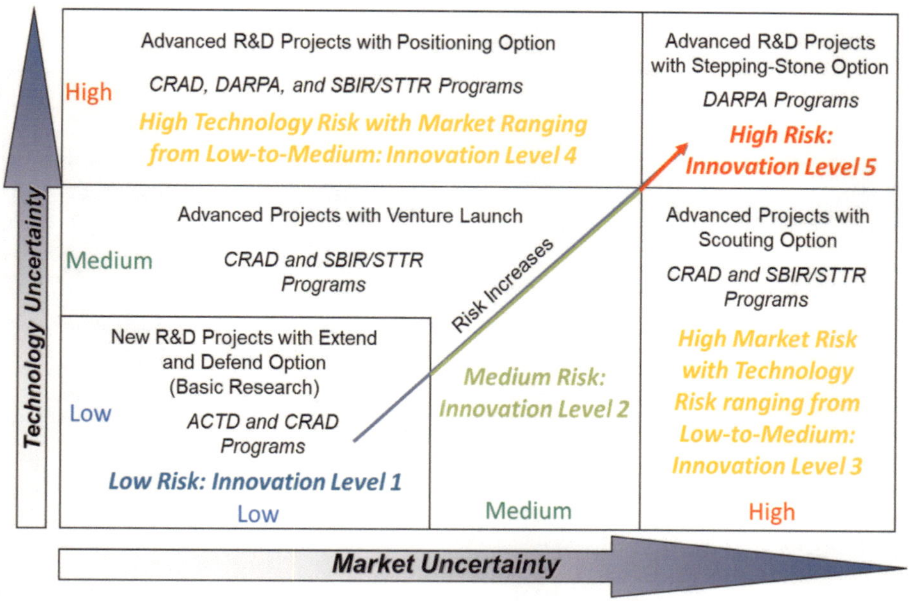

Figure 3.
Newly proposed simplified cooper chart for quantifying the innovation indicators.

then mapped onto the simplified Cooper chart depending on their assigned risks. The mapping of the industry IRAD projects and government ACT programs/projects shown in **Figure 3** is performed using **Table 3**.

In practice, from the PaFoPE perspective, the industry IRAD projects are usually planned and managed by PaFoPEs to align with the national goals and agencies' objectives. If this alignment is done properly, it will help PaFoPEs to (i) prepare their proposals for biding the BAA/RFPs/ SOWs to be released by DOD agencies, (ii) effectively address the government requirements described in their released BAA/RFPs/ SOWs, and (ii) increase the probability of winning the bids. From the government perspective, understanding of the technology and market risks will help the program managers to better plan the budget and prepare the BAA/RFPs/SOWs.

6. Program management: balancing cost, technical, and program management risks

As discussed in Section 4 above, there are only ten or eleven out of twenty program management discipline areas that required the program managers to address during the program planning and execution phases. A good program manager must know to balance cost, technical, program management risks during the planning and execution phases. An effective PPM plan must carefully address the three key program management discipline areas including cost, schedule, and program risk planning and management. To do this the program manager must understand the key ACT program risk types and identify all associated risks for each type. Based on our experience, there are four key ACT program types, including technical/technology risk, non-technical risk, people/staffing risk, and program management risk. Based on our research in public domain concerning the risk type [1–34], a generic list of risks for each of these risk types is provided in **Figure 4**. Understanding of these risks will help the program

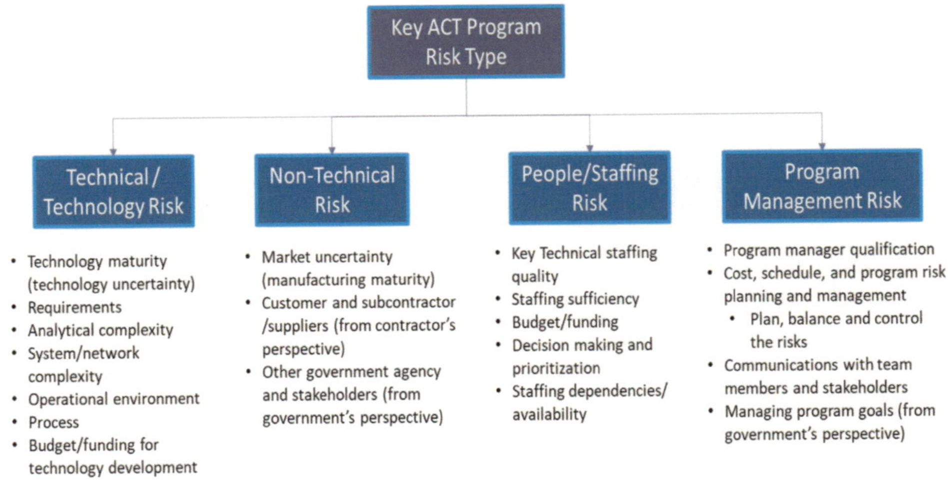

Figure 4.
Understanding the key ACT program risk types.

managers to balance the cost, schedule, and program management risks when executing the ACT programs. As an example, if the technical risks associated with technology maturity and system complexity are high, the program manager must (i) identify a subject matter expert and a technical team who are familiar with the identified technology and related TEs, and (ii) allocate appropriate budget to mitigate these risk in the program plan.

Understanding of the ACT program risk types and associated risks will help the program manager to identify the risks and develop an effective program plan to mitigate and balance out the identified risks. Depending on the PM's perspective, the ACT program risk types and associated risks (see **Figure 4**) usually have different impacts on the program planning and execution. Based on our experience, to effectively develop a PPM plan for executing and managing the program during the post-acquisition phase, the program manager requires to understand all PPM activities throughout the ACT program life cycle illustrated in **Figure 2**. From the government perspective, **Figure 5** describes these PPM activities from the concept phase through the pre-acquisition phase with related source selection planning-and-execution and to the post-acquisition phase. For the concept phase shown in **Figure 5**, the planning actives must address the following tasks: (i) understand the agency objectives and national goals, (ii) understand the user needs and align the user needs with agency objectives and national goals, (iii) identify the required technology and related TEs to provide desired operational capability that meet the user needs, and (iv) conduct the (industry) market survey to understand the technology and market uncertainties on the identified technology and related TEs. For the pre-acquisition phase, the planning activities must address the following tasks: (i) analyze, assess, and quantify the program risks based on the (industry) market survey results, (ii) identify the technical and programmatic challenges based on the market assessment results, (iii) identify and generate required technical tasks in the form of the work breakdown structure (WBS) to address the identified challenges, and (iv) conduct and perform cost, schedule, and program planning and analysis to fit the allocated budget and scheduled timeframe and generate the government program plan to be described in the BAAs/RFPs/SOWs. For the source selection planning-and-execution phase, the activities must address the following tasks: (i) generate and release the BAAs/RFPs/SOWs to

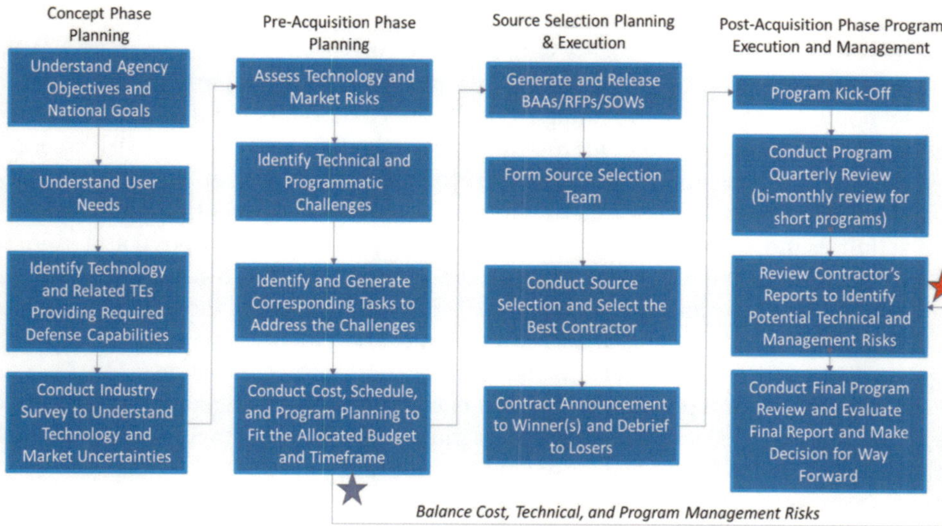

Figure 5.
A new perspective on the understanding ACT program planning, execution, and management activities from government perspective.

public domain requesting the bids from industry, (ii) form a source selection team with subject matter experts on both technical and program management areas, (iii) conduct source selection and select the best contractor for executing the government program plan, and (iv) announce the contract award winner(s) and debrief the losers. Finally, for the post-acquisition phase and program execution- and-management, the activities must address the following tasks: (i) plan and conduct program kick-off and work with the selected contractor to finalize the program requirements and request the contractor to present their final execution program plan at the kick-off meeting, (ii) conduct the program quarterly review (should be bi-monthly for short period of performance program), (iii) review contractor quarterly reports and identify new and/or potential technical and programmatic risks and update the cost/schedule/and program plan to add new risks and retire the old ones, and (iv) conduct final review and evaluate final report to make final decision on the way forward.

Similarly, from the contractor perspective, **Figure 6** illustrates the desired PPM activities from the pre-acquisition phase through the source selection planning-and-execution and to the post-acquisition phase. Unlike the government perspective, the contractor perspective does not have the concept phase planning activities. For the pre-acquisition phase illustrated in **Figure 6**, the contractor planning actives must address the following tasks: (i) receive and review[7] the BAAs/RFPs/SOWs from the DOD agency of interest, (ii) form a CCT[8] to prepare the proposal and start the bidding process[9], (iii) conduct the contract requirement flow-down, (iv) identify the key

[7] In practice, the capture or (and) program manager(s) is (are) usually the initial reviewer(s).

[8] For program with budget of 5^{+}M USD, CCT team includes a capture manager, PM, and a program chief engineer, who will oversee engineers and staff with required experience.

[9] In practice, industry bidding process is a gate process deciding if the BAA/RFP/SOW is aligned with PaFoPE's interest with high probability of win. The chapter assumes that the BAA/RFP/SOW is of PaFoPE's interest. Note that PaFoPE is the acronyms of private and for-profit enterprise.

program requirements and associated technical and programmatic challenges, (v) tailored system engineering process with required program tasks and generate a WBS addressing the overall program requirements and challenges, (vi) analyze program cost, schedule, and program planning to fit the allocated budget and schedule within specified timeframe, (vii) conduct program cost, schedule, and program risk assessment, and (viii) revise and finalize the WBS to address cost, schedule, and all technical and program risks. For the source selection planning-and-execution phase, the PPM activities must address the following tasks: (i) generate the proposal and prepare the cost volume for the bid, (ii) work with the government PM to gain better understanding of ACT program requirements, (iii) refine the proposal and cost volume as needed, (iv) submit the proposal and cost volume, and (v) when requested, respond to government source selection team and wait for the contract award decision. Finally, for the post-acquisition phase and program execution- and-management (assuming the contract is awarded), the PPM activities must address the following tasks: (i) work with the government PM to plan and conduct program kick-off and finalize the program requirements and present the final execution program plan at the kick-off meeting, (ii) work with the government PM to prepare and execute the program quarterly review (should be bi-monthly for short period of performance program), (iii) respond to government PM's requests, and (iv) prepare and execute final program review and address all government PM's requests.

Figures 5 and **6** describe the recommended PPM activities that can potentially help the program managers to develop an effective PPM plan with a good balance between cost, technical, and program management risks for both government and contractor perspectives, respectively. From the government perspective shown in **Figure 5**, the act to balance the cost, technical, and program management risks occurs between the pre-acquisition planning phase (see blue-star) and the post-acquisition phase (see red-star). In practice, the blue-star captures the government PPM plan, while the red-star captures the progress of the plan during program execution phase. This is the time

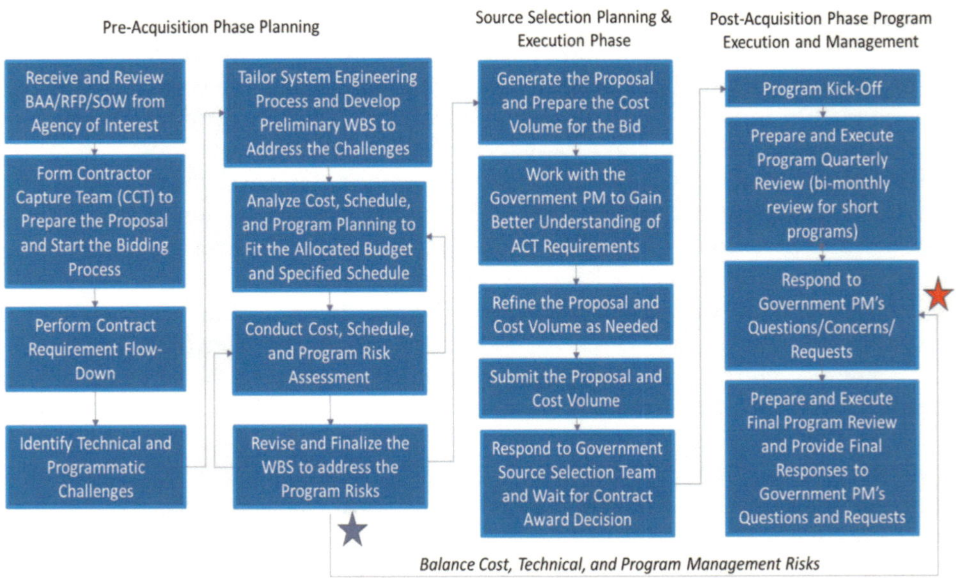

Figure 6.
A new perspective on the understanding ACT program planning, execution, and management activities from contractor perspective.

when the government PM can balance the cost, schedule, and program risks based on contractor's performance. The PM will (i) add new risks and retire the old risks, and (ii) adjust the PPM plan to balance the risks. Similarly, from the contractor perspective, the act to balance the risks also occurs between the blue-star and the red-star shown in **Figure 6**. It should be noted that, for a small ACT program, the PPM only requires the WBS, and a schedule plan. For large budget program (typically 20⁺M USD), the PPM plan requires an integrated master plan (IMP) and integrated master schedule (IMS) [26, 27].

7. Earned value management system for tracking and managing risks

In practice, both government and contractor PMs use the Earned Value Management System (EVMS) to effective track and manage the program risks. As described in [29, 30], the term "EV" is defined as an objective measure of the work done expressed in terms USD or hours that representing the value of the work done. The "earned value management (EVM) process is defined as the process of defining, planning, and controlling the scope of work, program schedule, and program budget. Thus, the EVMS is the integration of EVM processes, EVM procedures, and related EV tools to comply with the ANSI/EIA Standard 748 [28]. He recommended EVMS is a combination of processes, procedure, and related tools [28–31], which can be used to measure and track the "earned value" (EV) against an integrated baseline plan (IBP) captured in the PPM plan. The IBP is the baseline IMP and IMS mentioned earlier. In practice, for defense ACT programs with contract value greater than or equal to 20M USD, the contractor PM is required to submit the integrated program management report (IPMR) to the government PM [29, 32]. The IPMR combines and replaces the Contract Performance Reports per DIMGMT-81466 and the Integrated Master Schedule per DI-MGMT81650 [33]. The IPMR report contains the EV performance data. Per DI-MGMT-81861 [32], the report provides required program status of contract cost and schedule performance according to the government required seven formats. The seven formats include Formats 1, 2, 3, 4, 5, 6, and 7. **Table 4** summarizes the requirements associated with the seven required formats.

IPMR format	Format requirement description
Format 1	Define and report cost and schedule performance data by a specified program WBS
Format 2	Define and report cost and schedule performance data by the contractor's organizational structure, e.g., Functional or Integrated Product Team (IPT)
Format 3	Define and report changes to the IPB or Performance Measurement Baseline (PMB)
Format 4	Define and report staffing forecasts
Format 5	Provide a narrative report used to provide the required analysis of data contained in Formats 1, 2, 3, 4, and 6
Format 6	Define and report IMS and changes
Format 7	Define and report time-phased historical and forecast cost submission

Table 4.
Description of required IPMR seven formats to capture EV performance data [32, 33].

Contract value (USD)	ACT program applicability	Remark and recommendation
<20M	Not required	Based on our experience, it's recommended the contractor PM to report IPMR Formats 1 and 5 for contract value between 10M and 20M USD. For Format 5, only Format 1 data analysis is required
≥ $20M and ≤ $50M	Required monthly IPMR report	Formats 2, 3, and 4 may be excluded at government PM discretion based on program risk
> $50M	Required monthly IPMR report	All Formats must be included in the IPMR report

Table 5.
Applicability of EVMS to ACT programs/projects [32, 33].

As indicated in [29, 30], US government has adopted the standard that defines the EVMS implementation requirements for tracking and managing risks for all defense programs. According to [29], the EVMS implementation is (i) a mandatory requirement for all defense programs with contract value greater than or equal to 20M USD, and (ii) not required for less than 20M USD. Per DI-MGMT81861A, for contract value between 20M and $50M, a simplified IPMR report may be allowed at the government PM discretion based on program risk. The simplified IPMR requires to report EV data according to Formats 1, 5, and 6 described in **Table 4**. For contract value greater than $50 M, a full IPMR report is required, including all formats described in **Table 4**. **Table 5** captures a summary of the applicability of EVMS to defense ACT programs/projects and associated contract values.

To provide a better understanding of EV data and related cost and schedule performance data, the remaining of this section provides an overview of the recommended baseline EVMS model. The model includes five key EV data captured the Budgeted Cost of Work Scheduled (BCWS), Budgeted Cost of Work Performed (BCWP), Actual Cost of Work Performed (ACWP), Budget at Completion (BAC), and Estimate at Completion (EAC) [28, 31]. The BCWS represents the planned EV of the work planned to be accomplished in a period of time. BCWS can be calculated using:

$$BCWS = \%Complete(planned) * ProjectBudget \quad (1)$$

BCWP is defined as the EV of completed work in terms of the work's assigned budget and calculated using the following equation:

$$BCWP = \%Complete(Actual) * ProjectBudget \quad (2)$$

The ACWP is the actual cost incurred and recorded for work completed within a specified time period. The contractor PM usually reports the cumulative ACWP for the WBS work package that have been completed. Finally, the estimate of BAC is established by the PMs during the program planning phase. From the contractor perspective, the contractor PM estimates the BAC during the pre-acquisition phase for every specified level of the WBS. The BAC value represents the total budget from which individual period BCWS values are derived and they are the benchmarks for assessing overruns and underruns at the end of the contract. The budgets for all authorized work must be captured within the BAC. The BAC can also be referred to as the "Total Planned Value" of a project. As indicated in [34], there is no formula for calculating BAC. The calculation of BAC requires complex cost estimating methods and associated tools [16, 34]. Popular estimating methods include parametric, analogy, engineering estimate, actual costs, and three-point estimate [34]. Popular estimating tools include SEER, aPriori Cost Estimating Software Tools, and DOD COCOMO Software [16].

The cost and schedule performance data are characterized by Schedule Performance Index (SPI) and Cost Performance Index (CPI), and the SPI and CPI data are generated using the following equations:

$$SPI = \frac{BCWP}{BCWS} = \left\{ \begin{array}{c} SPI > 1 : \text{Indicates an ahead} - \text{of} - \text{schedule condition} \\ SPI < 1 : \text{Indicates a behind} - \text{schedule condition} \end{array} \text{plan}| \right\} \quad (3)$$

$$CPI = \frac{BCWP}{ACWP} = \left\{ \begin{array}{c} CPI > 1 : \text{Indicates a favorable cost efficiency condition} \\ CPI < 1 : \text{Indicates an unfavorable cost efficiency condition} \end{array} \text{plan}| \right\} \quad (4)$$

The PMs track and monitor the SPI and CPI data manage the execution teams according to the reported SPI and CPI values. As an example, when both SPI and CPI indices are equal to 1, the execution team performs their work according to schedule time and allocated budget. For instance, if the SPI is .8, it means that the team is behind the schedule and that only 80% of the scheduled work has been completed, not the 80% of the total planned work. When the CPI is .8, it means that for every dollar actually spent by the execution team, only 80% worth of work was performed. For this case, the execution team might have spent 20% of the budget on the re-work.

The EAC is also an important EV parameter that required the PMs to track and monitor. The EAC value represents the forecasted total budget that is required to complete at a given time during a project. The EAC value can be computed using BCWP, ACWP, SPI, and CPI using the following equation:

$$EAC = ACWP + \frac{BAC–BCWP}{CPI * SPI} \quad (5)$$

Other related EV parameters are the percentage of the Cost Variance (CV%), percentage of the Schedule Variance (SV%), and the Variance at Completion (VAR). The CV%, SV%, and VAR can be calculated from the EV data using the following equations:

$$CV\% = \frac{BCWP - ACWS}{BCWP} \quad (6)$$

$$SV\% = \frac{BCWP - BCWS}{BCWS} \quad (7)$$

$$VAR = BAC - EAC \quad (8)$$

From Eqs. (6) and (7), the Cost Variance (CV) and Schedule Variance (SV) can be written as follow:

$$\begin{aligned} CV &= BCWP - ACWS \\ &= \{CV > 0 : \text{Indicatesthecostunderrunplan}||CV < 0 : \text{Indicatesthecostoverrun}|\} \end{aligned} \quad (9)$$

$$\begin{aligned} SV &= BCWP - BCWS \\ &= \{SV > 0 : \text{Indicatestheschedule} \text{isaheadplan} || CV < 0 : \text{Indicatestheschedule} \text{isbehind}|\} \end{aligned} \tag{10}$$

In practice, the level of effort (LOE) cannot have a schedule variance because BCWS and BCWP are always the same. The PMs can use the EV data to check and correct for anomalies associated with the program "health." Typical anomalies are: (i) actual budget that is required to complete at a given time during a project should never be greater than EAC at the same given time, and (ii) you cannot earn more than what is budgeted, i.e., BCWP cannot be greater than BAC.

8. Conclusion and recommendations

The specific nature of ACT program characteristics requires the PMs to have a good understanding of the PPM activities to develop effective PPM plans. As discussed above, the plan will be developed depending on the PM's perspective, i.e., contractor vs. government. In general (regardless of the perspective), a PM, who is responsible for the planning and executing an ACT program, must have a good understanding of the challenges and issues associated with ACT program characteristics, acquisition life cycle, program cost/technical/management risks, desired PPM activities for balancing cost, technical and program management risks, and EVMS methods and tools. The above sections, Sections 2, 3, 4, 5, 6, and 7, have provided an overview with sufficient details on each of the challenges and issues mentioned above. To help improve the preparation and development of an effective PPM plan during the concept and pre-acquisition phases, the chapter recommends (i) a tailored Zachman framework for PPM planning, (ii) an innovative approach to quantify the technology and market risks associated with ACT programs using the innovation indicators and simplified Cooper chart, (iii) a set of PPM activities for balancing cost, technical and program management risks, and (iv) the EVMS applicability for tracking and managing the identified ACT program risks.

Recently, based on [16, 34–45] has proposed an approach to integrate data and decision sciences into PPM. The proposed integration approach for PPM planning and execution leverages big data analytics (BDA) technology with BDA data acquisition and data curation TEs, and ML-AI TEs. The recommended ML-AI TE's include (i) data mining techniques and tools (DMTT), (ii) data exploitation using multi-objective reinforce learning and adaptive neural network (MORL-ANN) tool, and (iii) predictive analytics techniques using MORL-ANN tool [34–45]. These ML-AI techniques and tools leverage related cost historical data bases, BDA framework with data acquisition and data curation models and tools to develop the program cost estimate and execute the EVMS plan to be included in the PPM plan. As pointed out in [35], there are many researchers and start-up companies developing algorithms, analytical models, and tools to apply ML-AI in program management. When this next generation ML-AI tools becomes popular and widely adapted by the decision makers (such as PMs and acquisition authorities), there will be radical changes that will disrupt the development and execution of a PPM plan [35] predicted that ML-AI will disrupt six aspects of PPM, including: (i) better section and prioritization, (ii) support for the project management office, (iii) improved, faster project definition, planning, and reporting, (iv) Virtual project assistants, (v) advanced testing systems and software, and (vi) a new role for the project manager.

In summary, this chapter provides an overview of the ACT program types and related program characteristics along with program risks and describes the acquisition life cycle from both government and contractor perspectives. The chapter also describes (i) the government recommended ANSI/EIA Standard 748 for the implementation of EVMS framework, procedures, processes, and tools, and (ii) the trends for integrating ML-AI TES into the planning and executing of the PPM plan. In addition, the chapter recommends an innovative approach to quantify the technology and market risks, and a tailored Zachman framework that can be used to enhance the efficiency of a PPM plan. A set of desired PPM activities is also recommended for balancing cost, technical and program management risks. Finally, the chapter discusses the applicability of EVMS to ACT Programs and recommends a simplified EVMS report should be provided for contract value between 10M and 20M USD. The simplified report with Format 1 data analysis is required to capture cost and schedule performance data by a specified WBS along with a narrative report to capture the required performance analysis.

Acknowledgements

The author wants to thank his wife, Thu-Hang Nguyen, for her tremendous patience and support during the preparation and writing of this chapter.

Conflict of interest

The author declares no conflict of interest. The opinions expressed in this chapter are those of the author and they are not endorsed by CSUF nor Aerospace Corporation.

Author details

Tien M. Nguyen
California State University, Fullerton (CSUF), California, USA

*Address all correspondence to: tmnguyen57@fullerton.edu

References

[1] DOD Acquisition Process. Acquisition Process Overview. Available from: https://acqnotes.com/acqnote/acquisitions/acquisition-process-overview

[2] DOD Directive 5000.01. The Defense Acquisition System. Office of the Under Secretary of Defense for Acquisition and Sustainment. September 2020, 2022. Available from: https://aaf.dau.edu/storage/2022/07/DoDD-5000-01-Change-1-2022-07-28.pdf

[3] DOD Instruction 5000.02. Operation of the Adaptive Acquisition Framework. Office of the Under Secretary of Defense for Acquisition and Sustainment. 23 January 2020. Available from: https://www.esd.whs.mil/Portals/54/Documents/DD/issuances/dodi/500002p.pdf

[4] William TC, Brian CR. A Guide for DOD Program Managers. Defense Acquisition Authority. Fort Belvoir, Virginia: Defense Acquisition University (DAU); December 2014. Available from: https://acqnotes.com/wp-content/uploads/2014/09/A-Guide-for-DoD-Program-Managers.pdf

[5] Department of Defense Risk, Issue, and Opportunity Management Guide for Defense Acquisition Programs. Washington, D.C.: Office of the Deputy Assistant Secretary of Defense for Systems Engineering; January 2017. Available from: https://acqnotes.com/wp-content/uploads/2017/07/DoD-Risk-Issue-and-Opportunity-Management-Guide-Jan-2017.pdf

[6] DoD Open System Architecture. Contract Guidebook for Program Managers, v1.1. Prepared by DoD Open Systems Architecture Data Rights Team. June 2013. Available from: https://www.acqnotes.com/Attachments/Open%20System%20Architecture%20%28OSA%29%20Contract%20Guidebook%20for%20Program%20Managers%20June%2013.pdf

[7] Tien MN. Program planning and management for defense advanced concept technology programs. In: Marinela M, Tien MN, editors. Project Management – New Trends and Applications. UKINTECH-Open Science; 2023

[8] Technology Readiness Assessment (TRA) Deskbook. Department of Defense. Director, Research Directorate (DRD). Office of the Director, Defense Research and Engineering (DDR&E). July 2009. Available from: https://apps.dtic.mil/sti/pdfs/ADA524200.pdf

[9] Mark P. Advanced Concept Technology Demonstrations (ACTD). Program Resources & Integration Office of the Secretary of Defense DDR&E/AS&C (Advanced Systems & Concepts). April 2006. Available from: https://ndiastorage.blob.core.usgovcloudapi.net/ndia/2006/science/peterson.pdf

[10] General Accounting Office (GAO). Advanced Concept Technology Demonstration Program Can Be Improved. Report No. GAO/NSIAD-99-4 Defense Acquisition. October 1998. Available from: https://www.gao.gov/assets/nsiad-99-4.pdf

[11] Federal Acquisition Regulation (FAR). Part 35 - Research and Development Contracting. FAC Number: 2023-04. 6 February 2023. Available from: https://www.acquisition.gov/far/part-35

[12] Defense Advanced Research Projects Agency (DARPA). About DARPA. DARPA Overview. Available from:

https://www.darpa.mil/about-us/about-darpa

[13] Mariella M. What you need to know about DARPA, the Pentagon's mad science division. 19 July 2019. Available from: https://www.engadget.com/2014-07-07-darpa-explainer.html?guccounter=1&guce_referrer=aHR0cHM6Ly93d3cuZ29vZ2xlLmNvbS8&guce_referrer_sig=AQAAAG7aYv4lhcRVQrluKAES5CkktaRD-IvxeYgYWZ0EswiLZappyWlwR8UoZhJftQc6fjFAUoJI76Ng5-_OL8R1c0N1R0tzVyVVCKjSp4CCwiTFDHTVq_0qOV4iQu1ugy0vyP0eOqec5zC5jjb8WHVF2QJZa2d-MHGQrjoOJ2HkM-cx

[14] Department of Defense. Small Business Innovation Research and Small Business Technology Transfer (SBIR/STTR) Programs. Available from: https://www.defensesbirsttr.mil/SBIR-STTR/Program/

[15] DARPA. The Heilmeier Catechism. Available from: https://www.darpa.mil/work-with-us/heilmeier-catechism

[16] Tien MN, John DTN, My TN, Charles HL, Tam N. Program management integrated with data and decision sciences. In: Marinela M, Tien MN, editors. Project Management – New Trends and Applications. IntechOpen. DOI: 10.5772/intechopen.109964. Available from: https://www.intechopen.com/online-first/86949

[17] Zachman JA. A framework for information systems architecture. IBM Systems Journal. 1987;**26**(3):276-292. DOI: 10.1147/sj.263.0276

[18] Hay D. The Zachman Framework: An Introduction. The Data Administration Newsletter. June 1997. Available from: https://tdan.com/the-zachman-framework-an-introduction/4140

[19] Marisa D, Knut B. Innovation indicators throughout the innovation process: An extensive literature analysis. Technovation (Elsevier). February–March 2019;**80–81**:3-29. Available from: https://www.sciencedirect.com/science/article/pii/S0166497217301402?via%3Dihub

[20] Ottinger R. Create Sustainable Success with the 4 Types of Innovation. Fresh Consulting. 2 April 2021. Available from: https://www.freshconsulting.com/insights/blog/the-4-types-of-innovation/

[21] Miner K. The four levels of innovation: Assess the time, effort, and resources necessary to join the ranks of innovation. Pepperdine. Graziadio Business Review. Entrepreneurship, Innovations. 2010;**13**(4):1-3. Available from: https://gbr.pepperdine.edu/2010/10/the-four-levels-of-innovation/

[22] Cooper JR. A multidimensional approach to the adoption of innovation. Management Decision. 1998;**36**(8):493-502. DOI: 10.1108/00251749810232565

[23] Sopheonblog. Innovation and New Product Development Q&A with Dr. Bob Cooper. Webinar with Dr. Bob Cooper, the Founder of the Stage-Gate® System. Available from: https://www.sopheon.com/blog/innovation-and-new-product-development-npd-qawith-bob-cooper

[24] Program Management Tool for Aerospace. Production, Quality & Manufacturing, Manufacturing Readiness Level (MRL). AcqNotes. Your Government Contract Vehicle Experts Website. Available from: https://acqnotes.com/acqnote/careerfie

lds/manufacturing-readiness-levelma nufact

[25] Manufacturing Readiness Level (MRL) Deskbook, Version 2.0. Prepared by OSD Manufacturing Technology Program in Collaboration with the Joint Service/Industry MRLWorking Group. May 2011. Available from: https://www.dodmrl.com/MRL_Deskbook_V2.pdf

[26] Program Management Tool for Aerospace. Program Management, Integrated Master Plan AcqNotes. Your Government Contract Vehicle Experts Website. Available from: https://acqnotes.com/acqnote/careerfields/integrated-master-plan

[27] Program Management Tool for Aerospace. Program Management, Integrated Master Schedule. AcqNotes. Your Government Contract Vehicle Experts Website. Available from: https://acqnotes.com/acqnote/tasks/integrated-master-scheduleschedule

[28] Program Management Tool for Aerospace. Earned Value Management, NDIA EIA 748 Earned Value Management. AcqNotes. Your Government Contract Vehicle Experts Website. Available from: https://acqnotes.com/acqnote/tasks/ansi-eia-748-earned-value-management

[29] Earned Value Management System (EVMS) Interpretation Guide (EVMSIG). DoD. Earned Value Management Acquisition Analytics and Policy. OUSD A&S (AE/AAP). 2019. Available from: https://www.acq.osd.mil/asda/ae/ada/ipm/docs/DoD_EVMSIG_14MAR2019.pdf

[30] Earned Value Management Implementation Guide (EVMIG). DoD. Earned Value Management Acquisition Analytics and Policy. OUSD A&S (AE/AAP). 2019. Available from: https://www.humphreys-assoc.com/evms/evms-documents/dod/DOD%20EVMIG-01-18-2019.pdf

[31] Program Management Tool for Aerospace. Earned Value Management, EVMS Equations. AcqNotes. Your Government Contract Vehicle Experts Website. Available from: https://acqnotes.com/acqnote/tasks/evms-equations

[32] Data Item Description. Integrated Program Management Report (IPMR). Number: DI-MGMT-81861A. OUSD (AT&L) PARCA. 2015. Available from: https://www.cms.gov/research-statistics-data-and-systems/cms-information-technology/earnedvaluemanagement/downloads/ipmr-did.pdf

[33] Integrated Program Management Report. ACQuipedia. 2017. Available from: https://www.dau.edu/acquipedia/pages/ArticleContent.aspx?itemid=274

[34] Earned Value Management. Budget at Completion (BAC). AcqNotes. Your Government Contract Vehicle Experts Website. Available from: https://acqnotes.com/acqnote/tasks/budget-at-completion

[35] Nieto-Rodriguez A, Vargas RV. How AI will Transform Project Management. Harvard Business Review. Project Management. 2023. Available from: https://www.dau.edu/acquipedia/pages/ArticleContent.aspx?itemid=274

[36] Iranmanesh SH, Zarezadeh M. Application of artificial neural network to forecast actual cost of a project to improve earned value management system. International Journal of Social, Behavioral, Educational, Economic, Business and Industrial Engineering. 2008:658-661

[37] Garling R. Artificial Intelligence and Earned Value in Project Management [Master thesis]. Charles Town, WV: American Military University; 2020. Available from: https://richgarling.com/?p=649

[38] Wauters M, Vanhoucke M. A comparative study of artificial intelligence methods for project duration forecasting. Expert Systems with Applications. 2016;**46**(15):249-261. DOI: 10.1016/j.eswa.2015.10.008

[39] Lee SH, Kim K-Y, Shin Y. Effective feature selection method for deep learning-based automatic modulation classification scheme using higher-order statistics. MDPI Applied Science. 2020: 1-14. DOI: 10.3390/app10020588

[40] AI vs. Machine Learning vs. Deep Learning vs. Neural Networks: What's the Difference? IBM Blog. IBM Data and AI Team; July 2023. Available from: https://www.ibm.com/cloud/blog/ai-vs-machine-learning-vs-deep-learning-vs-neural-networks

[41] Valohai. MLOps Basics. Valohai Blog. Available from: https://valohai.com/mlops/

[42] Kirenz J, Gröger C, Lutsch A. Data Platform Architectures & Machine Learning Operations (MLOps). Stuttgart: Hochschule Der Medien. pp. 1-19. Available from: https://www.kirenz.com/slides/data-platform-mlops.pdf

[43] Kreuzberger D, Kühl N. Machine Learning Operations (MLOps): Overview, Definition, and Architecture. pp. 1-13. Available from: https://arxiv.org/ftp/arxiv/papers/2205/2205.02302.pdf

[44] Liu Y, Ling Z, Huo B, Wang B, Chen T, Mouine E. Building a platform for machine learning operations from open source frameworks. In: 3rd IFAC Workshop on Cyber-Physical & Human Systems CPHS 2020. Beijing, China; 2020. DOI: 10.1016/j.ifacol.2021.04.161

[45] Munir M. How artificial intelligence can help project managers. Global Journal of Management and Business Research: Administration and Management. 2019;**19**(4):29-35

Section 4

Project Management Interface within a Project Life Cycle

Chapter 7

Inter-Organizational Integration, Transition, and Collaboration in the Project Front-End, and Project Initiation Phase

Rajenlall Siriram

Abstract

Project management is a complex process involving different stakeholders within and outside the firm. These stakeholders involve among others, the client who has the initial need, and establishes the project requirements and boundaries; the sales teams involved in developing the initial solution and sealing the contract with the client; the project management practitioners responsible for executing the solution as per the contractual requirements; different organizational units, such as engineering, finance, supply chain, health, and safety; and other stakeholders, such as sub-suppliers, legal authorities, consultants, and funding agencies. These stakeholders have different perspectives and objectives that make project management a complex process. In this chapter the challenges, benefits, and opportunities of inter-organizational integration, transition, and collaboration within and between firms in large complex projects are explored. The scope of this chapter is on the interface between the sales front-end phase and the project initiation phase because it is in the sales front-end, where the strategic and operational direction for the rest of the project is set and agreed. A better understanding of this interface may provide opportunities for improvement in project management success.

Keywords: integration, transition, project life cycle, collaboration, coordination

1. Introduction

Project management has received much attention in the last several decades. This attention is largely driven by the state of project management in many firms. Many firms have reported projects that have failed due to numerous reasons, among which include at least the following—scope creep, cost overruns, schedule slippage, poor planning, lack of proper risk management, inferior quality control systems, poor procurement processes, gaps in meeting technical specifications and performance, inadequate resources, poor integration between the different stakeholders involved in the project life cycle (PLC), poor teamwork, poor communication, lack of collaboration, nonadherence to quality standards as well as other project processes, and poor monitoring and control, etc. This list is not exhaustive but gives a good overview of the complex challenges facing project practitioners.

In response to the poor state of project management, there has been much research in the area of project management with the main aim to improve project success. The research is aimed at improving the project management body of knowledge with the end result of improving project management practices and in so doing improving project success rates. While there are numerous academic journals, conferences, and books aimed at contributing to the project management body of knowledge, it is worth mentioning ref. [1], which is an exhaustive text providing a fully comprehensive methodology for managing the PLC. In the private sector, many firms have also responded with initiatives primarily aimed at reducing project failures and improving success. The internet provides many examples of such initiatives, to mention at least PM@Siemens, which is a fully comprehensive project management methodology aimed at improving project management practices within the Siemens group of companies [2].

Project Management Institute [1] sees project management consisting of five steps, namely—initiation, planning, execution, monitoring and control, and closure. Taking a systems engineering view to project management, Blanchard and Fabrycky [3] view project management as consisting of two parts, namely—the acquisition part and the utilization part. The acquisition part includes conceptual/preliminary design, detailed design and development, production, and/or construction. The utilization part consists of product use, phase-out, and disposal. Blanchard and Fabrycky [3] do include conceptual design as part of the project management phases; however, they do not include the project concept phase. Blanchard and Fabrycky [3] include the feasibility study as part of conceptual design; however, this feasibility study is specific to the design and focuses on design-specific issues, such as needs analysis, system and operational requirements, system maintenance concepts, functional requirements, and project planning as well as the project specifications. In this chapter, the project concept phase is seen as part of the project front-end phase and it includes the project scope, requirements, boundaries, the initial solution and alternatives, specifications and performance measures, resource commitments, timelines, costs, business case, the funding requirements, contractual terms, and conditions as well as the formalization thereof, and the go/no-decision, etc. The project concept is much more than the technical design concept; it includes the entire business case, all the various organizations, the various mechanisms and arrangements involved in the inter-organizational relationships [4]. Project Management Institute [1] also does not see the project concept phase as part of the initiation phase. In Ref. [1] the project initiation phase commences once the project is handed over from the sales front-end team to the project team; it excludes the sales front-end. The project concept phase is part of the project front-end phase; this refers to the activities that are performed before the actual start of the project [5]. This project concept phase occurs before the PLC; note that according to Project Management Institute [1], the PLC commences at the project initiation phase and extends until project closure, which is when the project is handed over to the client. Therefore, it is emphasized that by only focusing on the PLC, we are missing the critical front-end part of the project [6].

Notwithstanding that there is an abundance of focus from both academia and a practitioner level on improvement in project success, many researchers and practitioners have identified that much of the failures in project management is because of poor inter-organizational integration, transition, and collaboration between the different stakeholders that are involved from the initial sales stage to the PLC phases.

Project Management Institute [1] defines the PLC to commence at the project initiation phase, which is when the project manager takes accountability and responsibility for project delivery. This is where the project manager's accountability and responsibility commence for the operational delivery of the project in terms of cost, schedule, and performance. However, the project has been committed much earlier in the sales stage where the sales team has already set the direction for the project. It is in the sales front-end stage where the initial project needs, as well as project requirements, are established, where the project budget is established, which is a function of the materials, equipment, resources, and time. It is also where the high-level project solution is conceptualized, which establishes the boundaries for the project specifications, criteria for the project performance, and where project sustainability is established. This is an important and critical phase, which requires sufficient focus and commitment to establish the correct foundation and future direction for the project.

The rest of this chapter is structured as follows—first, an understanding of the interface between the sales front-end and the project initiation phase is provided; this is followed by the relevant definitions and terminology, challenges, project success, and governance requirements. Thereafter the mechanisms to improve integration, transition, and collaboration are provided, which is then followed by the benefits and opportunities of inter-organizational integration, transition, and collaboration, and finally a conclusion highlighting important lessons for project practitioners and managers is provided.

2. Understanding the interface between the sales front-end phase and the project initiation phase

For further clarity in terms of the interface between the sales team and the project team, consider the following generic example. Firm A has a need for some type of infrastructure development project; let us refer to firm A as the client. The client will conduct an initial analysis in terms of project scope, project timelines, project budgets, etc., to ascertain the feasibility of the project. Client A may perform this work internally or appoint external consultants to perform this piece of work. Whichever option client A chooses, the work is multidisciplinary in nature and involves many internal and external stakeholders. This is the initiation phase of the project from a client perspective. From their perspective, most of this work is performed by the client's project team. Once the client is satisfied with the feasibility study, the client will then proceed with the next phase, which includes the client issuing a request for proposal (RFP) to the market. Other organizations will respond to the RFP: Let us just consider one service provider who supplies a lump-sum turnkey project. Let us refer to this service provider as contractor B. The contracting firm will then respond to the RFP. The contracting firm will have its own initiation phase that includes the project scope, project time, project budgets, feasibility analysis, etc. From a contractor B perspective, this work is also multidisciplinary in nature and most of this work is led by the contractor's sales team.

The are several steps that include discussions, documentation exchange, and negotiations between client A and contractor B before a contract is awarded. There are also other discussions, documentation exchanges, and negotiations with other contractors, say C, D, E, etc. These contractors are the competitors to contractor B. These contractors were not successful in advancing to the award stage. In this chapter, the focus is not on the engagement between client A and the competitors to contractor

B. Let us assume that contractor B is successful in being awarded the work by client A. Note that most of the engagement between client A and contractor B was driven by the project team from client A and the sales team from contractor B. The project team from contractor B was to a substantial extent led by the sales team, where in most cases involvement from the project team is limited.

In preparing the value proposition for client A, the sales team from contractor B is also involved with many sub-suppliers and other stakeholders internal and external to contractor B. These sub-suppliers are an integral part of the value proposition. These engagements typically define the value proposition to client A and it also is prone to potentially high-risk levels if not correctly managed. In these engagements, important decisions are made by the sales front-end team that commits to the future direction of the project. These engagements have long-term consequences for contractor B. Therefore joint involvement between the sales front-end team and the project execution team will be beneficial. Sales teams sometimes place far too much weight on decisions and choices based on costs. They do not always give the right amount of focus on other factors, such as technical capability and performance, and this could be detrimental to the firm as well as the project. Joint involvement between sales and project execution teams offers the advantage of the four-eyed principle. Where the best options are evaluated by both the sales and project execution teams, better-informed decisions are made. This alleviates risks and sets up the project for success. **Figure 1** gives a graphical representation of the interface between the sales and project execution teams.

Once the project is awarded, the sales team from contractor B hands over the project to the project team in contractor B. This is the handover process between the sales front-end team and the project execution team. Once handed over, the project team takes accountability and responsibility for the project. The project team then kicks off the project and several activities are triggered, for example, project kick-off meetings, setting up of the project charter, project organizing, planning, resource allocation, carrying out the work, project closure, etc. The project charter is extremely important as it is a document that reinforces the project costs, scope boundaries, schedules,

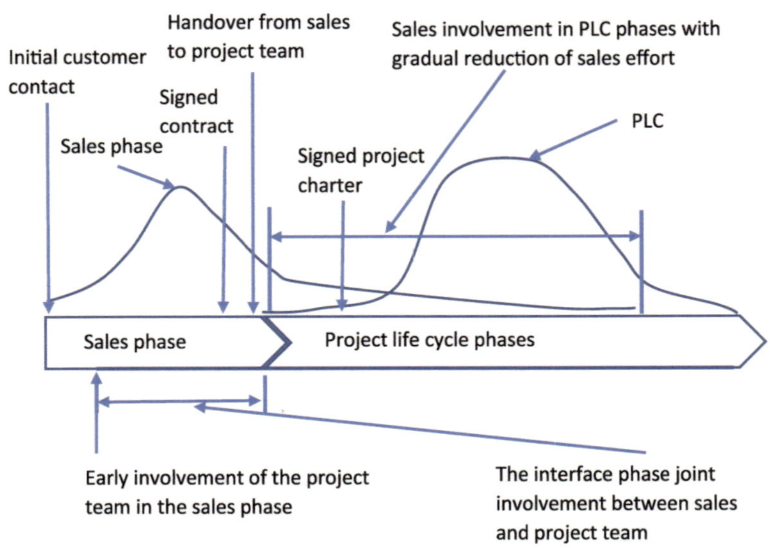

Figure 1.
Interface between sales and project teams.

quality control aspects, project deliverables, resource allocations, escalation mechanisms, etc. The project charter is an agreement between the project team from contractor B and client A. It is an essential part of the project initiation phase because it aligns the commitments made in the sales front-end phase to the commitments that will be adhered to and followed throughout the PLC. The project charter is a key milestone document that sets the direction for the rest of the project. Note that in this example the project deliverables have already been communicated by client A when the RFP was issued. This may have been quantified and/or qualified further during contract negotiations. Any changes must be reflected in the contract when awarded. This implies that the initial concept design, project timelines, costs, schedule, etc., which have already been committed during the negotiated sales phase are now further clarified and agreed. The project charter reinforces these commitments, highlights and records any additional changes that have now come to the fore, such as changes in scope, deliverables, schedules, and costs. An integral part of this phase is revisiting and assessing project risks that were initially identified during the sales phase.

Prior to the official award of the contract by client A to contractor B, there are numerous discussions, documents exchange, etc., before mutual understanding is finally reached that eventually leads to the contract award. During this period (interface and exchange between Client A and contractor B), there is a rapport which is built, and a mutual trust relationship is established. During this phase, the sales team from contractor B was predominant in managing the relationship between client A and contractor B. They were also instrumental in putting together the technical solution, and finalizing the price, which is dependent on inputs from many other firms internal and external to the contracting firm. These inputs include, for example, engineering for the technical solution, procurement for the cost inputs based on engagements with external sub-suppliers, health and safety for legislative requirements, finance, etc., with some and often limited involvement from the project team regarding resource allocations, timelines, project risks, etc. It is, therefore, imperative that for continuity from sales to project execution there is a properly documented handover between the sales team and the project team. Note that during the sales front-end phase there is tacit as well as explicit knowledge. The explicit knowledge is recorded in documents and is easier to transfer, tacit knowledge is not recorded and is difficult to transfer. The handover over process must take cognizance of both tacit and explicit knowledge. Siriram [7] highlighted the importance of a proper handover from the sales team to the project team. He also highlighted that those promises made at the sales stages of the project are not often carried to the project phases and this has the potential to result in project cost overruns. Based on at least this example, it is evident that the transition (and interface) between sales teams and project teams is of utmost importance. Therefore, it is key to contextualize the integration, transition, and collaboration in terms of the PLC.

To better understand the dynamics in terms of these interactions between the sales and project teams, it is important to explore the integration, transition, and collaboration dynamics between the sales and project teams.

3. Definitions and terminology: integration, transition, collaboration, the project front-end, and the project initiation phase

Firstly, before diving into the dynamics of integration, transition, and collaboration, it is important to define and understand these terms.

In terms of integration, there is a requirement for both technical and nontechnical integration. Technical integration deals with the technological interfaces between different disciplines, locations as well as interfaces between different systems and sub-system components [8]. Nontechnical integration deals with the communication, behavioral and social influences among people, organizations, and the external environment of the project [8]. Integration may also be viewed as the coordination of activities across the PLC. However, integration has been approached from a more mechanistic rational approach, in other words, a systematic approach, which is management by objectives approach. This is a short-term view to integration across the PLC, neglecting a more systemic holistic approach. The latter integrates the project from a wider systems context taking a longer-term view. This view takes into consideration the project's wider organizational and strategic perspective as well as its future sustainability and the co-existence of the project in the wider environment. The longer-term view is a more strategic approach compared to the shorter-term view, which is more operational. It is also worth noting that the strategic longer-term view is established in the project front-end, which is driven by the sales team, while the operational shorter-term view is embedded in the PLC stages, which is driven by the project team and their project goals. There are two separate parts—the sales front-end and the project execution part.

Transitions may be defined as how the project moves from one phase to the next; it specifically addresses the mechanisms for the handover, for example, between the sales front-end phase and the project initiation phase. It is important to understand that there are certain activities that are used to trigger transitions. For example, a signed contract by client A and the sales team of contracting firm B is a key milestone and is a trigger to commence the project initiation phase. Other examples of such triggers include, for example, signing of the project charter that indicates alignment between client A and the project team from contractor B; completion of the project technical design, indicating that project execution may commence, etc. Triggers are mechanisms to initiate transition activities, indicating that the project can advance to the next step and may also trigger payment points. Transition activities or milestones are sometimes celebrated through ceremonial events. When a signed contract is in place, the firm may choose to celebrate this event. It must, however, be pointed out that transitions are temporary events that are used to govern the PLC at certain points in time. It must also be highlighted that while the triggers for transition, such as signing of contracts, project kick-offs, or project milestones, are well known and practiced in the project management environment, there has been little emphasis on the social and symbolic aspects of transition activities (celebrations) [9]. Celebrations may be used to trigger transition activities, but they must be used with caution to celebrate key milestones and should not be overdone. Celebrating transitions through ceremonial events can be an effective way to ensure that the transition has occurred. However, one must caution against false celebrations that are a cover-up for throwing things over the wall from sales to project execution without the face-to-face interface discussions, negotiations, and agreements.

Collaboration may be seen, as a mechanism to cope with uncertainty and ambiguity in the project environment. Collaboration facilitates teamwork, information flow, and knowledge-sharing, and enables communication, resource flexibility, a good working environment, etc. The importance of collaboration within the project organization is well recognized. However, collaboration outside the project organization involving the different stakeholders might be neglected. There are formal means of collaboration as well as informal means of collaboration. Both types of collaboration are a means to enable information and knowledge sharing across the project environment from sales to project execution. Collaboration is also a function of trust where higher levels of trust give rise to better collaboration. Collaboration is a mechanism to ensure integration and transition. Formal means of collaboration include organizational structures, processes, documentation, systems, etc., while informal means of collaboration include meetings, workshops, and other social gatherings.

The project front-end refers to the sales and business development phase of the project. It is one of the most critical phases of the project as it is where the initial analyses of problems, needs, and client and stakeholder requirements are conducted. It is in the front-end where the initial solution alternatives and choices are positioned to the client [6, 10]. It is there where the business cases, target benefits, and their realization are set out both for the client and contractor. It is important to note that there are two sets of business cases—the first being the client's view in terms of the project scope, feasibility with its benefits, and realization. The second is the business case from the contractor's perspective for the project scope and feasibility with its benefits and realization. These are two separate initiatives done by two different firms—the client and the contractor, respectively. The project must make business sense for both firms, it must be a win-win situation to make the project a success. The front-end is the most critical phase of the project; it is where critical decisions are made. However, the front-end is not seen as part of the domain of the PLC and is outside the domain of the project manager [1, 3].

The project initiation phase is the start of the project from the execution perspective; it is the first phase of the PLC. Note, however, that the project has commenced much earlier in the sales front-end. The project initiation phase is when the project manager takes over accountability and responsibility from the sales and business development team. The project manager is now accountable and responsible to ensure that the project is delivered according to the project budget, schedule, and specifications that were established in the front-end and mutually agreed upon signing of the project charter. The project initiation phase is when accountability and responsibility have transitioned from the front-end.

4. Challenges associated with integration, transition, and collaboration between the project front-end and the project initiation phase

Challenges associated with integration include how well the project activities are coordinated across the different functional units as well as the coordination among the different stakeholders. Integration is a function of how well activities are coordinated. Integration demands at least the following alignment, documentation, coordination, communication, monitoring and control, and competencies as well as capabilities. Alignment includes strategic alignment in terms of the project's long-term and short-term perspectives, clear objectives, and in terms of project scope, client expectations, cross-functional team involvement, quality and risk measures, technical specifications and performance, etc. Documentation and coordination include well-documented and coordinated processes that are inclusive of ensuring adherence to processes. Communication includes clear guidelines and instructions on what is required and what is not allowed, how to access information and processes, and where to seek guidance if in doubt. Communication must allow for a two-way process that is not dictatorial but seeks to improve information flow and knowledge transfer and as such, improve processes and improve the adherence thereto.

Monitoring and control speak to the adherence in terms of process as well as how to handle deviations to process and their associated nonconformances. Competencies and capabilities are a fundamental requirement of the individuals involved in developing and executing the project and these are inclusive of both the front-end sales team as well as the project execution team. Unclear objectives, lack of coordination among activities, lack of well-documented processes, poor communication, poor adherence to process, lack of trust, lack of formal documentation specifying the interface between functional organizational units as well as system component parts, etc., are some of the challenges facing integration. Other challenges associated with integration include the mechanisms to improve coordination among the different activities in the project network. These are associated with how well activities are coordinated; poor coordination leads to poor integration.

Challenges associated with the transition from the front-end to the project initiation phase include at least the following—the shift in thinking from long term to short term. The front-end team is concerned with the long-term sustainability of the project, which includes factors that have social, environmental, and economic impact, coupled with client relationship management that extends beyond the scope of the current project, and it also includes project decommissioning. The project team, however, is concerned with short-term project benefits that include, cost, schedule, and performance of the project measured against what was sold to the client. The focus from the sales front-end team is geared toward the long-term sustainability of the firm, while the focus from the project team is focused on the successful delivery of the project. Therefore, one may view the front-end view as more strategic and the project view as more operational. This difference in thinking is a major challenge that needs to be overcome during the transition phase. Further to this, the transition process is also faced with other challenges like differences in performance metrics between the sales front-end and project teams, others like refs. [11, 12] also include the personalities, backgrounds, locations and responsibilities, lack of support, and proper organizational structures as additional challenges facing the transition. Others like ref. [13] also include a lack of management attention during the transition phase as a challenge. Specifically, executive management's attention in the transition process is key to removing obstacles and enabling a better transition process.

Challenges associated with collaboration include the uncertainty and ambiguity that arise because of the project environment, which includes multiple stakeholders, conflicting objectives, trust, the means, frequency, and quality of communication as well as resource constraints. Project resources are revenue generating and as such, they generate money for the firm. Removing them and reallocating them to sales activities that are nonrevenue generating is a challenge, as it hinders the firm's revenue-generating capability. Project resources are essential for revenue and profit. They are normally utilized to full capacity, especially the project manager, who is in most cases already committed to other projects. Availability of project resources is, therefore, a constraint that is a challenge for collaboration. The sales team, however, is nonrevenue generating; they are also constrained as they often work on multiple sales initiatives, and therefore, coordinating the availability of sales and project teams may also pose a challenge for collaboration. Collaboration is also a function of trust; higher trust leads to better collaboration and lower trust leads to lower levels of collaboration. The better the collaboration the greater the coordination, which leads to better integration of activities.

These challenges need to be overcome to improve project success. It is, therefore, necessary to understand what project success means both from a firm perspective as well as a project perspective. The interface between the project front-end and the project initiation phase is the most critical interface required for project success, and it requires special managerial attention. It is, therefore, important to understand what is required to improve management and governance to ensure project success.

The project execution team is more concerned with hard deliverable realities, while the sales team is more concerned with meeting the client's expectations and wishes, which sometimes may not be realistic, but to win the order, sales teams may make certain commitments. In preparing the solution for the client, the project team is risk-averse, while the sales teams are risk-taking. Should these two not tie up, there are gaps, which may lead to conflict with the client that will also then hamper integration, transition, and collaboration efforts. This is an undesirable situation. Therefore, proper governance is required at the onset to effectively manage the interface between the sales front-end and the project initiation phase.

5. Project success and governance

From a project management perspective, project success is viewed as meeting the project objectives in terms of the project budget (cost), schedule (time), and performance (specifications). This view of project success is a short-term perspective; it is management by objectives view, and it is a rational mechanistic and systematic view. In this view, the long-term wider more strategic and systemic perspective is neglected. The short-term view needs to expand the current view of project success to include project sustainability, which is the life of the project beyond its completion, the relevance and effectiveness of the project, extending to the longer-term goals of the project that were set in the front-end phase. These two perspectives on project success, namely the short term and long term, need proper management and governance. The project success criteria must include both long-term and short-term metrics.

Project governance mechanisms need to be put in place to manage both the short-term (operational, tactical, and systematic) and long-term (strategic and systemic) objectives of the project. Project governance mechanisms include organizational structures, the incorporation of processes, systems, regulations, as well as formal and informal mechanisms that can improve communication, integration, transition, and collaboration across the life of the project. Such mechanisms must also include the appropriate organizational structures to support cross-functional alignment in project environments, which is inclusive of well-documented processes. In terms of process, emphasis is placed on a proper handover process and documentation from sales to project execution. Other governance mechanisms include cross-functional teams to improve communication, information and knowledge sharing, and collaboration between the front-end and project execution phases. Attention must also be devoted to cultivating a symbiotic relationship between sales and project execution teams. Careful and continuous risk management, and risk mitigation processes early on, commencing at the sales front-end phase with continuity through to the project execution phases, should not be neglected. Project execution teams must be included in the front-end and have significant input in pricing the solution and sales must be involved in project execution as an oversight function, etc.

Such mechanisms improve collaboration, but integration is not well addressed by cross-functional teams. Collaboration may help improve communication, information flow, and knowledge sharing between the different functional units, but it does not enable integration. Integration can only be achieved through the alignment of goals, objectives, and performance metrics. This is mainly because organizational boundaries exist between the different units. These divide the different organizational units into different entities that have different goals and objectives, each having its own responsibilities and tasks that are measured by a separate set of performance metrics. For example, the sales team is measured on order intake targets measured in financial terms (e.g., dollars), while the project execution team is measured in terms of meeting project deliverables, such as cost, schedule, and performance. Procurement is measured on a range of factors, for example, cost of input items, lead-time, and delivery reliability of suppliers. The sales team should not only be measured on order intake targets, but profit margin should also be a criterion that will safeguard against accepting sales orders that have poor margin quality. Project execution should also be not only be measured on criteria, such as cost, schedule, and performance, but also on criteria, such as long-term sustainability of the project and client satisfaction. Procurement should also be measured not only on cost target measures but also on supplier reliability, delivery, flexibility, etc. These types of overlapping metrics enable better integration, transition, and collaboration between sales and project execution teams. Close alignment of performance metrics between the different functional units will improve integration from the sales front-end to project execution.

6. Mechanisms to improve integration, transition, and collaboration

Transition activities go beyond the structural dimensions that are required to ensure how well participants in both sales and project execution teams adhere to defined integration and collaboration mechanisms. It extends beyond adherence to organizational structures, processes, and adoption of systems; it is inclusive of mutual trust and understanding between the different stakeholders. This mutual establishment of trust must be developed early in the project; typically in the sales front-end phase and such trust will aid in developing a symbiotic relationship between the sales and project execution teams.

Integration is a means to facilitate the transition. There are different types of integration, namely vertical and horizontal integration. Vertical integration focuses on integration within a single unit through centralization, standardization, formation, and on systems. Horizontal integration focuses across organizational units, for example, through mechanisms such as cross-functional teams and job rotation [14, 15]. The question arises which types of integration mechanisms are appropriate for successful project completion. When there is the complexity that gives rise to elevated levels of uncertainty, people become inundated with different alternatives, making choices difficult. In such cases, more informal means of integration that facilitate information and knowledge sharing enabling a big picture approach are preferred. Informal means are more interpersonal and tend to bring different stakeholders together in a calmer environment which may facilitate better communication, which is critical in complex environments [16]. However, this does not negate the importance of formal means, such as organizational structures, standardization of processes and systems, which are also crucial factors. In terms of processes, an effective way to ensure adherence is to "hard wire" them; that is, automate processes where possible. In the digital era, it is not uncommon to automate processes and in so doing, deviations can be tracked and escalation paths trigged automatically. However, common business sense must prevail, and automation must be used cautiously; it must be used as a mechanism to improve efficiency and effectiveness while at the same time not hampering business operations and team productivity. Both vertical and horizontal integration mechanisms are required to facilitate integration and transition.

In terms of organizational structures, processes, and systems, it is not sufficient just to have them, but to also have the right ones. Different projects have different complexities, depending on the size, duration, number of resources, complexity, etc. Therefore, some categorization is required and as such, each type of categorization may need different mechanisms, organizational structures, processes, and systems. For example, consider the following:

There are three types of projects namely:

a. Class A: High cost, long duration, many resources, and complex.

b. Class B: Medium cost, medium duration, medium resources, and less complex.

c. Class C: Small cost, short duration, few resources, and little to no complexity.

In class A projects, we have time on our side to fix problems when they occur. The high cost, duration, number of resources, and complexity require more rigid organizational structures, detailed processes, and robust systems.

In class B projects, we have less time than in class A projects. Time is still on our side, so the project has some flexibility in terms of recovery from potential problems. The organizational structures, processes, and systems, however, to a considerable extent are like class A projects but with some allowance for flexibility in the implementation.

In class C projects, we must pull the trigger on day one; there is no time factor on our side and every-day counts, so we must start the day the order is received. The project cannot be hurdled by complex organizational structures, long-drawn-out processes, and complicated systems. Therefore a much reduced but effective level of organizational structures, processes, and systems is required.

Based on this simple example, it is apparent that we need to have different organizational structures, processes, and systems for diverse types of projects—one size does not fit all. We need to have organizational structures, processes, and systems that are fit for purpose. The same applies to governance mechanisms, they should be fit for purpose to control and monitor adherence to the organizational structures, processes, and systems.

Similarly to the categorization of projects, we also need to categorize project managers. For example, consider the following:

There are also three types of project managers namely:

a. A superstar who takes an already good project (e.g., high margin quality, no major schedule/time constraints, and not many risks) and exceeds delivery expectations from a cost, schedule, and performance perspective. Such a project manager is also able to take a bad project (e.g., low margin, major schedule constraints, and with many risks) and always wins no matter what.

b. Average project manager will deliver the project as sold with no radical improvement or innovation in delivery.

c. Mediocre project manager makes no difference if it was a good project or a bad project at the outset, this project manager often will allow the project to suffer, and it may not be recovered.

Therefore, it is important that the right level of project manager is appointed to the right project. It would be significantly beneficial to include the project manager responsible for the project execution during the sales front-end phase. However, this may not always be possible due to project resource constraints already discussed. However, in high-risk projects, every endeavor should be made to involve the project manager early in the sales front-end phase. Superstar project managers should be given the opportunity to excel; they should be coached and exposed to more class A type projects. Average project managers should be coached and mentored with the intention to turn them into superstar project managers. Mediocre project managers should be given the opportunity to develop, failing which, tough decisions should be made regarding their future as project managers.

Another important mechanism is executive management participation and their capital allocation responsibility early in the sales front-end. Capital in this context is everything that is required in terms of resources, such as people, funds, factory, and space. Executive management involvement in the sales front-end can help alleviate challenges and mitigate risks early in that phase. They can also assist with the challenges associated with, for example, collaboration, coordination, resource availability, conflicting objectives, etc. It will also be beneficial to appoint a project sponsor or project "godfather" from the executive team, whose responsibility is to provide high-level leadership and guidance from the sales front-end through to the PLC phases.

It is also important to reinforce the discussion on processes at the handover stage. Processes need to be the right fit for the project category. The project execution team must take accountability and responsibility for the handover processes. The project execution team needs to be the process owners, they must own the handover process. For a proper handover, the sales teams must adhere to requirements set by the project execution team. The project execution team may have "dark fears," therefore, the handover processes need to be driven by the project execution team and not the sales teams, sales teams are participants. Project execution teams must own the process, they must be accountable and responsible for putting the process in place, as well as monitoring and controlling the process. Consider the handover process as a client-supplier relationship where the project execution team is the client and the sales team is the suppliers. Joint involvement from both sales and project execution teams in costing and estimating, in face-to-face discussions with the client in the front-end will only reinforce integration, transition, and collaboration. Pricing finalization needs to be a joint effort between sales and project execution. Noting that the project manager and project execution teams are risk-averse, they need to be realistic and simply including mechanisms to eliminate or reduce risk unrealistically will over price and over constrain the solution. This would be an undesirable situation resulting in the solution being rejected by the client, leading to order failure.

On formal handover between sales and project execution, the project manager has the final say in terms of signing off, by indicating that a proper handover has taken place from sales to project execution. The project execution team must indicate that they are, or are not, sufficiently satisfied with the handover from sales. However, measures must also be put in place to safeguard against the project execution team being too rigid and unrealistic in rejecting handovers from sales to project execution. At the end of the day, the project must be delivered to the client and internal processes between sales and project execution must align to client deliverables and not hamper the client.

A post-mortem should be done at the end of the sales front-end phase before the commencement of the PLC phases. This is at the project initiation phase so that

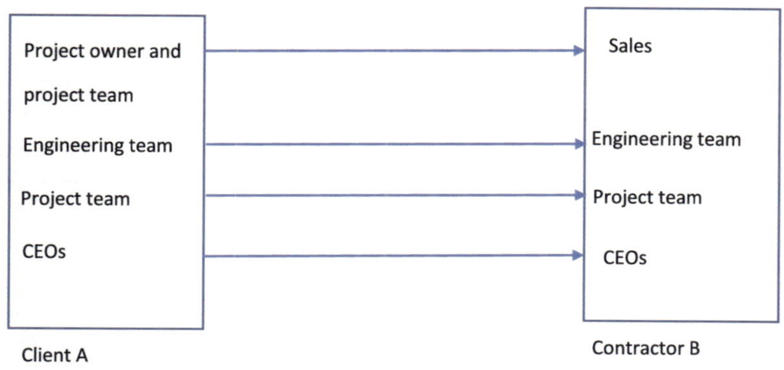

Figure 2.
Key account management structure.

anything that has been missed can be highlighted and proper risk management can be put in place to mitigate the risks identified, as well as enable lessons learned for future projects. Ideally, one consolidated document needs to be part of the handover process and this document must be signed by both teams as such agreement is reached. The post-mortem ideally will precede the project charter. In this way, there is internal alignment between sales and project execution teams before aligning with the client.

Having the correct integration mechanisms is not sufficient, one also has to have the right governance structures to facilitate the integration. This will lead to a better transition between the front-end and project execution teams. There are many options when it comes to governance structures. A key account management structure is sometimes adopted by large firms. This type of structure enables the front-end and project execution teams to effectively engage with the client. It allows for multiple levels of engagement with the contractor and the client. **Figure 2** gives a typical example of such a structure. For example, the sales team from the contractor engages with the project owner and project team in the client firm; the engineering teams from both firms interact with each other; the project teams from both firms interact with each other; the CEOs can also have a one-to-one engagement, etc. This allows multiple levels of engagement that enable better information and knowledge sharing and continuity across the PLC as well as across the entire firm. Key account structures may also offer some flexibility to alleviate the resources constraints from both the sales front-end team as well as the project execution team. Key account management structures only make sense for large firms and large projects. For smaller less complex projects and for smaller types of firms more informal means like appropriate organizational structures, cross functional-teams, meetings, face-to-face communications, etc., are more appropriate. It must, however, be noted that organizational structures, standard processes, and systems are an integral part of the governance mechanisms, key account management structures and other informal means do not negate their importance.

7. Benefits and opportunities of inter-organizational integration, transition, and collaboration

The benefits of a well integrated, transitioned, and collaborated project include at least the following:

Alignment of stakeholder requirements, as well as a unified understanding and acceptance of measurements and milestones. Moreover, it puts both the sales team and project team on the same page. It helps reduce risks and potential conflicts, it also facilities information and knowledge sharing and enables continuity from the front-end to project execution phases. There is also continuity in terms of risk management from the project front-end to the PLC phases, allowing the team to collectively manage project risks and identify opportunities for improvement. Benefits lie in lower risk because both sales and project execution teams are jointly involved in developing the client value proposition. This joint involvement ensures that both sales and project execution teams are aligned in terms of the deliverables, which is required in meeting client expectations. Furthermore, the commitments that are made have a much better chance of being achievable because of the joint involvement. The collaborative efforts result in more accurate budgeting, costing, and planning, which provide greater confidence in bringing the project within budget, schedule, and specifications. The end result is a happy client.

The handover process between sales and project execution is much smoother. This leads to better teamwork and cross-functional collaboration in the later stages of the project. Better alignment leads to the sales front-end and project execution teams working collaboratively to meet client expectations. This improves the chances of project success from a project budget, schedule, and performance perspective. A close working relationship leads to better team satisfaction and a good atmosphere enables the team to work in a more collaborative manner to overcome any hurdles that may occur.

A baseline understanding of the project deliverables has been established between the sales and project execution teams. The transition from the front-end to the project execution formalizes the change in accountability and responsibility from the sales team to the project team. Now that the transition has occurred and accountabilities and responsibilities have changed, and the clock has started ticking from a project schedule perspective, the milestones and measurements now need to be regularly tracked. This is required to ensure adherence to the project budget, schedule, and specifications that were committed during the sales phase. It is also important to note that transition occurs throughout the PLC, potentially at every "go/stop" gate (if a Phase-Gate process is used). Accountability and responsibility change at certain gate points where the project is handed to a new team. This must also be coordinated with the contractual phases of the PLC.

A well integrated, transitioned, and collaborated project results in higher-margin quality as well as lower risk in project execution. This also improves team morale, as general staff works better on a project knowing there is upstream potential to improve on the project deliverables. This is a lot better than trying to recover a project with high risk, which is often the case in projects that are not well integrated, transitioned, and collaborated. There is also a better understanding of the limitations, mutual understanding, and clarity in terms of meeting client expectations and project deliverables.

Integration, transition, and collaboration also imply information and knowledge sharing, which ensures that everybody on the projects knows what is required. This leads to better alignment between all stakeholders. It must also be noted that transition is not a once-off event, it occurs throughout the PLC. Just as the project execution team needs to be involved in the front-end process, so too do the sales team need to be involved in an advisory or oversight capacity in project execution, to ensure that the work is completed to the agreed requirements both from an explicit and tacit perspective. When sales and project execution work together the transition is smooth and seamless. As the project evolves sales team involvement is reduced. However, it is not a hard stop from the sales team, the transition is a process of information and knowledge sharing and continuity with a gradual reduction in sales involvement.

While the benefits are numerous as outlined herein, both sales and project practitioners must be cautioned against at least the following:

Acknowledging that while information and knowledge have been shared between the sales and project execution teams, one must ensure that tacit knowledge, which has not been documented, is also transferred across to the project execution team. This is possible through the gradual reduction of the sales team involvement, which will ensure information and knowledge transfer and continuity.

The project scope and limitations must be understood and adhered to as per the contractual documentation and risk management need to be a continuous process throughout, commencing at the sales front-end through to the PLC phases.

Acknowledging the transition from sales to project execution, the latter needs to ensure that the correct resources at the right capacity and capability are allocated to ensure that the project milestones and deliverables are met.

Resources now need to be committed and the project is now in execution mode. It is important that the scope is correctly managed by the project execution team and any deviations need to follow due process, otherwise, the project can be hampered by scope creep, which could lead to cost, schedule, and specification deviations that will be detrimental to the project.

8. Conclusions

Project management is not a single functional unit operating in isolation. It involves different functional units like sales and marketing, tendering, engineering, procurement, logistics, health, safety, etc. Therefore, successful project management requires proper integration, transition, and collaboration between the different functional units as well as the different activities. Projects are complex structures, mainly because of the complexity that arises from managing different stakeholders with different objectives. These stakeholders are both internal and external to the firm. There are also technical and nontechnical aspects of the project that need to be integrated and managed. Technical integration for example includes different technologies, perhaps from different suppliers, which all need to be integrated to create a complete solution, as well as the integration of possible different project locations. Nontechnical integration refers to the communication, behavioral and social influences between the different people, firms, and the internal and external environment.

In this chapter, the shortcomings in project management have been highlighted. Attention is specifically drawn to the integration, transition, and collaboration between the front-end and project execution phases. The front-end is predominately managed by the sales team, in some cases with limited involvement from the project execution team. The interface between the front-end and project execution phases is not understood well and requires special attention. The front-end is where the scope of the project is established, where the initial solution is defined, and where the rapport with the client is established. It is, therefore, important to ensure continuity between the front-end and project execution teams, failing which will be detrimental to the future success of the project. The front-end does not fall under the scope of project execution, but it is a crucial phase that sets the strategic direction for the future success of the project. It is emphasized that the front-end requires more involvement from the project execution team and it must be a joint effort between the sales and project execution teams. It must, however, be noted that project execution resources are expensive, and they are also limited. Therefore these constraints need to be recognized; however, every endeavor should be made for joint involvement as the benefits outweigh the costs and risks.

To improve understanding of the integration, transition, and collaboration between the sales front-end and project initiation phase, it is important to better understand this interface. Therefore in this chapter attention has been devoted to understanding this interface, by reinforcing the definitions and terminology associated with integration, transition, and collaboration. Thereafter, the challenges, requirements for project success and governance, mechanisms for improvement, and associated benefits are highlighted. This chapter draws attention to this crucial interface and ensures it receives the right amount of management attention. It also highlights that the current scope of project management focuses on the PLC, which does not include the sales front-end phase. Therefore, to improve project success, there needs to be a concerted effort dedicated to integration, transition, and collaboration between these two phases.

Notwithstanding the points already highlighted, it is important to point out that the basis for integration, transition, and collaboration is trust. Trust between all stakeholders needs to be established early on in the front-end. Without trust, the mechanisms will not be successful and the benefits will not be realized. It is also important to highlight that tacit knowledge transfer is an important item in establishing trust, as not transferring tacit knowledge could create the perception of a poor trust relationship, which is detrimental to the project. Integration is a function of the coordination of activities. Higher levels of trust lead to better collaboration, which leads to better coordination, and better integration, which leads to better transition.

Finally, as a reminder, the importance of having the right organizational structures, processes, and systems that are fit for purpose, and the monitoring and control of these organizational structures, processes and systems cannot be over-emphasized. Having organizational structures, well-documented processes, and expensive systems that are not adhered to, is simply a waste of effort and time.

Acknowledgements

The author recognizes the contribution made by Thomas Eichbaum, Bohdan Pylypczak, Jacobus Johannes Smit, and Dave Evans for reading the initial drafts of this chapter and providing valuable comments on editing, as well as further insights, which helped improve the content and quality of this work. The author is grateful for their valuable contribution.

There were no funders involved in this work.

Author details

Rajenlall Siriram
Department of Mechanical, Industrial and Aeronautical Engineering, University of Witwatersrand, Johannesburg, South Africa

*Address all correspondence to: raj@alpha-concepts.com

References

[1] Project Management Institute. A Guide to Project Management Body of Knowledge. 5th ed. Pennsylvania: Project Management Institute; 2013, p. 616. https://www.pmi.org/learning/library/siemens-initiative-organizational-project-management-8378 [Accessed: 17 December 2021]. Available from: https://repository.dinus.ac.id/docs/ajar/PMBOKGuide_5th_Ed.pdf

[2] Mittelstaedt A, Lebsanft K. Use and support of the PMI® OPM3® standard in conjunction with Siemens internal maturity in project management (MPM) assessment protocol and project management best practice methodology, PM@Siemens. In: Proceedings of PMI® Global Congress EMEA; 19 May 2008. St. Julian's, Malta. Newtown Square, PA: Project Management Institute; 2008

[3] Blanchard BS, Fabrycky WJ. Systems Engineering and Analysis. 4th ed. New Jersey: Pearson, Prentice Hall international; 2006. p. 804

[4] Miller R, Hobbs B. The complexity of decision-making in large projects with multiple partners: be prepared to change. In: Williams T, Samset K, Sunnevag K, editors. Making Essential Choices with Scant Information. Basingstoke, UK: Palgrave MacMillan; 2009. pp. 1-34

[5] Nobelius D, Trygg L. Stop chasing the front-end process—Management of the early phases in product development projects. International Journal of Project Management. 2002;**20**(5):331-340. DOI: 10.1016/S0263-7863(01)00030-8

[6] Samset K, Volden GH. Front-end definition of projects: Ten paradoxes and some reflections regarding project management and project governance. International Journal of Project Management. 2016;**34**(2):297-313. DOI: 10.1016/j.ijproman.2015.01.014

[7] Siriram R. Project management assessments. South African Journal of Industrial Engineering. 2018;**29**(1): 108-127. DOI: 10.7166/29-1-1675

[8] De Toni AF, Pessot E. Investigating organizational learning to master project complexity: An embedded case study. Journal of Business Research. 2021;**129**:541-554. DOI: 10.1016/j.jbusres.2020.03.027

[9] Van der Ende L, Van Marrewijk A. The ritualization of transitions in the project life cycle: A study of transition rituals in construction projects. International Journal of Project Management. 2014;**32**:1134-1145. DOI: 10.1016/j.ijproman.2014.02.007

[10] Williams T, Vo H, Samset K, Edkins A. The front-end of projects: A systematic literature review and structuring. Production Planning & Control. 2019;**30**(14):1137-1169. DOI: 10.1080/09537287.2019.1594429

[11] Griffin A, Hauser JR. An international publication of the Product Development & Management Association: Integrating R&D and marketing: A review and analysis of the literature. Journal of Product Innovation Management. 1996;**13**(3):191-215

[12] Song XM, Neeley SM, Zhao Y. Managing R&D-marketing integration in the new product development process. Industrial Marketing Management. 1996;**25**(6):545-553

[13] Artto K, Valtakoski A, Kärki H. Organizing for solutions: How project-based firms integrate project and

service businesses. Industrial Marketing Management. 2015;**45**:70-83. DOI: 10.1016/j.indmarman.2015.02.021

[14] Trautmann G, Turkulainen V, Hartmann E, Bals L. Integration in the global sourcing organization—An information processing perspective. Journal of Supply Chain Management. 2009;**45**:57-74. DOI: 10.1111/j.1745-493X.2009.03163.x

[15] Turkulainen V, Kujala J, Artto K, Levitt RE. Organizing in the context of global project-based firm—The case of sales–operations interface. Industrial Marketing Management. 2013;**42**:223-233. DOI: 10.1016/j.indmarman.2012.08.004

[16] Kokkonen A, Vaagaasar AL. Managing collaborative space in multi-partner projects. Construction Management and Economics. 2018;**36**: 83-95. DOI: 10.1080/01446193.2017.1347268